Social Work with Lawbreakers of Society

Social Work with Lawbreakers of Society

Volume 2

S. K. Bhalla

MD Publications Pvt Ltd
New Delhi

For information:

MD Publications Pvt Ltd
'MD House', 11, Darya Ganj
New Delhi - 110 002
Phone : +91-11-41563325 (Customer Service)
+91-11-41562846 (Editorial)
E-mail (orders): contact@mdppl.com
Website: www.mdppl.com

ISBN: 978-81-7533-157-0 (Set of 2 Vols.)
978-81-7533-159-4 (Vol. 2)

Published and Printed by Mrs. Rajni Gupta on behalf of **MD Publications Pvt Ltd** at Times Press, New Delhi.

CONTENTS

Preface

The criminal justice system has three major components: law enforcement, the courts and corrections. If these components are seen on a continuum, corrections encompasses the latter end of the continuum and deals with individuals who have been convicted of a criminal offense. Prisons and jails are the most visible correctional facilities for adults. However, probation, parole, and other alternatives to incarceration also fall under the aegis of corrections and account for more than two-third of the adult correctional population.

The social work profession's involvement in the justice system began in the area of corrections. In the late 19th and early 20th centuries, much social work activity was directed toward institutionalized adults and juveniles, as well as to individuals on probation. Prior to the 1970s, during the years when rehabilitation was a more accepted correctional philosophy than it is now, social workers were visibly employed in probation, parole and correctional facilities.

As social work has continued to evolve, however, it has largely abandoned the field of corrections. Several reasons have been offered for the profession's move away from this field. Predominant among these is the coercive nature of corrections, which is contrary to the social work profession's emphasis on client self-determination. Similarly, within direct social work practice the emphasis is on providing care and treatment to clients from a nonjudgmental stance. Within the field of adult corrections, the emphasis in one's approach to offenders is primarily on control and punishment from an authoritarian stance. These basic philosophical differences between social work and corrections have discouraged social workers from active involvement in correctional settings. Even though social work as a profession is not as active within the field of corrections as it once was, there is substantial evidence that the need for the profession's involvement is greater than ever.

The need for social work involvement is apparent in both the fields of juvenile justice and adult corrections. To this end, social work education should include content in both areas of practice, training students in multiple methods for work with juveniles or adult offenders. However, the correctional philosophies, needs, and intervention strategies within each field differ significantly.

The number of individuals under some form of correctional control continues to increase. At year end 1998, just under 3% of the U. S. adult population, or about 1 in every 34 adults, was either incarcerated, on probation or on parole. Over two-third of the individuals under correctional control, well over 4 million adults, are supervised in the community. These individuals and their family members often need the services provided by social workers in a wide variety of agency settings, as do the large number of individuals who cycle in and out of jails and prisons.

There is a great deal of overlap between offender populations and the individuals and families with whom social workers come into contact in other settings. For example, about 16% of male and 23% of female jail inmates have been identified as mentally ill. The rate of confirmed AIDS in the prison population is more than five times the rate in the general population. Almost 60% of female state prisoners report experiencing prior physical or sexual abuse. In addition, over 75% of prisoners are alcohol- or drug-involved offenders.

Racial and ethnic minorities are disproportionately represented behind bars and comprise over 65% of the prison population. The lifetime likelihood of going to prison is 29% for black men, 16% for Hispanic men, and 4% for white men. As social workers strive to address societal practices and policies that adversely impact certain groups, the disproportionately high number of nonwhite inmates in correctional populations deserves attention.

The incorporation of content on offenders and corrections into existing curricula will not, of course, provide students with the depth and breadth of information that an entire course or specialization in the topic would. Concern has been expressed that areas of specialization that require work with involuntary clients, including corrections, decreased within schools of social work from 1979 to 1989. As more students pursue career opportunities that offer the possibility of private practice and third party payments, the primary focus of social work has been moving away from working with at-risk and disenfranchised groups. This should concern the profession. Indeed, if social work hopes to make a significant impact on the field of corrections, there must be a much greater presence of relevant content in the profession's accredited academic programs. The vast majority of offenders belong to at-risk and disenfranchised groups. A beginning step to strengthen students' interest in fulfilling their professional responsibility to address the needs of at-risk groups is to ensure that the curriculum includes material about these groups.

However, as needed and beneficial as specialized courses in corrections are, many schools do not have the faculty expertise or the space in their curricula to provide them. Recently, social work educators have addressed the incorporation of diverse content areas into social work curricula, including content on violence, family reunification and legal issues. The integration of content into an existing graduate social work curriculum is a good alternative to adding a new course and provides relevant information to a majority of students when lack of resources precludes other options.

These benefits indicate the positive outcomes that could result when content on offenders and corrections is integrated into the social work curriculum. Integration of material may be useful in increasing student awareness of relevant values, concepts, and strategies underlying work with offenders and in helping students understand the complexities of a social problem. Benefits could also include expanding students' knowledge of practice with diverse populations, encouraging interest in an avenue of social welfare, and providing specific examples of practice to which students can apply their more general social work training.

Several key principles should guide the incorporation of material on adult offenders and corrections and be made explicit to students when discussing work with offenders. These guiding principles are widely accepted within the social work profession. However, because of the stigma attached to offenders, these principles bear repeating. Even within the field of social work, some clients tend to be considered more "worthy" of assistance than others, and criminals are often at the bottom of the list. The following principles are considered essential for effective work with offenders inside or outside of correctional settings. They are set forth as basic assumptions that should guide educational efforts within social work curricula.

The value and worth of all individuals must be upheld. In part this means embracing the assumption that given the right supports and services all individuals have the potential to succeed. Society might not be willing to expend the resources that are necessary for success; indeed, society might not even know what is needed many times, but the individual human potential exists. Both educators and students must be open to examining their own value systems and beliefs about the worth of all individuals, even those who commit heinous acts.

Activity on behalf of offenders, inside or outside of correctional settings, fits with the professional social work mission to "enhance human well-being and help meet the basic human needs of all people" described in the National Association of Social Workers (NASW) Code of Ethics. Indeed, "a historic and defining feature of social work is the profession's focus on individual well-being in a social context and the well-being of society". The problems experienced by offenders touch not only their lives but also the lives of their families and communities. Thus, positive results with offenders benefit society. In addition, according to the Code of Ethics, "social workers also seek to promote the responsiveness of organizations, communities, and other social institutions to individuals' needs and social problems".

I am very much grateful to Mr. Pranav Gupta, Director of MD Publications Pvt Ltd, for his kind cooperation and support for this book.

S. K. Bhalla

9

Intervention, Service and Treatment for the Community Welfare

Introduction

Agencies may have several tasks and we have seen how schools, protective agencies, and courts develop specialized ongoing services appropriate to their institutional functions and relationships with people.

Situation finding and case finding bring under the community spotlight a wide range of neighborhood, group, family, and individual phenomena. It is possible, quite frequently, to deal with the vulnerable, the exposed, those in clear danger at a point prior to the development of fixed antisocial patterns or personality symptomatology. But it is also necessary, and on a very large scale, to act with and on behalf of those whose lives are considerably disorganized, whose values may be distorted, and whose patterns of response and relationship are identified as forms of mental illness.

No one term describes adequately all the actions called for in the interest of the larger community, neighborhoods, groups, or individuals concerned. There are those who would talk of "planned change," a helpful concept if broadly defined. Perhaps the word "intervention" is a most useful way of suggesting purposeful action to interpose new influences into an ongoing situation or to seek new directions. Some actions, particularly those involved with the provision of specific resources or facilities, are best encompassed by the term "service," whereas professional efforts to arrest, cure, or change pathological processes are called "treatment." These are hardly well-defined or mutually exclusive categories of action; indeed, the boundaries between them are not at all sharp and to an extent the terms refer to differences in perspective rather than in operations. Nonetheless, they serve to suggest that children in trouble and their families are served and helped in a multiplicity of ways by many types of program and many categories of people.

We have already presented the range of required interventions, treatments, and service specializations which come to the fore following competent case and situation appraisal. Deferring, for the moment, the components of a diversified system of facilities for those children who must be helped away from home and noting that protective services have had special attention, there remains a long list which ranges from psychiatric clinics and family agencies to vocational guidance, group services, in-patient and out-patient medical care, probation, big brothers and big sisters, religious guidance, homemakers, foster care, public assistance, neighborhood self help and so on.

Clearly, the present chapter must be somewhat different from most of the others. We shall not be able to describe and to review current standards for all major forms of intervention, service, or treatment since this alone would require a full volume. Nor shall we be able to look at any one city's total service network as it affects clients and patients. A somewhat different approach is appropriate and possible.

We shall consider *the most promising currents in philosophy, theory, and method as they are relevant to the major programs serving those who are here in focus.* We shall illustrate from efforts throughout the country, not necessarily giving special attention to New York. That which is familiar, widespread, and traditional will not be mentioned not out of negative evaluation but rather to conserve space for newer approaches which require description.

Particularly since World War II, new directions and emphases in a variety of agencies and programs have added considerably to the potency and range of the armamentarium available for coping with the problems at hand. In fact, to some degree, developments of the past two decades have for the first time led to definition of certain types of individuals, families, and groups as candidates for hopeful intervention, whereas they were once seen only as "hopeless" or "uncooperative." We shall, therefore, begin with a review of some of the new notes struck in professional philosophy and some of the more promising emerging components of theory and method which reflect this new attitude.

In a sense, of course, some of the relevant themes have already been sounded, if briefly, in discussion of such specific programs as probation or the "open door" in the family agency. There is place, however, for a more systematic review.

Need for a Post World War II Breakthrough

The developments here under discussion did not all begin at one specific point or in response to one specific influence. Some go back to earlier points in American social science or in the histories of social work, psychology, and psychiatry. Minor themes which once occupied only a few individuals or agencies found new support. Nonetheless, for the most part, it remains true that the approach in the 1960s to children and families in trouble is different from the approach in the early 1940s. As we outline the major sources of pressure for change and the components of the new approach, the strokes must perforce be broad and countercurrents and exceptions will not be given adequate attention. This may perhaps be justified in the interest of the main ideas which must be conveyed. The validity of the basic analysis is strongly confirmed by any review of professional literature of the past twenty years.

Psychoanalytic emphasis. Why, then, were changes inevitable? First, perhaps, because the "psychoanalytic deluge" of the period immediately after World War II offered a method of intervention not suitable to many of those who needed to be helped. Social work had welcomed psychiatry early and gained much from it, beginning in the 1920s. A variety of external pressures tempered the absorption of psychoanalytic concepts and methods into environmentally oriented services and methods: the depression, the refugee situation, the war emergency, the postwar adjustment. Nonetheless, by the end of World War II, the number of psychoanalytically trained social workers had increased several fold, the supply of psychiatrists available as consultants or as team members had risen, and psychiatric clinic work or psychoanalytically oriented family casework was the high-prestige activity in social work. While there were many more untrained or partially trained workers dealing with clients than there were those who had full professional training, which included preparation for work in a clinical team, the professional literature, supervision, and role models reflected what must be described as a "deluge."

All of this certainly added to the effectiveness of work with neurotic patients, yet a large component in the public assistance caseload in times of high employment is a diagnostic group most recently called the "character disorders." "Character disorders" are also a predominant diagnostic group in families which abuse or neglect children and in which there are high rates of other disordered behavior.

Similarly, whereas the psychoanalytic emphasis added much to intervention with middle-class clients, it did not do as much for those in the working class, the source of the bulk of delinquency and neglect cases now in the courts and agencies. Psychoanalytic therapies had been shown to be valuable for the well-educated, but could they be expected to reach the new arrivals or those whose social or cultural patterns did not encourage them to talk about their problems, to formulate them in abstract terms, or to share them with outsiders? Perhaps, most important of all, no matter how effective psychiatric service might be where delinquency or neglect was a matter of intrapsychic factors, it could not hope to reach—at least at a reasonably early stage—those many situations where group, neighborhood, and cultural factors were at work. Thus, there was need for a shifting of balance.

Individual emphasis. Some of the troubled and the vulnerable could not be served by the treatment emphases of the early 1940s because of the assumption that intervention is necessarily on the level of the individual. The entire structure of case finding, particularly that associated with individualized justice, is a force in this direction. If one tries to understand influences and motivations, while protecting fully the rights of each individual, one tends to emerge with a "remedy" oriented to the individual case and a methodology which is conceived in individual terms.

Yet certain *types* of problems, at specific *stages*, are not affected on this level. For example, the member of the teen-age antisocial gang who is not yet in the hands of the law has problems in the realm of values and goals which are probably best approached as part of an approach to the group. Later, perhaps, he may require individual help or guidance. Albert Cohen, to illustrate, has pointed out that the delinquent gang member he has studied finds it difficult to change without group support and is more readily reached as part of a change-effort directed at group values.

Similarly, even in the instance of intrapsychic problems, there may be specific age or diagnostic categories which respond best to interventions organized on a group basis.

Finally, it may be, as we shall suggest, that neighborhood "self help" approaches are the method of choice even to change *individuals* under some circumstances. Resistance as an intrapsychic problem. An emphasis on the individual under all circumstances and a psychoanalytic orientation combined to create a situation in which agencies and services tended to interpret most client nonparticipation, noncooperation, withdrawal, or hostility as a psychiatric problem in "resistance." Explanations would be sought in developmental and personality terms.

In one sense, this was an old "charity organization" moral evaluation in new dress. For the early nineteenth-century friendly visitor tended to differentiate the "worthy" from the "unworthy" poor in part on the basis of their ability to take advice and to follow prescribed courses of conduct. The "unworthy" were left to the "poor law authorities." Modern psychiatry provided diagnostic categories which offered no hope ("constitutional psychopath") and the "resistance" concept which placed the problem in the client rather than in the therapist. Or, at least, there were many who felt able to use the explanation "client will not cooperate" to mean that there was present a degree of client resistance beyond agency ability or responsibility to affect.

Not adequately encompassed by such formulation is information about the ways in which social, ethnic, and cultural factors influence perception and cognition, or about the ways in which background affects role expectations, ways of perceiving problems, manner of asking help, and so on. Clearly, the entire "resistance" and "non cooperation" concept required reanalysis.

Authority as precluding a helping relationship. On the level of ideology, the most serious obstacle to the adequate development of casework services in probation, parole, institutions, and juvenile police programs was a very limited concept of the role of authority in a helping relationship. This stemmed in part from an era of "passivity" in casework technique, a reflection of the early psychoanalytic influence in which the caseworker sought to facilitate client "catharsis." More basically, it was a natural result of a treatment model in which a voluntary, self-motivating client came in search of personal insight and all deviations were taken as lacking the essence of treatment. It was assumed that casework could not be practiced in an authoritative setting and that the historical separation of "charities" from "corrections" had been wise. Caseworkers who persisted in probation work were considered to be outside of the professional mainstream.

But a few inventive workers refused to give up so vast a field of practice and insisted on looking at the matter as an unsolved issue: "Can casework be practiced in such settings?" they asked. Ultimately however, the concept of authority itself required analysis and reconsideration before the field could be opened up to hopeful work. Social work, psychology, and psychiatry had to learn that all professional helping relationships have authority components and that these must be understood and dealt with in specific ways.

Building-centered programs. Other types of breakthrough were also necessary. With some exceptions, the group services field had tended toward a building-centered approach in its programming. This was certainly not the tradition, since the earliest settlements had not been "houses" in the modern sense, and they had been characterized by broad experimentation. Yet professionalization had brought standardization of method and structure.

The prefabricated clinic unit. Another, still potent, stereotype must also be mentioned among those undermining the effectiveness of agencies. Once the child guidance clinic became a unit with defined professional roles and some reputation for therapeutic success, the assumption gained currency that it could be attached in its one pure form to a variety of settings which would thereby become effective treatment centers: schools, courts, children's institutions. We have already discussed consequences in schools and courts. In the children's institutions, social workers, psychologists, and psychiatrists acted as though they believed that daily life and education could continue on their own, in rather neutral fashion, while an occasional "fifty-minute hour" became the most salient of initiators of change. In daily reality, of course, the clinic was rendered very weak and ineffective by isolation from daily living. This, too, had to be taken into account.

Forces on the Side of Change

The need for a breakthrough or a series of changes was inherent in the outmoded and inadequate assumptions and consequent problems of existing programs. It received its impetus, too, from the rate of failure, recidivism, withdrawal, and non eligibility for existing services at a time that rates of reported delinquency, neglect, disorganization, and personality disturbance continued to rise and the public sought greater effectiveness in return for its increasing investment.

There were also a variety of other developments which contributed to change. Most important, perhaps, was the new impact of social science on social work and on psychiatry. This occurrence has been described and analyzed in other contexts. For present purposes we might note that social work had been rooted in late nineteenth-century social science and had deserted it when, as social philosophy, it offered little by way of dynamic analysis of the clients' current situations and provided few clues to planned intervention and change. The social science to which social work could "return" after World War II had gone through a period of empiricism. It had been called upon to address itself to current realities. In some of its branches it was emphasizing concepts and levels of abstraction which made it useful to professional practice. Moreover, some of its most creative practitioners were willing to concern themselves with problems of social practice. To illustrate the new "availability" of social science we mention mid-century work in social stratification, small groups, the family, organizational (bureaucratic) theory, urban sociology, contemporary cultures, criminology, and penology. The emergence of functional sociology and anthropology offered an approach to theory familiar to those trained in Freudian psychodynamics. Strong support to this entire development came from the program of grants, internships, research, and publications of the Russell Sage Foundation, in particular, and later from other foundations and the National Institute of Mental Health. The psychometricians, too, began to serve clinical situations by the imaginative development of projective techniques. In general, social science could be integrated with rather than opposed to the dynamic psychologies.

Professional inventiveness during World War II, spurred on by manpower shortages, had led to a variety of types of experimentation with therapeutic groups. Inevitably, psychiatrists, psychologists, and social workers continued the pattern of innovation on their return to civilian life. Since these steps were now backed by strong social science underpinning, treatment would never again be conceived of only in individual terms.

There were other forces. Within "corrections" itself, there were impulses toward professionalization, as there were in many emerging fields in the modern world. Several disciplines were suggested as the base for this field of practice. After a period of debate, leadership groups, including the National Council on Crime and Delinquency (then the National Probation and Parole Association), defined probation, parole, and certain roles in the detention and correctional administration field as within the province of social work. Given such identification, and offered opportunity within the National Association of Social Workers and the Council on Social Work Education, a small group of well-equipped correctional personnel began to effect basic orientations toward this work and, in turn, all social work service. On the governmental level, after World War II, a special juvenile delinquency project in the U.S. Children's Bureau also supported and accelerated this development, eventually to be replaced by a permanent delinquency division which develops and publicizes standards, encourages innovations, and seeks to help solve personnel needs.

Within the field of psychiatry itself, there were internal dynamics which led to more attention to ego problems a subject which might take us far a field. Important here is the fact that this, too, affected concepts of client and therapist role, goals, and methods and gave status to objectives which in an earlier era would have been defined as "too superficial." What is more, ego psychology provided a bridge between the psychoanalytic and the cultural, offering an approach toward the integration of the older clinical wisdom with newer social science emphases. At the same time, these currents in theory and their own practice experiences were leading some psychiatric practitioners to concentration on family dynamics where once the diagnostic and the treatment unit was the theoretically isolated individual.

Ideas and creative leadership gave rise to experiments and demonstrations. Among the most influential have been the St. Paul Family Centered Project, the various innovations of the New York City Youth Board, the work of Otto Pollak at the Jewish Board of Guardians in New York, several "detached worker" experiments in major cities (Los Angeles, New York, Philadelphia, Chicago, Boston, Detroit, Cleveland), the Chicago Area Project and Hyde Park Youth Project, Nathan Ackerman's family therapy experiments, and a number of institutional programs.

Professional Currents

Seen together, these new factors in the situation suggest new formulation of goals and pose new requirements. While we must be quick to admit that much of the thinking still requires validation through results and translation into method and professional training, the new currents can no longer be ignored. To the extent that their programs for children and families in trouble are organized only on the models of 1940, communities have reason for serious concern.

What, then, are the themes which have already established themselves as deserving attention and consideration? The variety of perspectives creates some inevitable overlapping. The following would seem to be a minimal list: (*a*) more adequate incorporation of the social dimension in diagnosis and intervention; (*b*) the use of "family diagnosis" and 'family treatment" wherever relevant and possible; (*c*) adoption of a "reaching out" philosophy in serving those unable to meet agencies on traditional middle-class terms; (*d*) use of group methods as appropriate; (*e*) use of neighborhood methods as appropriate; (*f*) formulation of goals in "value change" and "means change" rather than "personality change" terms, where appropriate; (*g*) assurance of integration of services around the case where more than one service is involved; (*h*) attention to total agency and institutional milieu; (*i*) assurance of a flexible and experimental orientation to intervention. Several of these matters are best elaborated in subsequent chapters (service integration and the therapeutic milieu, for example), but the remainder may be briefly reviewed. We shall also discuss the much-publicized so-called multiproblem family.

The social dimension. In one sense, all of the professional tendencies summarized in the remainder of this chapter reflect the new ways in which social science is being drawn upon by the "helping" professions. As we specify some of the current contributions which must be absorbed and built upon, however, the extent of adaptation and professional innovation will be noted.

The basic point is simple and, once made, inevitable: it is not valid to conceptualize only in intrapsychic terms causation of and intervention in a broad range of maladjustments, depredations, problems, and tensions. Current theory of delinquency has evolved in what may be a helpful manner. In seeking to intervene, one cannot ignore the social backgrounds, peer-group pressures, and value systems which affect aspirations, view of reality, attitudes toward constituted authority, presence or absence of guilt, and concepts of adequate family life and of parent-child relationships. Where ethnic derivation remains salient in family life, the caseworker or settlement worker, for example, must also take account of the ways in which Jewish, Italian, Negro, Puerto Rican, Irish Catholic, or Mexican family culture (to cite only a few) defines adolescent boy and girl roles and parent-child relationships.

Already a substantial body of professional literature, too extensive for summarization, has evolved to suggest and to illustrate how social factors should affect the helping professions. One collection stresses social science concepts in the following categories: family structure, ethnic patterns, social roles (age, sex, occupation, associations), values, social stratification, bureaucratic theory, theory of deviance as a group property. In the most comprehensive effort to the present point, specifically to illustrate the incorporation of social science concepts in child guidance treatment, Otto Pollak has emphasized a limited number of concept clusters: family of orientation, i.e., growing up (to assure attention to the father, siblings, relatives in the household, etc.), social interaction (to bring into focus all forces having impact on a child outside the therapeutic hour), social role (to contribute to realism in goal setting and to enrich family diagnosis), culture conflict (client culture and therapist professional culture both affect diagnosis and treatment).

Concepts such as these lead to a reevaluation of the entire impact of "social environment" on the client—or what the psychiatrist would classify as "social reality." In an earlier era, the therapist would seek to neutralize negative impact of these "externals" or to achieve that environmental stability which would permit the intrapsychic change processes to work. Today we know that the very complex and many-faceted interpersonal, social, and cultural environment is relevant to problem identification, need for and interest in change, setting of goals, perception of self, perception of the helping profession and the agency, ability to participate, and mode of participation in a given kind of change process. Practitioners everywhere are now seeking to absorb fully the implications of these notions, while professional schools attempt to broaden the basic social science preparation of coming generations of workers.

The application of sociology, social psychology, and anthropology to the analysis of professional culture and organizational structures has yielded new perceptions of professional blind spots and of the ways in which *administrative and service structures* affect the usefulness of agencies. Valuable insights are being derived relative to agency size, communication patterns, relationships between professionals from different disciplines, and the extent to which total agency impact rather than professional interview sessions alone is important in achieving the effects sought.

The emphasis on the *ego*, where treatment personnel were once preoccupied substantially with superego (conscience) and id (impulse) problems, has provided a way to conceptualize connections between the intrapsychic and the social reality realms. The ego serves this mediating and integration role for the individual. Some would, in fact, substitute the broader social science concept of interpersonal competence. This total development has pointed to the validity of advice giving, educational approaches, and retraining where these were once frowned upon as superficial techniques. Clarification of social realities, training which changes understanding and perception, reinforcement of skills for coping all these have their substantial validity. As a result, new opportunity for experimentation and flexibility in program and method is opened up. Only beginnings are being reported as of this time.

To illustrate specifically, one might mention the "children who hate," a group whose problems are tied up with direct disturbance of ego functions. In some instances there is a deficiency and helplessness in ego functioning. In others, an overdeveloped ego "serves the wrong masters" and defends impulse gratification at any cost. These children are said to need a "supportive design to strengthen the deficient ego functions and a counter-delusional design to dissolve their defenses before any of the well-known channels of therapy can be tried on them."

Social science concepts have provided the basis for a reanalysis of the nature of *authority* and the recognition that various intervention and social treatment situations are characterized by differences of degree of authority, rather than by mere presence or absence of it. This was a necessary development if serious progress was to be made in technique. Elliot Studt, who has given this subject special attention, points out that fully to understand an authority "event" one must look at the social organization in which it occurs, the two positions related by authority, and the two persons in these positions. Authority is, to her, "legitimized power"; in correctional settings, for example, the workers must make explicit what the client's subordinate role requires. In all settings, apart from the "power" deriving from statute and agency structure, the worker draws upon what may be considered professional "authority" the power deriving in a relationship from demonstrated competence. His effectiveness with a client probably increases as, in the course of a relationship, a shift occurs in the type of authority which predominates. For those who work with offenders of all ages, the authority relationship implies certain control over behavior and decision making which demands both skill and self-awareness.

In relation to the last item, in particular, professional workers in authority roles are often tempted to avoid their responsibilities as unpleasant. The exercise of the role reflects personal history, broadly conceived. Given the view that many delinquents have had unfortunate experiences with authority figures, the case for providing a new and constructive type of relationship with authority is strong.

The new social theories about deviance suggest new approaches to prevention and intervention, too. While these theories are being tested empirically, there would be validity to action research which seeks to determine whether changes in the legitimate opportunity structure will, in fact, decrease the frequency of antisocial gang membership or the forms of gang activity. Special attention is being given to vocational counseling and placement for youth in disadvantaged neighborhoods, community work projects, job training opportunities, well-led boys' club and center programs, ways of broadening and widening cultural horizons, and intergroup programs. Similarly, constructive leisure-time programs assume new importance. While all of these approaches have existed in the past and while so-called character-building agencies have always represented themselves as important in delinquency prevention, the "opportunity" emphases may suggest special target populations for the programs and may help ensure sharp focus where there is now a diffuse "shotgun" offering. It is of interest that the Ford Foundation is currently supporting a variety of preventive programs which base themselves on an opportunity-enrichment strategy. In the words of a foundation spokesman:

> *Successful prevention means recognizing the increasingly frustrating conditions of life of low-income youth in our cities, and trying to provide more jobs, more educational possibilities, and more of the normal opportunities for recognition and achievement possessed by other youth. Experts are realizing that much gang activity results from the fact that youth in slum areas see little chance of achieving status and recognition except through antisocial activities.*

Family diagnoses and treatment. The current family emphasis, at its best, is, in/act, a specific case of the return and deepening of concern for social variables. Florence Powdermaker has put it in these vivid words:

> *No man is an island, no member of a family is free from the impact of all the other members. When we treat a child or young person, indeed any member of a family, we put all of the burden of change on him despite the fact that as he endeavors to change, he remains in the situation in which his problem arose and in which the impacts continue. Thus, while he is trying to modify the behavior that defeats him, members of his family often cannot sustain him. They are not aware that his behavior is frequently the result of an interaction with them and between them-indeed the patient himself may not know it in all its subtlety.*

Porter Lee said as far back as 1919 that "the individual members of a family cannot be successfully treated without treating the family." However, the child guidance field continued to give lip service to the notion while working with the mother to a limited degree as "social environment" and almost completely ignoring the father's role. Even the family service agencies, presumably the center of a family orientation, were making individual diagnoses, were treating individuals, and had to begin to experiment with family-oriented diagnostic conceptualizations and family treatment procedures in the mid-1950s. The process has only started.

To some extent, the family diagnostic orientation has served to counter an excessively intra psychic tack in case evaluation. Inevitably, it raises social role questions and calls attention to interaction within the family. It alerts one to the siblings as well as to the child who may have occasioned a referral. It may suggest the importance of grandparents who are in the home. It has certainly highlighted those ethnic and cultural patterns and values which may be at the core of interpersonal tensions or conflicts or which may block adjustment. It has shown how shallow are diagnoses which do not consider family factors. It has guided experimentation with family-oriented interventions.

However, the decision for family diagnosis and treatment poses many problems. Is there any way to suggest boundaries and limitations? Obviously, every contact of an individual with a social service does not demand a family appraisal or involvement of all household members. When does it? There has been some tendency to defer this issue and to get on with experimentation: reestablishment of the importance of the home visit; diagnostic interviews with the family as a group; assignment of all family members for clinic treatment to the same professional worker where "case division" was once the norm; alternation of individual and two-parent interviews.

Helen H. Perlman proposes that social workers keep their professional footing by letting the "job for which we and the family have met" determine how one moves. One might be selective by looking particularly at the interaction "with the problem in the center of concern." She hastens to add that whereas the diagnostic value of family interviews has been shown, little is known about the treatment used or effectiveness of such interviews. Perhaps, she comments, increasing insight from the "small group" field may change this. In the psychiatric field, too, it will require considerable imagination and innovation to move from conviction about a family approach to the formulation and teaching of principles and techniques.

Multiproblem families. Spurred on by the family diagnostic emphasis as well as by social planning concerns, there developed, particularly through the 1940s and 1950s, a considerable amount of interest in what have variously been called multiproblem, hopeless, hard-core, or problem families. The development has both useful and misleading features.

The starting point is clear: since the time of organized social services and the compilation of administrative statistics it has been known that there are certain groups of families which make heavy demands upon community resources and facilities. It has also been known that within this group there are those particularly "resistant" or "unhelpable" families (to cite both American and British terms) who absorb services and funds but do not seem to change and who continue patterns of living which arouse community concern or fury, as the case may be.

In England, it is reported, there was heightened awareness of this group when the wartime evacuations and the resultant problems which arose occasioned considerable attention and the assembling of data. In this country, there was widespread interest in Bradley Buell's findings in a series of American communities that 6 or 7 percent of the families absorbed half or more of health and welfare services and that too often one could cite only "services rendered," rather than "problems solved."

Perhaps, inevitably, there has been a tendency in many quarters to act as though the multiproblem family is a diagnostic entity. Charity and social welfare have known the Victorian "undeserving poor," Booth's "submerged tenth" of the 1890s, and the "unhelpable" of the turn of the century and there has always been some tendency to seek a unified interpretation of that condition, sometimes in moral and at other times in diagnostic terms. Thus, it is not surprising to find in the professional literature of social work of the 1950s (some of it contributed by psychiatrists and social scientists) a substantial number of analyses which imply or accept the notion of group homogeneity and the existence of common psychiatric and social dynamics. Even the most sophisticated of professional workers have not been able to avoid the trap of discussing the characteristics and causes of what is assumed to be a real group. It is as though study has revealed a new disease entity known as "multiproblemitis."

The amount of confusion which this has generated has been considerable. Moreover, the less sophisticated practitioners are given one more stigma-evoking label to overcome in rendering service. One is not surprised at the comment of a British health officer:

> I never did like the term "problem families" and think that it has the most unfortunate effect upon the staffs of any Social Services, who have the habit of using it. There is, of course, no clear-cut division between responsible citizens and those whose habits make them a nuisance and a burden to the rest of the community I should be glad if I never heard the term again.

On the positive side, however, we must take note of the extent to which the "multiproblem" concept has contributed to much needed professional innovation. To mention a few results, we might list the Family Centered Project in St. Paul, Minnesota; several Youth Board programs in New York City; Bradley Buell's Winona, San Mateo, and Washington County experiments; and (more recently) a long list of special efforts variously called "reaching out," "programs for multi problem families," "operation outreach," "family centered casework," and so on.

The response to what has been learned about the multiproblem phenomenon has given particular support to family diagnosis and treatment, "reaching out" (see below), group treatment methods, experiments in combined individual and neighborhood work, and new devices for service integration. Agencies have been brought together in a variety of cooperative undertakings. In addition, having discovered that a very substantial proportion of the families which make such heavy demands on community services are, in fact, already known to welfare departments, Community Research Associates, the organization headed by Bradley Buell, has undertaken to introduce a series of administrative, training, and family diagnostic procedures. The outcome of many studies, including considerable attention to family diagnosis, these new procedures are now being tested on a large scale throughout Minnesota, in San Francisco, in four Pennsylvania counties, and in Omaha, Nebraska. It is expected that an emphasis on family diagnosis, prognosis, classification by level of service needed, in-service training, periodic evaluation, and follow-up may increase problem solving, in contrast to mere continued service in welfare agencies.

The St. Paul Family Centered Project, which had considerable influence, summed up its own special features as follows: (*a*) going out to a family; (*b*) use of home visits; (*c*) use of social diagnosis and an original profile for evaluation of family functioning; (*d*) the caseworker as the coordinator of services. Especially interesting in the context of discussion of increased attention to social dimensions of problems is a scale developed by the project for the evaluation of family functioning. Attention is paid to such areas of family functioning as child care; individual behavior; family relationships; social activities; relationship to the caseworker; use of community resources; family economic practices; health practices and problems; home and household practices. Many of these categories were ignored in the earlier "all-psychodynamics" era. In the most rigorous evaluative study as yet available in this field (but lacking a control group) the project's research team found, after two years of service, that there was some slight movement in two thirds of the cases. This is an impressive record if sustained, in view of the degree and complexity of pathology involved.

Particularly heartening is the fashion in which the experiences of special projects increase professional confidence in the potential for accomplishment and change. Buell speaks with conviction of the potential for improvement in recidivist, multiproblem families. All of the St. Paul reports cite the evidence of strengths in deprived families. In the words of the manual: "Multi-problem families are far better treatment risks than had been assumed. We have learned that improvement in social functioning is possible even with serious personality limitations."

Wiltse, who joins in the view that there is no such thing as a "hopeless" family, and who emphasizes that a variety of diagnostic entities are involved, nonetheless chooses to call attention to those families (many of whom are on public relief) who are completely controlled by events around them. They are too disorganized to be ignored but may not offer one major problem as a point of attack. The caseworker must often take on a "parenting" responsibility while developing a partnership with his client. The helping relationship demands teaching by precept and example, supervision and setting limits, offering both warm support and an ego ideal, mobilizing needed resources and facilities. In a sense, there is need for new "role training." Family diagnosis and work with the family as a unit are fundamental.

Settlements, neighborhood centers, family agencies, and child guidance clinics are among those developing special programs for what are called "multi problem families." In addition, there are some beginnings in this country in the testing of a European approach, the development of housing units for the training and education of families in need of special help in adjusting to the standards and demands of social living in urban areas.

As one examines reports and surveys it becomes clear that the multi problem concept has, in fact, had a variety of effects:

- The tendency to think of this as a new diagnostic category or social label has, among the less sophisticated, created confusion and promoted undesirable attitudes affecting both workers in the field and the public at large. One large city spoke hopefully of listing, "isolating," and quarantining the group.
- The emphasis on multiproblem families has made it possible to win support from public authorities and community chests for a wide variety of new programs.

- Many of the developments which we have already pinpointed as post-World War II professional breakthroughs have been promoted, accepted, and developed under the "multiproblem program" label (family approaches, reaching out, social science emphasis, etc.). In actual fact, however, these new orientations are not limited to work with any one client group or in any one type of program.
- Most of the more elaborate ease coordination experiments (service integration) win support as ways of dealing more decisively with these special problem groups.

"Reaching out." The ideology of "reaching out" has provided the dynamic force behind a significant portion of the initiative and innovation associated with the work with "multiproblem" families, antisocial gangs, and disorganized neighborhoods. Such terms and concepts are associated with this approach as "aggressive casework," "assertive casework," "operation outreach," and "going out." The New York City Youth Board has played a leading role in demonstrating and publicizing this ideology in action.

In the perspective of more than a decade and a half of experience, the basic theory is clear and obvious: Because of differences *among* the various cultural, ethnic, and social groups in need of social services, one cannot and should not expect members of all groups to conform to one model of the agency client. Furthermore, in view of the personality variations *within* each social-culturalethnic group among those in need of help, one cannot expect all to conform to one model of the agency client. The degree of introspection about one's problems and the tendency to "structure one's distress" in personal or interpersonal terms, for example, vary among the social classes. Self-referral and cooperative appointment-keeping at social agencies must be expected to vary with education, to take another illustration.

Social science insights, as already suggested above, thus lead to modifications of application procedure. They make it clear that the caseworker, at least under certain circumstances, must be willing to undertake a considerable amount of home visiting. Client "non cooperation" is seen to represent much more than psychological resistance related to treatment dynamics. The insights of ego psychology suggest ways of conveying an image of a helping person and developing a helping relationship appropriate to a person's situation and problem, not necessarily conforming to the hour-a week-in-the-worker's-office pattern. Material help and guidance in relation to daily routines may be offered quite appropriately and actively not only to meet urgent family needs but also to develop a starting point for relationships on which future work may be built.

Similarly, if antisocial groups or groups of youth under high hazard are to be found on the street corners and not in the community centers, it becomes reasonable to assume that group workers, now "detached" from their buildings, will "go out" to them and will invent new ways of establishing contact and demonstrating the desire to be helpful.

"Reaching out" sometimes requires physically moving the service closer to the potential users. Economics and administrative dynamics have created a tendency toward centralization of social agencies in recent decades, but the new philosophy has counteracted this to a degree, stressing service outposts in settlement houses, new public housing, and store fronts.

For "operation outreach" assumes that if one analyzes the total social situation one comes to understand that it is often the agency, rather than the child or parent client, which is "hard to reach" or "self-defeating." Those doing this work are convinced that programs which are inventive and flexible can be effective. In fact, so varied are the current innovations that "reaching out" may best be characterized as an ideology supporting inventive and flexible approaches which seek to bring needed services to those who are not served by the more traditional agencies or professional workers.

A British effort with a particularly good record is a program which began during World War II. In 1942 a Liverpool pacifist service unit sought to help "hopeless" cases abandoned by existing services. The following description is of interest:

Conscious of their inexperience, they began by offering the humblest services and attempting to find a sound basis for their relationship to the families. Cleaning, decorating, removing, repairing and disinfecting were the first forms of service and on this basis the rest was built. Friendship was made the foundation of the work a relationship of mutual trust and respect as between equals.

The experience of these units and their professionalization led to the creation of the Family Service Units in 1948. While it has continued to reflect the dedication and flexibility of the earlier units, the current effort has been fully identified as a social work program to be staffed by trained social caseworkers. Its philosophy and methodology have merged into the general "reaching out" approach to multiproblem families.

Faced by the need to work intensively and flexibly with the most complex and disorganized of client situations, both public and voluntary authorities have welcomed the Family Service Unit effort. Particular attention is given to those "unable to maintain proper standards of home and child care without proper assistance." The emphasis is as much on avoiding family disintegration as on comprehensive efforts at family rehabilitation. As the need for this work has been appreciated, public authorities in Britain have been willing to support expansion of the program through subsidy in many localities. By 1959 there were thirteen units throughout Britain plus four in London. Other authorities have assigned so-called intensive workers for similar work as part of the public social welfare program. It is not yet clear whether the program will remain under voluntary auspices or eventually will be fully absorbed as a public service. In the meantime, it continues to contribute to refinement of philosophy, theory, and method and to the development of content for training programs.

Of specific interest in the history of these units is the emphasis on neighborhood self-help to parallel work with individuals. To strengthen the spirit of friendship and identification between staff and client, the former are usually expected to live in the area, often in the center which houses the unit. While it is now rare for the workers to become involved in apartment clean-up and renovation, the heritage of that practice remains in the form of an emphasis on role training and concrete services as the point of departure.

There is some evidence, too, that the Quaker background of the program, the close neighborhood identification, and the group feeling in the staffs which is fostered in each unit provide even the fully professionally trained with a sense of "cause" which supports staff in innovation and persistence despite obstacles. A similar, almost missionary zeal was sensed in the group which originated New York's Services for Families and Children and the St. Paul Family Centered Project. Stong identification with a unit and staff stability are essential in this work also because of the likelihood that work with a given family must be long-term and requires a continuity of outlook. Thus, if the absence of a given worker or his departure means continuation with a unit member who is well informed, rather than a basic change in orientation, the service is more likely to be effective.

Although American programs have used the language of "reaching out" only since the late 1940s, the philosophy and practice did exist earlier. The well-known Cambridge-Somerville Youth Study, for example, found that relatively untrained staff, by today's standards, could establish relationships in all but 10 percent of the cases, whether or not invited in by the client, and could remain as long as the program objectives required.

Current philosophy is expressed in a recent report:

To offer help through words may be a service that is incomprehensible to some families, while the offer of a practical service be it a pair of shoes, a promise to visit the school or make a clinic appointment may make concrete to the family what we mean by our abstract term, "relationship." The goals we set for all families will be a reflection of our commitment to help, and not merely an opportunity to exercise our skills in treating in depth. The decision to meet the needs of the ever-increasing multiproblem families will be a reflection of our dedication to help people who need us, and not only those who meet our requirements.

Given this kind of commitment on the part of the caseworker, agency policy must support and encourage it. Thus, "we question selecting clients on the basis of the presence or absence of motivation or self-awareness."

It is artificial to carry on a discussion of "reaching out" without mention of the problems of ethics and authority. This entire tendency is premised on the professional resolution of conflict about authority which we have described in a previous section. "Reaching out" is possible only as the agency and staff members are prepared to assume a greater degree of responsibility and to exercise a greater degree of initiative when case appraisal shows this to be vital to family-child protection and rehabilitation. This is neither legally nor psychologically possible for a staff unless they are backed (as appropriate) by law, agency charter, or community values. Nor, given skilled "reaching out," must the client ultimately be deprived of the right to "close the door"; the agency is obligated to turn to the courts if that "closing" exposes children to hazard. Given an adjudication, the worker has new leverage to extend service.

While we shall discuss at a later point the approaches which may be taken to integrate services involved in a given case, it is of some interest to note the convergence in planning case integration of: a reaching-out philosophy, full understanding of the problems of so-called multiproblem families in many categories, and social science insights. Thus Buell, on the basis of the San Marco effort, stresses the importance of the caseworker's "historic role" of mustering, focusing, and coordinating a multiplicity of special resources and services needed by a family in relation to the totality of family problems. At the same time, clinicians lead one to the view that both family psychodynamics and social science concepts establish the necessity for spelling out a method of case integration. Once the total interaction is understood, it becomes obvious that fragmentation actually defeats family and child welfare efforts.

Group methods. We have already suggested above those limitations of an approach focused only on an individual and those potential advantages of group techniques which encouraged the post World War II breakthrough. Psychiatrists, social workers, and psychologists who had experimented with group methods in the armed forces welcomed the opportunity to transfer their explorations to civilian settings. At the same time, a variety of impulses set in motion by the field of progressive education and by social science merged with casework development in social work to suggest new group methods.

1. Group therapy: Today, a wide range of interventions is substoned under the general titles of "group therapy" and "group psychotherapy." Leaders in the field and writers in some of the professional journals make fine distinctions among the several approaches and define the requirements of sound practice. They are gradually evolving a system of theory, much of it based in psychoanalytic psychology. Although small group research and group dynamics have yielded impressive laboratory-type findings, they have not for the most part been translatable into professional practice. While the rationale is sociological, the session-by-session process resembles certain psychologically guided group therapies.

The many concepts and applications of group therapy are now demonstrated in programs in child guidance clinics, schools, settlements, courts, family agencies, adult mental hygiene clinics, health centers, and elsewhere. At times the group therapy represents the total intervention; in other situations it is integrated with individual therapy or with a variety of social services. Among those served are young children, adolescents, either or both parents, entire families as a unit, tenant groups, and client groups in many social service programs. Staffing and leadership are found on a team basis or in the hands of personnel who may be trained in psychiatry, education, psychology, social work, or social science. Many of the reports of specific therapeutic undertaking are impressive and encouraging.

For present purposes, it might perhaps be appropriate to sum up with the observation that the experimentation with group therapeutic approaches has now reached the point of need for codification. Some methods must be more suitable than others, some professional workers best prepared for specific roles. However encouraging some of the anecdotal records reproduced in professional journals, more rigorous validation of programs should be sought so as to facilitate choices and planning. People live large segments of their daily lives in association with family members, peers, neighbors, and associates; there is every evidence that groups of various kinds, purposively formed and professionally controlled, are effective change media. However, the time has come to systematize criteria for group formation, techniques, and setting of objectives; not, it must be stressed, to "freeze" the field of group therapy but as a step toward rendering it more specific and responsible.

2. "Detached workers": "Reaching out," a group focus, and emancipation from the fixed building converge in the "street club" programs in large cities. Of all the program developments described, none has caught the public fancy as much as has the work with antisocial gangs, some on the verge of "rumbles." The stage, television, novels, the daily press, and popular periodicals have acquainted all Americans with the group worker who moves out to the "hangouts" of youth on corners, in poolrooms, and in candy stores, establishes himself as concerned with their welfare, offers certain direct services (for example, help in the search for work), and attempts gradually to introduce sound goals and direction. At times, as an interim objective, he attempts to bring an antisocial group into membership in a center, settlement house, or especially established teen-age lounge. Where street fights threaten, efforts are made to head them off; sometimes there is mediation between rival gangs.

Although public awareness of these programs is a matter of approximately a decade, they have a somewhat longer history. All the earlier efforts were sponsored by voluntary agencies. The roots are probably in the Chicago Area Project, launched by Clifford Shaw over twenty-five years ago. A number of variations, on a relatively small scale, emerged in several large cities which became concerned with antisocial gangs as World War II ended: Los Angeles,

Cleveland, Detroit. Two small New York City programs were encouraging the Central Harlem Street Club Project and the Tompkins Square Project. When the New York City Youth Board was launched, it financed expansion of the former undertaking and sought to base a larger effort in a group of neighborhood centers. A variety of problems developed and the Youth Board decided to organize, supervise, and coordinate the program directly as a public program. Each major gang outbreak for a period of several years was followed by an expansion of this work. In the ten-year period from 1950 to 1060, the authorized staff grew to 120 field workers working out of the 10 units of the Council of Social and Athletic Clubs. There is liaison with many groups but workers are formally assigned to 130 groups with "membership" of 8,000. Approximately 40 of the groups are reported to be conflict groups of "considerable concern."

Most of the direct service in the New York City program is rendered by street club workers (a noncompetitive civil service category which has no educational requirements) and senior street club workers (who hold a social work M.S. degree, or some combination of other M.S. training or a B.S. plus relevant experience). There are well-qualified supervisors and coordinators and a program of in-service training.

The Youth Board reports an impressive record of "incidents averted," "mediations," social and athletic activities arranged, participation in lounge programs, referrals for medical-job-educational social services, and direct services rendered by its own staffs. It has also published a variety of descriptive reports which seek to clarify gang-member motivation and methods of intervention. It has not undertaken more rigorous measurement of effectiveness or systematic formulation of theory.

The following capture the spirit of the street club worker's approach:

> *I was standing next to the orchestra when Shorty came over with a relatively large youngster whom I had never met before. There were two other kids behind him whom I didn't know. Shorty said, "I want you to meet our boss,*

the big man. This is Ringo." I had heard a lot about Ringo but had never met him. Ringo shook hands with me and then said, "I hear you're supposed to be working with us. I just got out of jail, but they told me down at the Tombs that somebody had been around." I told him that I had been around for the last month or two and that I had heard about him and I was very glad to meet him. Ringo said that if I were to take on his crew I would have my hands full because they were a bunch of wild kiddies, the roughest in all New York. I told him that that was one of the reasons why I had been assigned to the group. I told him that I didn't know many of the fellows and I was awfully glad to meet him because I was certain that I would have to get to know him. I then invited Ringo over for a soda and he introduced me to the other two fellows who didn't say anything, but just looked me over. One was Bobby and the other his brother, Walter. While we were having soda Bobby began to comment on some of the girls at the dance, calling them real bags. He did this good naturedly and pretty soon we were laughing and joking, and I suggested to Ringo that probably now that he was out of the Tombs he might need a job. Ringo said he was wondering if I could help him do that. I told him by all means I would be able to. I gave him my telephone number and told him to stop around the next morning if he could and we would see what we could work out. Ringo thanked me and I terminated the contact at this point because I didn't want to let it drag on too long.

After the game we hung around outside the settlement shooting the breeze for a while until it was time to go. When I got back to my car it was in a mess. Somebody had taken a knife and ripped and cut the back seat so that the material was scattered everywhere. I was shocked. I went back to the settlement to see where the fellows were and the only one I met was Abe. I told Abe about it and he came to the car and both of us cleaned it together and then I went back to the block. All the fellows were gathered around and there was a great deal of talk about it, wondering what the pitch was since nothing had been taken. I recall that Manny had not been at the game nor had I seen him around all day. I didn't think that this was the kind of thing in which someone I didn't know at all would be involved. After speaking to the supervisor on the phone, we both agreed that I ought to look up Manny. I left the fellows and walked up to Manny's house. He was standing on the stoop by himself with a funny grin on his face. I exchanged greetings with him and told him what had happened. He still didn't say anything; he sort of looked at me. I told him that the reason

I had come over to see him about it was that I thought that he was the one who had done it, and if he had I wanted to find out why. Manny didn't say anything for a long while. I talked to him about the way his game was coming and we talked about girl friends and then I told him that frankly the car was three years old already and it could be repaired but it would cut down the amount of money I got when I traded it in. He then very quietly began to curse at me. He said that I was no good. He said that I thought that I was smart; he said I thought the sun shone only on me, that he didn't like the clothes I was wearing, the way I tried to con him all the time, the way I acted as if I could play basketball better than he could. In a word, he really tore into me and after a while he was no longer quiet, but was really very, very furious. I listened to him and then I began to get mad, because here Manny had destroyed the back seat of my car and I was being bawled out for it. So I lambasted him. I told him I thought it was a stupid, crazy, mixed-up thing to do and he should drop dead. Then he started to laugh as if he wanted to hurt me; he was glad I was mad. At that point I decided that this was getting a little bit complicated and I wasn't understanding all the things that were going on. So when he asked to see what the damage was, I consented, frankly because I didn't want to continue this kind of talk. We walked over to the corner where I parked the car. Manny looked at it and was still laughing. Then all of a sudden he stopped laughing and very seriously told me that he was sorry that really, before I had come around, he had been crying. He didn't know what had gotten into him. He thought that one of the things he wanted to do more than anything else was to be like me and he said he didn't feel he had a chance at all. Then he got to the point where he just hated me for being what I was. He wanted to do something to hurt me, hurt me bad. Then we got into the car and drove around while Manny began to try to tell me why he did this and what it meant?

Lerman has analyzed a similar pattern of work with what he calls "Youth in Conflict" in Chicago as demanding:

i. active communication that the worker cares about the group's problems;

ii. active demonstration that the worker is nonjudgmental;

iii. a willingness to sympathize with members' weaknesses and to support their strengths;

iv. overt expectation that they can cope with their problems;

v. flexibility, openness, imagination in the role of the helpful adult;

vi. the worker's coming to grips with his own system of values, his social class biases, and his own personality components.

Effective intervention also requires a worker who is trained to understand internal peer-group dynamics, the predominant surrounding value system of the adults who are significant to the group, the behavior and values of the sources of authority, and other salient social realities.

While there are variations in the terminology, most sources report similar emphases and concepts. A conference group of experts called upon the staff member to analyze groups and their members from a variety of perspectives and to follow two general principles:

First of all he is a representative of adult society and he is obligated to uphold the code of ethics to which he subscribes as a member and representative of a law-abiding, democratic community. He knows that the code is imperfectly practiced. He also knows that the code was evolved over a long period of time and that it can be changed, but only by the efforts of people who can understand it and restrain their judgment while they work for change. The worker becomes the bearer of values to youngsters who have pretty good "hunches" about what is right and what is wrong but they want their "hunches" corroborated by an adult in whom they trust.

The second principle is that the worker sets limits and sticks by them. If such limits are interpreted objectively and enforced impersonally, yet consistently, the group members sense the conviction behind them and develop a feeling of steadfast support. They feel that the worker is saying: "I like you but I don't always like what you do. I meant it when I said I'd do everything I could to help you but if I can't get your cooperation then I can't help. If I know you have a gun, I'll have to call the police. If you have, use, or sell narcotics, I must inform the police. But, if you honestly try to change, I'll understand and we'll work things out together."

The street club worker transmits his values and set limits in a way that makes him different from other adults these youngsters have known. The worker is a "different" adult one who represents something strong and solid. He has no need to punish them, to make them feel small, or to change them into replicas of himself?

The worker's chief program objective is to help the group to undertake activities which would not be undertaken without his support. To the extent that they are able to perceive new possibilities in their lives, members are en route toward more successful adulthood.

In one of the most perceptive analyses of the type of work in the professional literature, Walter Miller describes the results of the Boston Special Youth Program, a three-year intensive, direct service undertaking with corner groups. Seven groups received the intensive service and seven less intensive service. The workers' direct objective was that of "redirecting the energies of group members into constructive channels." Of special interest is the manner in which the arrival of the street club worker affected the relations of younger boys to older gang members and the relation of all the boys to influential local adults. Moreover, when the groups which had received the intensive service began to shift their value systems, so that "rep" derived from winning in sports, running dances successfully, and conducting legitimate enterprises, the "neglected" gangs began to attack. They were jealous of their rivals' successes. Miller notes the need to work with all groups in what he calls a "community relational system" if success with some is not to increase conflict initiated by others. Workers in other cities have arrived at similar conclusions. Where conflict groups are involved, the New York City Youth Board finds it necessary to ensure liaison with all major fighting gangs and to establish an elaborate staff communication network to head off conflicts, end inflammatory rumors, and facilitate mediation. The question may be posed as to whether at this latter point the street club program is not attempting to be, to do, and to promise more than it should. Its basic pattern of seeking out street clubs in the neighborhood, establishing relationships slowly, and offering program-guidance services is appropriate for the group workers assigned and for a social service. Beyond this, and the responsible reporting of information about danger, weapons, and antisocial activity, the street club program is in the realm of law enforcement. It cannot possibly have the city-wide coverage, the mobility, and the communications system essential to adequate community protection. While, in the short run, the public image of a force in readiness to protect the community may lead to support for the program, there must inevitably be disillusionment which is not related to the sound core of the program. In the early period of this work, staff members had considerable difficulty with the problem of maintaining their responsibility for cooperation with law enforcement authorities while seeking to develop a relationship of trust with group members. To some degree the problem still remains Nonetheless, major programs report that deep relationships may develop and effective work may be carried out while adhering to the fundamental principles:

1. That workers in implementing their role never consciously violate the law nor aid and abet anyone else in so doing.
2. That work with an individual gang member, or with a gang as a whole, is always done within the framework of the well-being of the total community and its members.
3. That in our work with individual gang members and the gang as a whole, when the well-being of the community, its members, the gang involved, and/or its members are in jeopardy. . . . we seek the active participation and assistance of law enforcement

agencies in the community, including the police, the district attorney and the courts. At the same time, while working in consort with the above mentioned agencies, we continue to exert our own efforts to the fullest to control the anti-social behavior of the gangs and/or individuals involved.

On the basis of these principles, detached workers find it possible to prevent and control conflicts, remove dangerous individuals from the community, remove weapons from gang members, and, generally, to control dangerous situations so as to create a climate in which positive results may be achieved. Workers in many communities report that gang members welcome release from the need to fight. Los Angeles has, in fact, staffed its program with probation officers and reports that this does not impede the gang work; research evaluation is now under way.

The discussion may create the impression that all gangs in all cities are alike and that professional workers are in complete consensus about the nature of teen-age gangs and the form to be taken by programs. This is far from the case. Some report elaborate gang organization and solidarity and a network of intermediate junior and "deb" groups associated with major conflict gangs. Other observers note gang instability and shifting leadership. To them the gang is only a "near group." Different age groups seem to provide the focus of antisocial activity in different communities. There are some observers who stress the threat of conflict gangs, while others see drug-using gangs as the major menace. A few observers call attention to gangs as channels of induction into adult rackets. Some consider the gang as "given" and to be worked with; others would break it up aggressively and would ridicule its leadership as "psycho." Most serious workers favor working with the gang structure and leadership even if the ultimate purpose is gang dissolution-in contrast to an attempt through punitive tactics to compel a gang to "break up."

The discrepancies are not the result merely of differences in perception. Clearly there are many types and degrees of youth grouping. A large portion seems to be on the fringe of antisocial activity, occasionally stealing, destroying, or fighting. Others are launched on well-organized delinquent careers. To the present point the evidence does seem to suggest that the general approach of the "detached workers" apparently has real merit *if conducted on a sufficient scale and so as to have impact on the total youth life in the community*. There is agreement that qualifications of staffs should be raised and training intensified.

Of some interest too are the variations in the work developed on behalf of female gang members (the "debs") and younger boys whose gangs are on the fringes of delinquency. Inevitably, the "ganging" patterns of girls are somewhat different from those of boys and result in changes in method. A report of Boston and Roxbury experience, for example, notes less local tolerance of girls who violate the neighborhood "code," more "hanging around" in the home, the need for greater worker program initiative, and early and frequent invitations to meet the mothers. Since there have been few reports of work with girl gangs elsewhere, generalization is difficult. New York City Youth Board reports describe some girl gangs as responsible for male gang fights but the evidence is limited.

There has been much interest in reports of work at the Henry Street Settlement in New York since 1956 with gangs of boys in the 8-13 year age range and with some girls as well. The Settlement has sought to break through the pattern whereby the juniors of a gang which is dissolved or the members of which end up in prison graduate to take over and continue the pattern. The unique feature of this program is an emphasis in the early stages on developing cooperative relationships with parents so as to stimulate interest in and concern for their children. While the particular parents do not tend to join the usual settlement groups, it is found that through persistent work it is possible to get them to meet with other parents to consider situations affecting their children. This is a "mobilization" of neighborhood adult opinion against juvenile delinquency but not against juveniles. Custom-tailored group work programs for the children offer positive and acceptable status providing experiences and a "socializing relationship with a group worker." One goal is to help individual children free themselves from overwhelming and unsound peer controls, so that they may pursue individual choices and preferences. The program offers a variety of forms of stimulation and direction.

In the words of the project director, "The children seem to thrive on the attention given them as the immediate adult community attempts to prescribe regularity and order. It would seem that when adults, particularly the parents, close ranks and stand together, the very ground these children travel from home to various parts of the neighborhood becomes more solid."

So promising is this approach that a major foundation grant has now permitted its expansion to a sizable group of New York City settlement houses.

In concluding this section we might also note that many of the programs have, in fact, combined their group work with direct work with individual gang members. At times the group leadership has been in focus. In other situations the worker becomes an all-purpose counseling and referral service for youth on the corner. Where the worker is clinically trained, he may be able to offer a refined and subtle therapeutic service to a few, thereby shifting the gang balance.

Neighborhood self-help, planning, and therapy. The street club work thus must be tightly integrated at the one end with services to individuals and at the other with general neighborhood self-help efforts. We have already noted the Roxbury experience which demonstrated that one could not abstract a few gangs from an area and work with them while ignoring others. And we have cited the Henry Street finding that to heighten parents' concern for their children and to back them in their sense of responsibility is to begin to change the community value system and thus to affect the youth.

It has been pointed out that the main limitation of the St. Paul Family Centered Project was its concern with cases scattered throughout the city. The project could integrate community welfare service but could not concentrate services on one neighborhood as such. New Haven's Neighborhood Improvement Project seeks to remedy this.

The hypothesis is offered that "if new opportunity structures are opened violence tends to be relinquished." The authors of this statement posit the theory that the form of gang which develops reflects the legitimate and illegitimate opportunity structures. One might broaden this hypothesis with the assertion that individual and family deviance is in part shaped by local neighborhood factors.

Although Clifford Shaw began his work in Chicago over twenty five years ago, it seems reasonable to state that the serious, large scale area and neighborhood work is only beginning in this country. In its largest dimensions and implications it is beyond the scope of our present volume: involved are all aspects of the attempt to make the metropolis viable and livable once again by reducing it to identifiable and unique neighborhoods with which people may become identified and which regain a form of stability and informal social control. This is truly a basic form of social reform and prevention which would affect rates of deviance. A *segment* of this general objective is the mobilization of local sentiment and energies in relation to specific needs, situations, and services which affect the young people or the character of family and neighborhood life. In this category one might list the Hyde Park Youth Project; the Chicago Area Project; New York City's LENA, "Neighbors United," or Riverside Youth Assembly; or many other similar undertakings throughout the country. Mobilization for Youth, a large-scale experiment, has begun operations in New York.

These are all beginning efforts, not in chronology but from the perspective of the size of the task, the need to develop professional methods, and the limited achievement. It is nonetheless fascinating to observe the convergence of group work and social planning and to note how self-help also becomes therapy. This requires explanation.

To begin with the Chicago Area Project, Clifford Shaw and his colleagues concluded in their studies that only a halt in neighborhood deterioration brought about through active involvement of residents would decrease delinquency. It was crucial, they felt, to reestablish spontaneous social control. They believed that local self-help enterprises of many kinds would create a sense of neighborliness and mutual responsibility, would increase resident concern about children, and would offer youth clear moral codes and much-needed controls. The self-help objectives result in a method which emphasizes local, "natural" leadership and as much local financing as possible. The work has been carried on in twelve areas. The neighborhood centers, which provide the core of the recreational and educational activity, do have both paid and volunteer professional staff; so-called indigenous workers are selected wherever possible, however. The project fosters and preserves the independence of local groups. The range of specific program content and form is as wide as that of the settlement. "Detached workers" have been included. Neighborhood committee members work with groups—but also work with individuals, seeking to "reincorporate" them into conventional groups. As the project is currently structured, much of the field service and research staff is supplied by public bodies, but the original private board remains in a coordinating role. Citizen groups and the Project Board raise close to half the annual budget.

The program is so complex that exact measurement of results has not been possible. Close observers testify that (*a*) it is possible, successfully, to encourage resident self-organization in low income areas and to establish stable and enduring community organizations; (*b*) it is possible to mobilize local leadership in the interest of children's welfare; (*c*) large proportions of the boys and girls in the "target" population use the facilities of the neighborhood centers; (*d*) it is likely (but not proven) that all of this does both decrease delinquency and help the reintegration of training school and correctional institution graduates into the community?

The Harlem Interdepartmental Neighborhood Services Center, also mentioned there, is an experiment in case integration which added a community organization component out of treatment considerations. Ways had to be found to reestablish contacts between disorganized families and their neighborhoods and to win local support for client efforts at self-involvement in community life. Staff community organizers took on these specific objectives in close contact with the casework program, but did not assume a general neighborhood organization task. Almost all very large cities now have programs which accept the premises of the Chicago Area Project and which seek ways of "normalizing" neighborhood life in order to decrease antisocial activity and enrich the futures of their youth.

Hillman, who summarizes many such programs which have been initiated by settlement and neighborhood centers, distinguishes what he calls "practical aspects" (getting new facilities, city services, police protection, urban renewal) from what he calls "idealistic aspects," the personal growth and satisfaction in being more than a pawn in civic life. He adds that it is "the practical side of citizen organization and action which accounts for the renewed current interest." There is substantial documentation of the expanded activity which includes many new types of endeavor. One wonders, however, whether the distinction between "practical" and "idealistic" is valid or whether the appraisal of their roles is correct. For, in broader perspective, these are aspects which are not only intertwined but also interdependent. All available theory and documentation suggest this. There are adequate, effective neighborhood mobilizations only as a community attains a sense of purpose and power and none of the practical achievements are properly implemented and accomplish what is sought unless the new buildings, parks, street lights, and recreation facilities provide an environment for people who are becoming ever more self directing.

If, to return to a term quoted in an earlier section, there are in the disorganized areas of our cities many "hopeless" families, then we may say that the mobilization for self-help is only successful as it achieves the material conditions for family rehabilitation but that it will not achieve this unless, in the process, the people themselves become better able to grapple with the factors affecting their daily environments. In this sense, then, *the self-help endeavor may be said also to have a therapeutic aspect.*

Astute observers of such programs all cite specific instances in which individuals have undergone major personal change as they have found useful roles in local action. Perhaps at some point in the future, in fact, we may be in a position to identify those types of people or situations for whom the self-help mobilization is the most suitable therapeutic medium, in contrast with individual or group psychotherapies. While noting this, we hasten to caution, however, that the mobilization has its own validity for all the "practical" reasons and that it does not achieve individual rehabilitation without accomplishing many of its practical goals simultaneously. Social welfare programs evolve from the custodial to the therapeutic to the preventive-social-planning phases. Successful citizen action and planning is the heart of prevention and ultimately decreases the need for therapeutic interventions.

Flexibility and Experimentation

Despite the length of this chapter, we have identified only major professional currents and have illustrated with reference only to a very few of many pioneering efforts. It may be appropriate to conclude on the note that while the process is underway it is by no means completed. Much that is only now begun or which will emerge in the next several years may achieve levels of effectiveness not currently known. Many of the theoretical insights are not yet reflected in most practices. For the problems are complex, the goals demanding, and current failure rates high.

The relevant professional literature contains many additional insights, leads, and suggestions which would seem to deserve attention, yet full summary is not possible and codification is premature. To illustrate very briefly and not at all comprehensively, we might note, for example, the evidence that a social worker with both casework and group work training may serve a group while focusing on individuals, and may reach a gang by involving its leadership in casework services. Or, to cite another illustration, those who work with probationers would find helpful the suggestions as to how one makes them aware of the realistic consequences of behavior while conveying concern. The objective is to "be effective, not popular." The context of such treatment is the definition of intensive treatment as a privilege, not a right. Many therapists also now join in the view that the therapist cannot help a patient to adjust socially unless he himself has a definite, if not too rigid, set of moral values which he is willing to impose. For all treatment directed at enhancing social functioning contains social control elements; strict therapist "neutrality" is not possible. A skilled practitioner avoids imposing idiosyncratic personal, cultural, and class values, while continuing to stand for social norms.

Many new treatment designs are needed, and the recognition of this will increase as the various subgroups among the delinquencies and the neglects are identified. The adaptive delinquent needs to be persuaded that he cannot, in fact, "get away with it indefinitely," while the maladaptive needs one of a variety of psychotherapies if he is not reached early enough on a preventive level. For those "children who hate," who are "beyond the reach of education" but below the grip of the psychiatric interview, other approaches need to be invented. Many technical innovations are needed, such as the life-space interview, an on-the-spot confrontation in private which follows immediately on salient experiences as a kind of emotional "first aid" which may also be exploited clinically.

Unless future results are negative, there is even validity in the pursuit of approaches which might seem at first glance to sacrifice indispensable values in the community posture vis-a-vis the offender. In this category we might include experiments in paying delinquents for "working" on a research basis, during which they become involved in treatment.

Special encouragement should go to many treatment innovations which would seek to take advantage of the milieu and staffing of the hospital-institutional type of setting while avoiding the pathologies of "institutionalism." In this category one would include day treatment centers (the child goes home to sleep), day schools in psychiatric hospitals (a special type of classroom plus individual therapy), night centers (the child goes to a regular school but his residence is the hospital or institution), and their variations. Such programs are only effective as they include concern for peer groups and inmate cultures as dynamic forces.

Finally, and in another category, we may return to the need to be inventive about community opportunity structures, for preventive purposes and to ensure service resources. Particularly in the interest of adolescents it is vital to be concerned with resources which guide in the preparation for work, resources which record the availability of temporary and part-time jobs, and resources necessary to remedy physical defects. New opportunity camps and apprenticeship programs are also being developed to advance these ends. Especially encouraging in New York have been several small, voluntary employment placement and counseling programs which have adopted a "reaching out" philosophy in the face of the knowledge that many youths in underprivileged groups are too fearful to venture out to centralized services. New York State has begun to support an expanded, decentralized Youth Employment Service (YES). The U.S. Department of Health, Education, and Welfare and the Department of Labor have begun to take the lead in suggesting new counseling, retraining, and guidance approaches.

A primary area of concentration in the first phases of this work must be clarification of just when a client or patient must remain in his own environment to be changed and when he must be moved. At times home and family pressures are overwhelming. At other times, only constant confrontation of an environment in which one's own responsibility for a problem is clear will contribute to change. These issues will be illustrated further in discussion of children's institutions.

10

Integration of Services in Social Work

Introduction

It has examined agency and institutional provision for case finding and for treatment with attention to all the intervening processes. Assumed throughout and described to a limited extent is the integration of the separate efforts in a context of community accountability. This notion requires further definition and the mechanisms for its implementation are yet to be specified. First, let us recall the problems here addressed. Efforts to deal with children in trouble are not nearly effective enough; exploration soon reveals that the resources committed to the effort are inadequate in quantity and in quality. As one seeks potent remedies, it is necessary to go beyond the question of the adequacy of individual programs, the sufficiency of resources in a given category, or even the qualifications of a given staff. Clearly, there are also problems relevant to the system of community services as a *system*. The following overlapping generalizations are central:

a. Cases are found, but opportunities are lost. "Services rendered" are too often considered as "needs met." Case finding may be followed by the minimum of service prescribed by an agency's function; by unskilled service or a failure to follow up consistently based on a limited concept of agency responsibility; by the dropping of cases because of resource lacks.

b. Far too much agency service and action is not based on adequate case appraisal or diagnosis.

c. Agencies often "drift" into case dispositions or make plans for services which are known to hold little promise of effectiveness. Conflicting philosophies and objectives operate at the level of case disposition, and punitive impluses often outweigh treatment strategy. Knowledge is in some instances limited; in others adequate staff is not available to make plans anchored in available knowledge. Resources may be in short supply.

d. Agencies are often in competition with one another for treatment resources; staff members within an agency are often in competition. Referrals are often made by "shopping," not through wise apportionment of available resources.

e. Agency service efforts in the individual case are not adequately integrated. Far too often agencies work with portions of families and segments of individual problems, and their efforts are unrelated except in the most superficial sense. Cases are "lost" in the gaps between agencies and services which do not "mesh." The complexity of many of the case problems, their family and community ramifications, is such that only the systematically interrelated efforts of the appropriate agencies will make an impact.

f. The sum total of agency prerogatives and rights and their implementation are such as to leave major gaps in the community pattern of services.

g. The deep and basic deficiency in the total community program, viewed as a whole, is in responsibility and accountability.

Of necessity, our efforts to specify the elements of a total community approach and to suggest philosophy and method which might be appropriate are general. A given community must translate guidelines, principles, and a large number of action proposals into priorities, specifics, next steps. Moreover, a given community requires mechanisms and structure for constant evaluation of its achievements and for review of policies and strategy in the light of changing problems, changing knowledge, and experience. Therefore, it becomes necessary, in the final phase of this present undertaking, to discuss community provision for planning, coordination, evaluation, and research.

Available experience suggests that the provision must be on several levels. First, there is the problem of ensuring the integration of services for the individual case in the context of the philosophy of accountability already discussed. Then there is the coordination and planning relevant to the neighborhood or the city subdivision. Finally, there is the provision for community-wide planning and coordination and the relationship of community-wide provision to the neighborhood structure, on the one hand, and to city and state structures on the other.

Context of the Problem

The sociologist would define much of what is here under discussion as a problem in bureaucracy. In a complex, industrial society, and particularly in its urban areas, the nature of population concentrations, the wide ramifications of needs, the multiplicity of skills required and services offered all lead social welfare programs to that inevitable formal organization (technically, "bureaucracy") which is characteristic of most organizations in the modern world. Wilensky and Lebeaux have reminded us that "red tape, buck passing, inaction, inflexibility," which are ways in which the layman would characterize many of the service problems, are actually pathological manifestations of some of the most basic and valuable features of modern formal organization. In their attempts to achieve efficiency, reliability, continuity, precision, and fairness, organizations are inevitably and increasingly characterized by *specialization* (within agencies and as between agencies); *hierarchy* (the distinction between workers and supervisors is especially important for present purposes); an emphasis on *rules* (activities are routinized where possible and all relationships are formalized); *assignment of roles to specialists* on the basis of assumed technical qualifications; and official designation of areas of jurisdiction for the several roles.

These are necessary features of social organization in our age, but they were unknown in the days of mutual self-help in simple, agricultural communities, nor were they in evidence in many of the social welfare programs which developed earlier in the history of the industrial revolution, when religious and humanitarian impulses, and not technical training or scientific knowledge, were the basis for action, and when specialization was almost unnecessary and unknown. Even today, there is far less bureaucratization in rural areas or in some of the smaller religious charities which have not professionalized and which have limited themselves to small subpopulations. Those who would solve the problems created by the pathologies of bureaucracy by harking back to the "good old days" ignore the facts of modern life, however. While some islands of simple and informal organization may continue to exist in social welfare, the matter of size alone size of client groups, size of agencies, size of staff demands formal organization for the bulk of public and voluntary provision. Solutions are needed for the problems which seem inevitably to arise, but it is fantasy to assume that social welfare alone, of all areas in modern life, will avoid this normal development.

Many specific problems already identified as present in individual programs dealing with children in trouble or in the total pattern of services are recognizable as manifestations of broader problems described by observers of social welfare bureaucracy. To the client, of course, they often appear as "obstacles and impediments."

Thus, the pattern of social work supervision may decrease the caseworker's initiative and independence just where it is most needed. Moreover, stress on eligibility and intake rules may keep services from people on irrelevant technicalities, or discourage those who are poorly motivated or not socially equipped to deal with the requirements. A high degree of specialization may lead to formulation of job requirements which eliminate most of those available for the jobs—and leave programs unstaffed. Or it may narrow the service given to that range sanctioned by the specialty, despite the needs of the case or the abilities and inclinations of the practitioner. Specialization, too, may leave gaps in service, may leave some client groups or social groups or geographic groups unserved, or may segment the client. Specialization of some kinds ("delinquents") also adds to stigmatization of some clients. A given service tends to define in quite specific ways how a client should behave (the reciprocal of the professional's role); people who do not fit into the mold may be dismissed as too poorly motivated to benefit from the service. Considerable assignments of resources are made to keep records and to provide formal devices (conferences, etc.) for communication between personnel within agencies; the investment represents a serious problem since it decreases the time available for direct work with clients; moreover, the communication routines and records often become ends in themselves, while the organizational machinery serves to decrease the sense of urgency in serving people. The greatest hazard, in brief, derives from the tendency to envisage the organization and its preservation as ends in themselves while the original objectives of service and help may become lost.

Some of these problems are obviously outside of the scope of the present work. Some are alluded to in connection with developments on the forefront of practice which address themselves to the correction of professional concepts and methods obviously unequal to some of the tasks posed. Another group of problems would be faced directly if there could be adequate provision for evaluation, planning, coordination, service integration, and case accountability.

The generalization of these problems both for social welfare as a whole and for all large-scale organizations serves an additional purpose, however. The analysis suggests that just as many of the defects of current programs are best understood as consequences of what might be called the ever-threatening psychopathology of bureaucracies, so must a substantial part of the solution be sought through organizational measures. This discussion addresses itself, therefore, to *organized means* for ensuring accountability and service integration.

On first impulse, one might be tempted to eschew more organization as both costly and likely to create its own complications, and instead to seek solutions through an appeal to professional ethics. This has a measure of validity. The true professions have codes of service which stress concern for the client. A major tenet in the social work ethic, for example, involves a stress on the identification and meeting of client needs. Social workers are much preoccupied with improving services, upgrading their skills, adding to their knowledge, breaking through unnecessary "red tape." Identification with the professional association and its ethics often supersedes the limited perspective of the local agency.

On the other hand, professionalization, not unlike formal organization, does encourage specialization; formalization of relationship; control of spontaneous emotional responses to people's problems; and emphasis on roles, qualifications, techniques, and procedures. Thus, while all that is possible should be done by educators and professional associations to solve some of the problems described through an emphasis on professional ethics and codes of service, organized solutions must be sought simultaneously.

Accountability and Service Integration

The agencies here in focus are instruments of public policy and social control. Their staff members are employed to achieve objectives defined in statutes, charters, and statements of purpose. The evidence is abundant and disturbing to the effect that where the objectives sought are not achieved, and this is quite often the case, the costs are high in destruction, waste, misery, and tragedy. In this context, the probation officer, medical social worker, social investigator for the welfare department, teacher or any of the others who might be mentioned—may not be regarded as individual practitioners whose actions and practices affect only themselves. They represent agencies carrying well-defined community responsibility and must, each of them, come to appreciate that failure to exercise that responsibility has serious community consequences. The term "responsibility" thus may describe community allocation of function to a given agency or service and agency allocation of role to a specific practitioner as well as the acceptance of such allocation by agency or individual practitioner.

It is helpful to consider devices for protecting or following the implementation of that responsibility with particular reference to the individual case. The concept of *accountability devices and instruments* may be useful in this regard. Put in slightly different phrasing: The case accountability device is a system or method designed to implement community responsibility by ensuring the continuity of work with the individual case until a point is reached at which community policy calls for case closing. (Implied, of course, is some assurance that the agency which maintains the contacts meets professional standards; this is a function of a variety of departments and of the planning machinery, perhaps, but is a burden too huge for any accountability system.)

An accountability system, by definition, must involve both some infringement on agency prerogatives and some increased invasion of an individual's privacy and of the confidential status of material about him known to social welfare agencies and others. Therefore, one would not wish a case accountability system so comprehensive that it would apply to all those who make use of social welfare, health, and educational services (i.e., most people). A "police state" atmosphere would not advance our objectives. Bather, there is need to define when and how a community should follow closely the service to members of the "high hazard" group in "clear and present danger" and how their rights are to be protected in the process. There is far less of a problem in the inclusion of those already subject to authoritative action because of their delinquency, neglect, or unlawful behavior as determined through court adjudication.

An acceptance of the accountability notion and the recognition that a major source of service failure is the fragmentation of services, fragmentation of clients, and loss of clients in the gaps between programs lead one to the view that *service integration* must be planned simultaneously with the creation of devices for case accountability.

It is helpful to differentiate between coordination in relation to the programs, policies, objectives, and plans of agencies, on the one hand, and coordination of the work *on the individual case*, on the other. The latter process, best identified as integration of services, involves ways of ensuring the meshing of resources and services for the individual client. It also includes concern for the consistency of approach and policies of various agencies or parts of agencies as experienced by the person for whom the service is designed.

Coordination devices, invented in the nineteenth century and introduced widely by the charity organization movement, had the potential for case accountability and the integration of services, but they were addressed to the problems of another era. Thus, the social service exchange long served the primary function of detecting those who sought and obtained relief in more than one agency. This problem has ended with the growth of public welfare. The social service exchange still makes it possible for an agency to know the names of other agencies which have had contact with a family; however, registration is selective and some communities have abolished the exchange because they did not consider it helpful or because the ethics of registration without permission seemed questionable. In addition, the volume of work, the inability to separate good leads from poor ones on a social service exchange slip, and uneven levels of staffing have limited the extent to which the exchange is regarded as useful. In some instances case summaries are requested; this may lead to some meshing of efforts. In even fewer instances, records are read or an exchange slip leads to telephone conferences or to actual full-dress interagency conferences. These may foster considerable integration of effort but generally are seen as timeconsuming and costly. It is doubtful that the exchange will ever become a potent service integration instrument unless it becomes more selective or is tied somehow to a system of case accountability. We shall return to this matter shortly.

The first charity organization societies of the 1880s were actually created in order to attain service integration (they did not, of course, use the phrase) where there seemed to be chaos. They soon discovered that the need for adequate relief and qualified service was greater than the demand for service integration, and they became today's family service societies. Several decades later, their heritage was seen in the community council movement, but here the major emphasis was on coordination on the level of agencies, not individual cases. Nonetheless, from time to time councils have sought to encourage case integration by promoting interagency understanding and communication, facilitating case conferences between two agencies working on a case, and conducting the kinds of workshops and institutes which lead to mutual clarification of function and greater readiness to work together. Most recently some councils have experimented with the new form of case conference described below or have initiated valuable projects.

The agency "merger" movement has also been in a sense a step toward case integration although actually a variety of motives are involved. Family agencies and children's agencies tended to join together after World War II. It was clear that efforts to maintain a family may be made more consistently and with greater skill before child placement begins; a protective unit requires close ties to a child placement service; etc. Attendance bureaus have joined with guidance and psychology programs to form more complete pupil personnel departments. Children's and family courts have been joined in one structure. There have even been a few instances in which child guidance clinics have become associated with in-patient treatment facilities.

Obviously the merger has important potential in case integration. The judge sitting in the children's case should have the family court record on the family. Without too much effort the psychologist should be able to review the experience of the attendance officer, and so on. Mergers appear to have achieved the desired effect where they were real, rather than mere paper actions, where staffs in the several components were on equivalent levels of status and skill, and where the programs were not so large as to demand formal integrating devices within the agency. The merger has obvious limits, however: one cannot achieve case integration in a large urban area by putting all the agencies under one organizational title and administration.

The case conference. While the older and earlier devices have not been adequate in their original forms, they have inspired recent developments which are encouraging. Central to these developments is a *new form of multiagency case conference* which serves both as an accountability device and an instrument for case integration. Cases are carefully selected for presentation because they represent "multiproblem" situations, a number of agencies are involved, and adequate progress has not been made. Agencies are represented by personnel on a supervisory and/or administrative level (augmented, perhaps, by the worker directly responsible for the ease).

This form of case conference involves a sharing of information and evaluations, culminating in a new case diagnosis or evaluation, as well as in an action plan mutually arrived at. Professional confidentiality of material revealed in the conferences is ensured through agreement. Particularly crucial is the agreement generally made as to which agency is to "take the lead" with the family and how the others are to support the effort (case integration). Furthermore, a "reporting back" date is set for review of progress and the making of further plans (case accountability). Once the case thus comes into the center of community attention, it is not so readily "lost."

From time to time this kind of practice has grown up in a community without much publicity or reporting, but it has had special attention in a number of communities in recent years as a way of dealing with families considered particularly difficult. Thus, to illustrate rather than to enumerate all developments, the Montclair Council of Social Agencies organized a case conference committee several years ago, one of several such in New Jersey, and emphasized "reporting back"; it stated that positive results could be documented. The Roxbury Family Project, working for several years in a Boston neighborhood, developed a similar plan. Oakland County, Michigan, is said to find a case conference "very effective."

The St. Paul, Minnesota, Family Centered Project promoted service integration through a continuous "workshop" for the special staff members assigned part-time by the agencies for purposes of the project. Because the project was a demonstration and research endeavor and staff were in a sense "loaned," if only part-time, it did not change the basic community pattern. The service integration emerged, in this instance, as a by-product of a joint study effort directed at the problem of designing treatment methods effective with so-called multi problem families. A *Casework Notebook* produced by the project defines the case conference as "the best device we have for joint planning." This project stressed that case conference effectiveness depends on the caseworker and his immediate supervisor; while policy agreements may be reached on the administrative level, or in interagency councils, servicc integration requires at least one meeting of those who will work together on the case.

A more limited device which is described as very effective is the case review committee in the Philadelphia schools. Top administrators of special services (medical services, pupil personnel and counseling, special education, etc.) are joined by experts where needed to confer on the most seriously disturbed and potentially dangerous young people in school. While the conference may decide on school exclusions or may initiate commitment, school transfers and special programs are also possible. Unlike some of the other case committees, the Philadelphia plan is not tied to ongoing treatment decisions and does not involve reporting back to review progress and make new plans.

Los Angeles reports that during 1958-59 there were 49 case coordinating committees associated with local community coordinating councils. During the one year, the committees considered 314 new cases and 476 ongoing cases, approximately hall involving a focus on children under 14. In a current Madison, Wisconsin, project a "case conference demonstration" is being used for general coordination and planning purposes and to create a climate for use of such conferences as part of normal service.

In England, most local authorities (93 percent) have some kind of coordinating machinery and half use the case conference device—mainly in the instance of work with children. There is emphasis on neglectful families. Younghusband's definition and advice is applicable on this side of the Atlantic as well:

> A case conference provides a setting for a limited number of workers directly involved in the case under consideration to assess the need, work out a plan of concerted action, and carry it out in cooperation with each other and with the person or family under discussion. It should be attended only by officers [involved] in the case under discussion, one of whom should take the chair.

She comments further that "the main problem is not so much multiplicity of visiting as multiplicity of independent and uncoordinated visiting."

Case conferences have been used in New York City in a number of special projects. In 1957 the Welfare Department pioneered with what became known as the Borough Committees of the Mayor's Interdepartmental Committee for Multi-Problem Families. Administrative or supervisory personnel from public departments (Education, Buildings, Health, Hospitals, Police, Welfare, two courts, Housing,

Mental Health Board, Youth Board) met monthly in each borough both to promote interdepartmental coordination in general and to ensure integration of services in the eases at hand. They constituted a permanent committee. All of the departments listed could refer eases. A conference sought to develop a plan of action for the particular case, to devise ways of cutting "red tape" and modifying directives where it seemed essential for the case being reviewed or for similar eases, and to designate the agency which would assume primary responsibility for service. Monthly reports of progress were required as a means of ensuring continued service integration as well as accountability. The total volume was small since only one case was discussed per meeting, but the effect on services and policies was said to be broader. While the plan was given up in the light of subsequent developments, its strength seemed to be primarily in the area of policy and program coordination. Unlike the practitioner case conference, the administrator and executive conference identifies action to be taken in definition of roles, filling of service gaps, and untangling of "red tape." It is not an efficient way to deal with many cases individually since the direct-service practitioner must follow through with the eases.

In 1958, taking account of expressed concern at the fragmentation of services as well as the gaps between agency services and the frequency with which cases are "lost," the Youth Board developed an experiment in one of its Referral Units. Under the plan, a highly resistive, multi problem family was selected for review and the project staff convened a meeting of an appropriate *ad hoc* committee which included representatives of all agencies, public or voluntary, currently or previously in contact with the family (usually four to ten in number). Prior to the meeting, the project staff prepared and circulated an up-to-date case summary. The Youth Board case conferences sought to attract the staff members directly concerned with the case, even though administrators were also welcomed.

At the meeting proper, the representative from each of the agenciès reviewed his agency's experience with the family and the total group then explored the situation, pooled evaluative judgments, and developed a plan and reasonable goals with the family. Although the initial picture of a case as it emerged in a conference was often discouraging, the "pooled" thinking tended to discover positive factors and to suggest possible "leverage." One agency was eventually requested to assume the lead in work with the family and to integrate the services of the others. Follow-up reporting was scheduled for a date three months after the meeting. So gratifying was the experience during the first year that the Youth Board determined to assign similar activity to all of its Referral Units. Preparatory meetings with all interested agencies met enthusiastic responses.

While the Youth Board experience with the case conference is substantially encouraging, organizational aspects have not been solved. A small community might achieve service integration and accountability through a "coffee-time" conference. Large cities need to staff many cases. What volume is possible? How are cases to be selected? Given considerable volume, what administrative devices are needed to implement accountability?

As will be seen, the unclear status of the Referral Units in recent years and their staffing difficulties have precluded the development of large-scale case conference machinery. In addition, the limited development of New York's "multiproblem' register has precluded its use for case selection. Yet the Youth Board conference experience suggests that it would not be at all unreasonable to expect a coordinating agency in a large city to use its machinery to organize and staff a network of case conference groups along the lines of the Youth Board pattern. Twenty-five or thirty such groups would be required for New York City, and they would staff two or three new cases each week and hear reports on eases previously staffed. This would bring about two or three thousand new cases into the accountability network a year—a reasonable total if the conferences are reserved for situations involving child neglect or delinquency, for cases with ramifications in a variety of agencies, for cases of considerable family disorganization and evidence that routine handling will not do.

Since the case conferences would generally not involve the same practitioners at each meeting, this kind of plan would not impose too heavy a burden on any staff member. It would depend in New York City on using Referral Unit staff resources or comparable staff to select the cases, prepare the conferences, and follow through. Other cities would need proportionately fewer conference groups. Organization of conferences on the basis of a neighborhood or city subdivision would seem desirable. Oakland, California, has set up a conference group for each of five high school districts and finds that both service integration and program coordination are possible. The Roxbury Family Project, which investigated the matter, stressed that coordinators and resource personnel involved in case conference procedures make their optimum contributions if they are "neutral," that is, if they do not have a direct service function.

Registers. The problems of case selection and administrative controis for this kind of machinery remain. A small community does not find it difficult to develop an accountability card index which is an integral part of a case conference system. It comes into play at the point of case finding. There must be some work done in advance to arrive at mutual agreement as to cases to be added to the register and scheduled for conference. (Among the possibilities, to illustrate: all cases of alleged neglect, all cases in which a child is temporarily separated from his parents, all adjudicated delinquency cases under certain types of circumstances, public welfare cases with certain interagency ramifications.) Following conferences and mutual planning, a simple process of notation of "return dates" would be adequate and would provide for the preparation of follow-up conferences at appropriate times.

The large-city roster is a more complex matter. Thus, despite frequent announcements of intent, the New York City Youth Board has not been able to use its roster for accountability purposes or for any other ongoing administrative operation even though some research use has been possible. Part of the problem is that of criteria for listing: cases have been placed on the roster on the basis of intrafamilial relationship patterns and parental attitudes, the outgrowth of Youth Board interest in the Glueck prediction work. However, the core accountability notion would be better served and the roster kept within manageable limits if a committee of experienced practitioners were to formulate criteria relative to problems, behavior, and, most important, the community agencies' experiences with the family.

Having solved the problem of criteria, the large city will have to use an electronic system to keep its roster usable and flexible. Cases could easily be coded by "conference group" (i.e., neighborhood), basic characteristics, agency ramifications. An electronic system could help select cases for conferences in the terms of predetermined priorities, while agencies themselves could add cases to the agenda in the light of their experience. The register could also provide, at appropriate times, suitable rosters of cases to be followed up, rosters of unreported cases, rosters of cases closed by an agency while core problems remained, and so on. Its costs, while important, would be small when weighed against current futile, uncoordinated, and pro longed services. Economies might eventually emerge if the social service exchange were properly to curtail its own activities in the light of the existence of the register. The community might, in fact, choose to place the register under social service exchange auspices and to merge it with the exchange. This is a matter of administration and financing, rather than a substantive issue.

The point is raised as to whether the use of a register does not abuse the client's confidence or stigmatize him. In some cases there is no question at all about the community's right to use a register as an instrument of intervention, since there has been either an adjudication which places the family or child under court supervision or protection or because the service is an outgrowth of a statutory charge to work with relief recipients (public welfare cases) or to help enforce the compulsory education law (many school-referred cases). Where the community's rights are not clear, discussion of the social service exchange and/or register should, under any circumstances, be a normal part of agency intake. The client accepts or rejects the register when he uses the service (or the decision may be deferred for reasons relevant to the case). Where the client cannot move voluntarily and children are endangered, the community may need to exercise its police power, which includes registration as part of the protective investigation process.

In fact, one may say of accountability devices generally what has been said of the register: if one limits cases listed to those which need to be in the forefront of community concern because of hazard, "clear and present danger," and complexity of interrelated problems, most cases will in fact present a legitimate basis for the partial invasion of privacy which is involved. Where such basis does not exist technically and the client rejects voluntary service, the protective services machinery may be called into action. If there is no legal basis for protective action and the client does not wish the service, his privacy should be safeguarded, despite the convictions of some professional workers that there are hazards involved—at least unless the predictions are validated by identifiable and justiciable "acting out."

"Intensive" workers. Accountability devices and service integration measures should ideally affect the practice of all agency staff members. A number of special studies and projects also have suggested the possibility of a degree of specialization with some families found to require particular and concentrated attention. Agencies often have several staff members particularly suited for intensive, rehabilitative work on the basis of understanding, experience, and skill. Why not reduce their caseloads, increase their prerogatives, and stress the integration of their work with other agencies? Recommendations for this work in a British study of *The Neglected Child* are also supported by American experience:

a. Caseloads should be small, consisting of not more than twentyfive families for each worker. With a larger number than this, the families that are passing through a crisis of some kind cannot be given sufficiently close attention unless other cases are neglected.

b. One worker should have responsibility for the whole family and for helping it in all its difficulties. Specialist workers will often have to be called in to deal with particular problems, such as poor physical or mental health. But one worker, from whatever service, must have full responsibility for the family, and others should visit only when necessary and only after first consulting with the worker in charge.

c. Help of this comprehensive kind must be available to a family as soon as its problems grow too complex to be dealt with by the functional services.

d. Those offering this help must be allowed to work in the same district for long enough to become well-known and trusted by the families they visit.

e. There must be close coordination of all services, based on fairly frequent discussions beth between those directing the services and (more important) between those actually visiting the same families. It matters little whether this is achieved through formal committees, over a cup of tea in the town hall canteen, or in other ways.

f. When the immediate crisis is over and families once more begin to lead a fairly normal life, it must be possible for someone to keep in touch with them for long enough to prevent a relapse.

g. People of the right character and experience should be chosen to undertake this personal service, and they should be encouraged to work in an independent and experimental manner and to develop new methods. This is the most important condition of all.

Perhaps, after a family comes into focus, the first attempts might be on the basis of careful integration between agencies. For it is not the multiplicity of visits per se but uncoordinated work which is so undesirable.

If this produced no improvement, one of these specially chosen workers would take full responsibility for the family after discussion between all the services concerned. Other visitors would not abandon the family altogether but would henceforth visit as little as possible and take no action without first consulting the person in charge. Which service would be chosen to assume responsibility for any given family would depend on which worker appeared to be in the best position to help. In most cases there would be several visitors already calling on the family; by discussion between them it could be decided who was likely to exert the most influence (owing to personality, function, pressure of work, or any other reason). That person would be put in charge and asked to report progress at intervals to other organizations interested in the case.

In this way most of the conditions necessary for effective personal service would be achieved without radical change. Families would merely find that one worker, whom they already knew and trusted more than others, was giving them more attention and was taking responsibility for matters upon which they had previously received calls from many people. Every organization would make its contribution. The distribution of casework would be decided not by theoretical arguments about the value of the different services, but by practical demonstration of their success in individual cases. No service would be condemned to limit itself henceforth to a narrow range of duties; each would be encouraged to think in terms of the whole family, and to gain a wider understanding of family problems. Good workers need no longer waste years of their time in dealing with the symptoms of trouble; they would be given a chance to tackle its underlying causes.

Several British health and social services have, in fact, assigned "intensive" workers. The St. Paul project, which defined its special staff members as "general family practitioners," sought coordination of treatment (what we have called service integration) by assigning them responsibility for working with families "to bridge them over to a more productive use of community resources"; developing better interagency collaboration in behalf of families; using their observations in order to contribute to community planning and social action.

In the St. Paul project, in New York's Neighborhood Services Center, and in many special units for multiproblem families throughout the United States, the case is transferred to a special unit and then assigned to an "intensive" worker who carries a variety of the ramifications. We have yet to experiment systematically with intensive workers who remain within their agencies and are unassigned to special projects—but whose job assignments permit the special intensive work on a selective basis. The California Youth Authority is launching intensive community treatment of delinquents along these lines.

Accountability and agency prerogatives. A community cannot develop service integration and keep families in focus via accountability machinery unless there is some surrender of agency prerogatives. Individual agencies alone cannot make final determinations about cases to list—or about when eases may be dropped. A conference should be able to decide who takes the lead, even if there is not unanimity. Community reports must be free to compare agencies on their "sticking" and "holding power."

All of this can be made possible by democratically conducted community planning and coordination machinery with local, neighborhood subdivisions in large cities. The agencies involved are either public services or voluntary programs supported by community chests or individual, tax-deductible contributions. In either instance it is legitimate to expect that an agency will cooperate with the community network, making its views known, participating in decisions, and supporting plans which are made. The *social* services are not the domain of individual entrepreneurs; those which act as such are hardly responsible in the sense in which the term is here employed.

In fact, once an agency accepts the philosophy here outlined, it will find its own ways of going even beyond the registers, conferences, and intensive units described. For example, a school system may develop a cumulative record system (or cumulative records plus confidential guidance files) to ensure continuity of service to a child from term to term, once his difficulties have identified him as requiring special help. The register must be in competent hands lest a child be stigmatized and forced into an unchangeable mold. The child health station offers similar opportunities to public health nurses and medical social workers.

Or, to illustrate further, a housing authority social service program might assign staff or obtain the help of public or voluntary casework services to maintain close contact with that "small hard core" of public housing tenants who require support and help lest their inadequacies produce new problems and lead to even further family disorganization. The Neighborhood Improvement Program of New Haven, Connecticut, places a casework unit which concentrates on multiproblem families within a public housing project. Within the unit are recreational and community organization personnel as well, offering a rounded program to casework clients and to the project as a whole.

Neighborhood Base

Staff members from a variety of agencies, responsible for cases in a given neighborhood, must eventually find ways to mesh their efforts. Any case integration system must therefore be brought down to the neighborhood level in some fashion. And this is just as well, since intensive knowledge of a locality is usually a prerequisite to successful service. This suggests the hypothesis that it may be useful to tie accountability and service integration provision to some kind of structure of neighborhood organization.

The Chicago Area Project, the model for many others, has had more than twenty-five years of experience and reports positive results. Its program in the neighborhood tends to lead to recreation provision, general community self-improvement endeavors, direct work with gangs—but not to service integration or accountability. On the other hand, the South Central Youth Project, in a blighted Minneapolis area, arrived at the agency case conference structure and assignment of one responsible worker per case as its major working method, but concluded in its report that "more community forces should be involved."

Given agreement to explore local organization in relation to service integration and accountability, several structural approaches would seem to be relevant. Any of these would require innovation and change, since much local organization in the youth field is concerned only with the provision of leisure-time and recreational resources. A proposal that there be some local ties to central planning and coordination bodies would win agreement in the abstract, but there would remain the need to define the realistic parameters of local initiative in fields in which decisions are made on city-wide or county bases. The question of the best possible relationships between social agencies, volunteer service groups, citizen self-help activities, and local planning bodies would still remain.

A search does not yield ready answers. Many patterns are obviously being considered, however, as urban areas seek to fill a vacuum created by the breakup of neighborhoods and the changes in urban political machines which in one sense provided for a degree of accountability of a sort. Many of the larger urban areas are, in fact, in transition in their patterns of neighborhood organization, as they take account of urban renewal, the problem of racial integration, and population mobility. Some special neighborhood organizations, created in order to deal with delinquency, are carrying out broad local improvements on the assumption that grass roots activity of this kind decreases antisocial orientations in the total community, creates needed services, and offers sound role models for youth.

This is, then, an area for tentative exploration and testing despite its urgency and substantive importance. The remainder of this section is devoted to brief mention of a variety of interesting developments. All aspects of local organization not immediately relevant are bypassed.

Oakland's "associated agencies." Oakland, California, in a plan under way since 1957, has created a coordination-service integration structure on a local basis by dividing the city into five high school districts. The executive of the program is based in the city manager's office and is called the "juvenile control coordinator." Costs are shared by the Board of Education and the City Council. Policies are made by an executive committee consisting of the executives of the agencies involved (schools, recreation, police, probation, Youth Authority, welfare, health). Each agency is represented on a coordinating committee, which is city-wide, and on the local district units. There is thus provision for joint planning, program coordination, and local case integration.

The heart of the program is the twice-monthly local district meetings which serve to ensure service integration and reporting back and to initiate new policies and provision needed to deal with emerging problems. All reports are positive. The effectiveness with which the agencies deal with local "emergencies" such as gang fights, as well as with individual cases, is impressive.

Coordinating councils. At one time the delinquency field was especially concerned with promoting the local coordinating council, a device for periodic meetings of local agencies or responsible local citizens concerned with delinquents. The movement's main development has been on the West Coast. Councils have lay and professional participation, generally combining both, and include a range of organizations, from law enforcement bodies to civic groups, schools, churches, and social agencies. They sometimes develop surveys or initiate activity to provide new resources. At other times they serve as informal centers for service integration. They are considered more effective in small communities and do not seem to meet an urban area's need for formally organized service integration and accountability involving large caseloads. Particularly lacking is a specification of roles appropriate to laymen and roles which should involve professional staff in order to protect confidentiality and ensure qualified help.

The New York City police-inspired precinct Youth Councils are like similar councils elsewhere. Theoretically, each police precinct (of which there are 78) has a council, but approximately one quarter are active. Local professionals, civic leaders, church leaders, and merchants join together to support PAL fund raising and to devise programs to meet special needs. The council is a means to organize some activity and occasional coordination, but is not structured either for accountability or integration. On occasion, it may have a vital, energetic program. The police are currently assigning professional staff to revitalize the councils but there is no city-wide policy guidance in relation to many areas in which other public and voluntary agencies also have youth councils and neighborhood organizations.

Washington, D.C., has given a larger task to its more than twenty boards set up in natural neighborhood areas, under the leadership of the Commissioner's Youth Council. Prevention, coordination, and some case integration tasks are undertaken by each local group.

New Jersey has juvenile conference committees in almost forty areas, having created them after a 1953 directive from its Supreme Court to local juvenile courts. A Monmouth County plan, which originated in 1945, was the model. Committee members are court appointed; the committees are designed to encourage the locality to come to grips with delinquency, particularly in the early stages. According to a recent report, thousands of citizens have actually served on committees. As New Jersey has sought to strengthen all of its services to youth in trouble it has had to look at the conference committees and to recognize that they have sought to carry out case evaluation, treatment planning, and case supervision, often in open committee, without diagnostic understanding or appreciation of what the experience could mean to participants, and without adequately qualified personnel. On the other hand, the committees have led to some effective screening and informal handling of cases which might otherwise have gone to court. They have channeled much constructive citizen interest in community services. As needed probation services and court intake structures expand adequately in New Jersey and as community social agencies offer alternative forms of informal help, it would seem likely that the direct case handling by conference committees would end and that these would become juvenile court advisory committees and local citizen committees concerned with planning. By their nature, they cannot adequately undertake service integration, which should be a function of an operating staff. The generalization applies to similar activities in many states.

The Baltimore area projects represent an intermediate type of development. They are, in effect, local community centers set up under the Welfare Department. The local community supplies all the needs of the project, but the Welfare Department adds clinical staff and a coordinator who encourages local organization to deal with local problems.

Precinct youth councils, juvenile conference committees, parentyouth aid committees, and their thousands of equivalents throughout the country are excellent recruitment grounds and orientation centers for "big brothers" and "big sisters" who may supplement professional helping services in valuable ways and who may act in lieu of such services for children referred through professionally qualified channels.

LENA. The Lower East Side Neighborhoods Association in New York City (LENA) is an elaborate and unusually imaginative effort in an area with a population of over 200,000. It was created in 1955, at a time of rapid neighborhood change, in response to local violence. It now joins together in a vigorous, effective, and in some ways unique organization five local neighborhood councils (four of which it initiated), community members, professional members, and 90 community organizations, from banks and trade unions to settlements and churches. Much of the work is carried on in divisions which have their parallels in the local councils: housing, health, education, youth, community arts, intergroup relations. Work is carried on in such a way as both to raise the tone and quality of community life and to deal with dangerous deviance. For example, the community arts program seeks through a summer concert program, dramatics, and a variety of offerings in the arts, plus a local "talent hunt," to enrich daily experience and to create pride in neighborhood—thus striking at one of the roots of its problem. Energetic self-help efforts are directed at problems and gaps in health, education, housing. Systematic work is done to increase contacts between diverse ethnic and social groups and to improve relationships.

There is much concentration on the youth. Neighbors, settlements, churches, schools, public departments are heavily committed to a two-pronged approach which includes a rich recreation and sports program (teams, leagues, competition, instruction, trips outside the area) and youth services. The neighborhood councils have their youth councils with similar emphasis and all give priority to grass roots volunteer-neighbor involvement and to youth participation and initiative. At the same time, a tightly coordinated network of area teams, consisting of professionals in local agencies, representatives of public departments, and neighbors, keeps its fingers on the pulse of youth gangs, meets immediately on call, and intervenes rapidly at the first signs of tension. Where constructive programs are possible, they are initiated; mediation is often undertaken; however, if danger threatens, the forces of the law are called into action at once.

Although more systematic testing of effectiveness is planned under the Mobilization for Youth project, being developed in a section of the LENA area, participants are convinced that the program has had considerable impact. Intergroup relations have been improved in the area, public services and housing have been brought more into harmony with need, closely coordinated agency programs-particularly social-athletic and social services—have ensured more complete coverage and have served many who were previously unreached. Particularly dramatic have been the successes in recent summers in heading off threatening gang violence and bringing together previously unfriendly groups.

While this description does not do full justice to LENA, it may serve as a backdrop for noting the extent to which an enthusiastic local self-help effort may both increase agency coordination on a neighborhood basis and approximate a system of accountability. As the result of the explorations and plans of local councils and LENA divisions, and as a natural by-product of the experiences which professionals and board members have in serving together in these activities, the public-voluntary coordination has been much enhanced. Public services in particular have often found new ways to adapt to local priorities and needs. At the same time, it has become routine, to take another illustration, for local settlements so to schedule their social and athletic programs as to provide the best possible neighborhood coverage for the entire week. Joint activities are common.

This total atmosphere, plus the activity of the area teams, increases the sense of accountability which is so important. Sometimes it is provided formally, as when LENA's Youth Service director helped meet a school suspension crisis by assuming responsibility for a group of 120 youngsters designated by the school officials as requiring concentrated attention. Local social service, medical, psychiatric, and educational help was rallied. At the same time, the district's best teachers cooperated in a Foster Teacher Plan to give special attention to a group of children with intense emotional difficulties.

Informal accountability and service integration develops particularly through the work of the area teams which keep attuned to the pulse of the youth gang situation and plan how to act in relation to specific individuals and gangs. This informal but intensive follow through is most impressive when contrasted with the anonymity and "crisis service" of the typical area. In a sense it becomes an urban neighborhood re-creation of the small town primary group relationships on which social control is based. Youth perceive that significant adults (parents, neighbors, church, social agency, police) know and care about what they do and will intervene if unlawful action is threatened. Unfortunately, not every urban area has the continuity and concentration of agencies and churches of the LENA area nor is it possible always to create such primary group controls.

Whatever the success of local organization (and it should have enthusiastic support), it will be necessary to ensure full coverage and to take account of intracity mobility through the establishment of some combination of formally organized case conference committees, "intensive" workers, and accountability registers or rosters. Perhaps there is a systematic way to relate these to a local neighborhood organization without violating confidentiality. A neighborhood service center may offer some possibilities.

Neighborhood service center. Early in its history, the New York City Youth Board experimented with a neighborhood "Department Store of Services," housing one of its Referral Units and also representatives of such public services as welfare, health, housing, employment, etc. The objective was facility in reaching the client, increased availability to him, and ease in referral by the Referral Unit, rather than service integration. Others have proposed local neighborhood service centers for some areas of large cities with services such as family casework, group work, work with gangs, day care, homemakers. Some would add a mental hygiene clinic, employment center, and legal aid and housing services. If this cross between a settlement and multifunction treatment center were created, it should obviously include integration and accountability devices of the sort already discussed. It should certainly encompass information and advice functions and a good referral service. The existence of a physical center would also facilitate its relationship to a "grass roots" self-help organization as well.

New York City has resumed experimentation with such an approach in a pilot Interdepartmental Neighborhood Services Center created in the spring of 1960 on a directive from the mayor. Unlike the earlier "Department Store of Services," which concentrated on case finding, information, steering, and referral, the new unit, in an area of high rates of social breakdown, actually seeks to provide wellintegrated team services and accountability focused on families and their members. It includes a modest community organization program. Service units of six workers each are assigned by two city departments (Education, Health) and the courts. In addition, the Youth Board assigns two Referral Units.

Defined as within the scope of the program are the so-called multiproblem or hard core families, but it has been difficult to develop clear criteria for referral in the absence of a roster of the sort described. Case characteristics stated in Glueck "delinquency prediction" terms, rather than service ramifications of the case, were initially the basis for the referral system. Later, complex cases not worked with elsewhere on an intensive basis were accepted; the bulk come from schools and the Welfare Department.

The cornerstone of the plan is the designation of one rehabilitation caseworker per case (an "intensive" worker in the sense used above), even though the family may be on the rosters of such departments as welfare, schools, courts, and health. Although on the payrolls of various departments as probation officers, attendance teachers, youth guidance technicians, or social investigators, the Center's staff members become "general" social caseworkers. Only the minimum of core statutory responsibilities remains vested in the originating agencies (such as Department of Welfare relief eligibility or probation reporting responsibility), while the Center worker assumes the task of providing a broad range of "reaching out," supportive, protective, and rehabilitative services. Some of this help is very concrete and some is treatment through a relationship, in an effort to get a family back on its feet. Health consultation and guidance in access to the services of other city bureaus (housing, licenses, etc.) are provided by specialists although there is evidence that health ramifications of cases are so extensive as to demand a more complete health plan.

A specialist is also assigned to a community organization program which has very modest objectives. The intent is to provide a bridge between the "below par" families and their neighborhood by involving them in local activities of a constructive sort and exposing them to more stable people. Local resources which they require are developed (for example, exchange of baby sitting). The thought is that this type of community organization support of the casework may help make more normal the environment to which children are exposed and may generally strengthen family life.

Initial response to the program has been encouraging. Of some interest is the fact that this particular three-year experiment is being conducted with some staff on the case-aide level and some who have full graduate social work training. All are experienced. In-service training and psychiatric consultation buttress the practice. A caseload of fifteen families per worker (several members may be seen regularly) is being experimented with; this permits one interview with a family member and two collateral contacts per week. The unit may serve 350-400 families at one time when fully staffed. Case turnover is very slow since extensive service is needed.

One might venture the suggestion that the creation of a neighborhood services center which also encourages local self-help activity and, inevitably, is staffed for intake provides an obvious opportunity to experiment with a broader "open door" citizens' advice and steering service (Ch. IV). This would be a particularly strategic development should the three-year experiment be deemed successful and permanent operation and expansion be decided upon.

Hyde Park Youth Project. Many of the elements already described were also joined together in Chicago's three-year action research program known as the Hyde Park Youth Project. Under the sponsorship of the city's Welfare Council and supported by a foundation grant the project undertook the following:

1. services to individual "behavior problem" children and their families
2. work with street clubs, corner groups, and street gangs
3. help to citizen groups and institutions in an effort to understand and alleviate community conditions considered the source of delinquency

4. coordination of all of this at the neighborhood level
5. research and description designed to make the experience transferable

The project was concentrated in a changing area of approximately two miles which included the University of Chicago. Its own staff was supplemented by a considerable amount of added support by "cooperating" agencies which accepted referrals or concentrated project cases into specific caseloads. The philosophy of reaching out was similar to that of the New York City Youth Board, the St. Paul project, and others. Great emphasis was placed on service integration and on bringing the program to the neighborhood level.

Rigorous measurement of total effectiveness against "controls" was not undertaken, but a variety of studies based on observation, judgments, and ratings were in a positive direction. The project's staff and sponsors urged that Chicago's Commission on Youth Welfare develop the type of program demonstrated in Hyde Park in selective areas of the city and that this long-term endeavor be publicly financed.

Forms of local organization. To some extent, the question of whether and how case finding and accountability should be tied to neighborhood organization must depend on the form which neighberhood organization takes. New York City, for example, is actually organized in many ways and on many levels by local settlements and centers, health councils, school-based councils, block organizations, precinct coordinating councils, neighborhood improvement groups, tenant organizations, parent organizations, social agency councils, the Youth Board, the urban renewal agency, the Commission on Human Bights. The pattern varies from area to area, functions both overlap and leave large gaps, and there are few means to interrelate these many efforts. Several of the larger agencies see themselves as potentially able to coordinate local organization but none actually does. The Community Council lacks resources for direct operations but has served as a clearance and service center for some of the many small, local groups.

It occasionally has been proposed that the schools serve as major local coordinating agencies in the delinquency field a role which would appear possible in relatively small communities. Schools have sometimes also taken initiative in promoting local neighborhood self help efforts, as in the instance of New York where the schoolcommunity relations program has given a rather open-ended charge to its staff of school-community coordinators (teachers with relevant background). They have joined existing local councils or health councils and have represented the perspective of the schools, have created school-centered councils in order to increase and channel community interest in school problems, and have created block organizations. Recently they have done much to facilitate racial integration in schools. The premise is that citizen involvement in school and community problems is constructive and should be promoted. While many of these projects are noteworthy, community interests will ultimately require a somewhat more rational structure. The schools will want to relate their neighborhood activity directly to school programs while other provision is made for the sponsorship of general self-help developments.

Another type of local self-help effort with special focus on delinquency is represented by past efforts under the New York City Youth Board, through its Department of Borough Planning and Community Coordination. Trained community organizers in borough offices served as borough coordinators. They had assistants and clerical help. Within the structure there were actually two types of relatively separate efforts: (*a*) Borough committees, made up of citizens of considerable prestige, served as advisors to the borough office in its relationship to the Youth Board's city-wide planning and coordination machinery. These committees had no administrative functions or prerogatives; the projects they suggested were considered centrally. (*b*) A local community organization program involved staff support and/or service to a variety of kinds of local and neighborhood councils and their youth councils as well as a program of frequent area meetings (in a variety of patterns) to tap neighborhood needs and problems and initiate community actions. These neighborhood councils and area meetings have been the center of substantial activity, the kind of local council organized depending in each instance upon the specific interests and resources of the particular community.

While the Youth Board program is in transition, a very similar pattern of organization and vital activity is found in many other communities under the voluntary auspices of local community planning councils. New York's pattern developed as the consequence of a vacuum left by a Community Council with limited resources. Basic questions are raised about publicly conducted local community organization in the Youth Board pattern since a local neighborhood organization must, perforce, direct its attention to public departments and local government from time to time. Are not staff limited by their status as public employees? Is such a structure not subject to political manipulation at some point in the future? The Youth Board's answer and the response of all those who see local organization as a legitimate public function was that councils which are organized by professional staff (whatever the salary source) are automonous councils. Moreover, public employees have knowledge of and easy access to public departments. Many of the concerns of local councils need to be addressed to such departments.

While the preponderance of opinion would tend at present to oppose publicly operated neighborhood organization, conclusive evidence as to alleged dangers does not exist. Urban renewal, public housing, and public intergroup relations programs are making more public resources available for such work. Some of these funds may be expended through voluntary contracts, as when a local community council accepts a contract associated with urban renewal. Other funds will be expended publicly. Perhaps attention should be directed at providing necessary safeguards for public operation and at ensuring the coordination of local organization in appropriate fashion.

Possible Patterns

As large cities make their decisions about responsibility for local organization and the coordination of such organization, they should simultaneously consider provision for local accountability case integration and its possible ties to self-help and to coordination structures. For the present, several lines of experimentation rather than final decisions would seem to be in order.

1. Creation of public units (such as the Referral Units in New York) as centers of accountability and service integration. These units would organize case conferences. They would require central registers. They should be decentralized.
2. Creation of accountability—service integration units under voluntary auspices, tied to broader local self-help activities, on the pattern of LENA. The LENA area teams are especially suggestive.
3. Continued separation of the three levels of function: service integration and accountability, local self-help, city-wide coordination. This would be the "most natural" pattern and would continue present systems. It would not eliminate the urgent need to rationalize and simplify the relationships of city-wide planning and coordinating bodies to local self-help organizations.
4. Continued experimentation with neighborhood-based treatment services staffed by "intensive" workers, on the pattern of the Interdepartmental Neighborhood Services Center. Experimentation in the use of community organization techniques as an adjunct to the casework should also continue. In addition, it would be useful to experiment with assignment of an "advice bureau" role to such centers. There is need for more rigorous criteria for assignment of cases to special units and intensive workers under this and other patterns of organization.

The leadership in such experimentation and planning must come from planning and coordinating bodies on several levels. Some of the possibilities are discussed in the next chapter.

11

Community Involvement in Corrections of Social Work

Introduction

The layman has been more than content to leave this grubby field to those public servants who care to work in it, and usually those public servants have been equally satisfied to be left alone. There still is, on the part of some correctional administrators, an anxious resistance to the idea of letting lay people take a hand in corrections in any way, but the realization is rapidly spreading that a systematic and genuinely active involvement of lay citizens can help bring to a correctional program the sort of support that the administrators will find wonderfully effective.

Such participation and support can take many forms and will need to be adapted very differently to different programs and even to different geographical locales. In the large cities there can now be found extensive and sophisticated programs for involving lay citizens in corrections work, but small towns and rural areas can do fully as well, depending upon the resourcefulness of the leadership available. Sioux City, Iowa, for example, a city of

91,000, has for several years been quietly supporting a home-grown project known as the Restoration Club, which brings parolees and a number of average townspeople into folksy and useful contact with each other.

The Restoration Club is the beneficiary of no government or foundation grants. It is not accompanied by any research and it is not conceived or directed by any well-trained professional. It is the product of the good will and imagination of the local parole officer who has an eighth-grade education and had many years' experience in police work before taking the parole job with the state.

A major asset of the project is the attack it makes on the problem of social distance between parolees and ordinary citizens. Experience leads us to believe that the apathy of the client about working to improve himself is often related to his sense of hopeless distance from the conventional middle-class community. At the same time the apathy of the community toward the general crime problem is related to the average person's remoteness from and complete lack of acquaintance with any real people in correctional caseloads. The Restoration Club attempts in a natural and informal way to reduce this distance and provide this acquaintance. It works because the parole officer is a man who has the necessary enthusiasm for the idea and the personal qualities needed to enlist the enthusiasm of other people.

The simple idea is that the Restoration Club is an organization in the town to which anyone can belong who is interested in probation or parole. The parole officer is the organizer and general sparkplug of the club and he lets his parolees know that he sees it as important for them to belong. Wives or husbands are also urged to attend. Equally important is the membership of some merchants, lawyers, ministers, and other average citizens who have become interested because they know the parole officer, respect him, and have become infected by his contagious interest in his work. Once a month the club holds a meeting in the local Y.M.C.A. with the parolees, their spouses, and the lay citizens mingling familiarly on a first-name basis. Part of the evening is taken up with a formal business meeting in which there is the usual reading of the minutes, old business, new business, election of officers, etc., etc. It is an opportunity for the parolees to have an experience in the sort of things that average, middle-class people do, and to see themselves with some satisfaction in that role. For the citizen members it is an opportunity to get to know a number of parolees on a friendly man-to-man basis and to discover the problems they have and the human qualities they bring to the solving of them. Between meetings there may be contacts also as a parolee may go to one of the citizen members of the club for some help or advice.

A California experiment in using local businessmen to help probationers find jobs showed the same happy results from getting easy rapport established between the two kinds of people. "The interviewers, most of whom are local businessmen, have many things to offer the probationer. First, as representatives of the community, they can give the probationers a sense of belonging. Where many probationers have felt like 'outsiders looking in,' they now have, perhaps for the first time, someone who represents the middle-class business community expressing enough concern to sit down with and try to help them."

The value of this kind of community involvement is difficult to prove even though any reasonable person would immediately recognize its probable usefulness. As compared with other Iowa parole districts, the area served by the Sioux City parole officer has had a lower rate of parole violations, though this could easily be due to the personal qualities he brings to his job aside from the use of the Restoration Club. But even if not one parole violation has been avoided as a result of the club there is still an important purpose that it serves. We have seen in recent years the general and immense gains made in respect to mental health and the problem of retardation because of a more enlightened public attitude. The most important issue has not been whether a citizen volunteer could go into a hospital and directly contribute to the recovery of a mental patient; the bigger gain has been that the improved understanding of the general public has provided a supportive context in which services to the mentally afflicted could be vastly improved. A better public attitude has produced more funds, both public and private, for research which has led to better treatment. More patients can be released early from hospitals and families today are more willing to take them home again.

Public ignorance of a social problem leads to public rejection of the people who personify that problem. This has been the condition of the public's relationship to crime and delinquency, and until we bring the public into a far more intimate acquaintance with it the new techniques we professionals develop will not achieve their full potential. The parole officer in Sioux City has an idea that should be taken to heart by many correctional programs that could be doing much more to create a community climate that would make their expensive professional operations more effective.

This program takes advantage of a community group, the Jaycees, that is already formed, instead of assembling a new group of individually recruited persons as the Restoration Club does. So the young men who become involved in SCORE are already organized to provide community services; they have some financial resources to contribute; and they are persons who have the advantage of youthful energy now and the prospect of being community leaders in a few years. With regard both to the present and the future this makes them an excellent group to be impregnated with knowledge and concern about delinquency and its treatment.

Of course civic clubs have always sponsored service projects, but the uniqueness of the marriage of SCORE and the Jaycees is that SCORE, by its essential nature, makes it imperative that the members of this organization become personally active in it. Nor is this just to save money by avoiding salary costs; but the active and very real participation of the Jaycee member himself is an integral part of the technique, and he knows that the project needs his personal activity and would not work with hired staff in his place. It is consequently one of the most honest devices for lay involvement that is presently in use.

Public Participation becomes Public Support

In an earlier chapter it has been mentioned that professionals in probation and parole tend to be fearful of any suggestion that they try working with their clients in groups. In view of this it is especially interesting that there is fairly extensive experience with using lay persons from the community to conduct group discussions. Michigan has been doing this since 1954 when lay persons were invited to visit and become acquainted with one of the state's penal camps. Some of the visitors were interested enough to want to help the program in a specific and personal way, so a lay group counseling program gradually evolved. It was given particular impetus when Camp Pugsley, a "probation" camp, was opened in 1956. Camp Pugsley was intended as a forestry camp setting for older teen-age boys who needed to be placed away from their own homes for a period of time but without commitment to the conventional training school. So it was envisaged as an open camp in which boys on probation might live. It would be hard to prove that the character of the institutional experience at Camp Pugsley is substantially different from that at many regular forestry camps to which boys are committed, but the volunteer counselors there give it a link with the community that is unusual in correctional programs.

When the camp was opened in its fairly remote rural area there were no nearby big cities or colleges to provide part-time professionals who could help with the counseling, so some businessmen from the nearest town, Traverse City, were enlisted as group leaders.

Although the plan originally grew out of an effort to acquaint the general public with correctional programs, it has become a means of obtaining actual service from lay people to an extent that once would not have been thought possible. Not only to Camp Pugsley, but to most of the correctional institutions in the state, the volunteers now come weekly and each meets with a group of eight to ten persons for an hour to an hour and one-half. Following the group session the volunteers stay for a session with staff members who review with them the dynamics of what seems to be happening in each group, and give them suggestions on technique. The group leaders are encouraged to work in pairs as coleaders so that the group can be more certain of meeting every week even though one leader may have to be absent.

Obviously, the use of this kind of leadership means that group therapy in the professionally sophisticated sense is not being attempted. But there are plenty of areas of discussion that the lay leader can handle adequately. The inmates in his group will someday return to the outside where they must find a job and in various other ways deal with the business world. The group leader, a man from the outside business world, can talk with them about job finding and job holding, the use of credit, and many other practical matters that will be crucial to the men when they leave, and, of course, these are subjects that the professional staff could not handle so well as these volunteers can. But also, there is real value in the mere fact of the businessman being present in the institution in this way. It reduces the inmate's feeling of rejection and increases his sense of belonging to the outside world if he can become comfortably acquainted with an average, everyday sort of person who comes to the institution week after week for no other reason than his genuine interest in being useful to persons he regards as human beings notwithstanding their incarceration.

Although the volunteer group leader will start his group counseling experience by keeping to safe and practical topics of discussion, it may, or course, lead to discussions in more depth. In some instances strong rapport will develop between the leader and his group, and if he is a perceptive and interested person he will learn much about counseling techniques from his experience and from the training sessions with the staff. So at times the counseling may become more personal and intensive. The experience in Michigan suggests that the feared dangers in this have not been as real as were supposed, and that the process can be kept in adequate control through competent supervision of the volunteers.

Most programs for the use of volunteers are, like this one, promoted and guided by the professionals who staff or administer correctional services. An exception was an unusual program in Toronto which was formed by several lay persons as an effort to help the parolee feel at home in the community. A group of citizens conceived the idea of having an apartment that could serve as a meeting and lounging spot for parolees and for volunteers interested in being useful to them. There was one social worker on the board that was formed to operate the project and an apartment was rented in the same building where she lived so that she could give it her frequent attention. There was no attempt to provide any structured program other than to get word to any parolees being released to that area that they could drop in at the apartment at any time. Interested volunteers were on hand in the evenings to greet any parolees who came and to help them, without pressure, to feel comfortable and to meet new friends. It was conceived as a very concrete way to make the parolee feel wanted and accepted in the community. The volunteers kept the refrigerator stocked and encouraged visitors to have snacks at any time. Some parolees occasionally cooked meals for themselves there, and sometimes a group of them would have a meal or a party. To a certain extent they talked about personal problems with volunteer counselors who were available, though more of the activity was social or concerned with practical personal matters. "One came regularly twice a week one night to play chess with a volunteer and the other to study with his help. One came for Sunday dinner only; some to watch television. Some learned to dance there with the help of enthusiastic volunteers, others to play bridge or scrabble. Some have found it helpful for laundry purposes or for a shower. One boy, without his own home since infancy, cooked all his meals in the flat but slept elsewhere. One man, for whom a sewing machine was rented, altered suits for several others. While it has not been satisfactory to have anyone living in the flat for long periods, since this limits its usefulness to others, it has been invaluable for a few days on release from prison or at times of illness or emergency."

Obviously it becomes important to select with care the volunteers for a project like this and one of the factors in selection that was originally underestimated was age. The majority of the parolees were young men and they showed a better responsiveness to volunteers who were near their own age than to those in the thirty to forty age group. This required selection of men who had the advantage of youth but also perceptiveness and dependably good judgment. The older volunteers continued to be fully useful but in more specialized ways rather than in general socializing.

The cost of operating the apartment varied from about $3000 to $4800 per year, depending on rent levels and the amount of use; and the board seemed to have little difficulty in meeting this expense through solicitation of cash contributions in the community. Though it was felt that the project was highly worth while it was discontinued pending reappraisal after two and one-half years.

The board's concept of the rationale for this type of service is a well expressed bit of philosophy that is not only supportive of the apartment idea, but is also pertinent to the whole process of helping offenders: "Most people involved in crime have lacked a steady home background. They are making mistakes as adults which more fortunate people made as children, but with a striking difference. When children from happy homes make mistakes they learn through the wise handling of the situation by their parents. They also take it for granted, when being disciplined, that the parent is there and will be there, still caring, when the discipline is over. The person involved in crime, however, who did not learn as a child and who, as an adult, is making the same mistakes, is disciplined by a prison sentence and there is often no parent figure there and no continuing relationship with someone who cares and who will help him learn from his mistakes. If this point of view is valid, then the apartment (which in a sense has been a home base giving 'parenting') can provide this continuing relationship."

Volunteer Probation Officers

The Toronto apartment was a fine joint effort by a sincere group of lay people, but often any noteworthy program for involving lay people in direct service to clients grows from and is dependent upon the special personality qualities of just one dynamic person who assumes the leadership. Bureaucracies, too, should deliberately structure and promote plans for community involvement but it is likely instead that any efforts of this kind are originated by an individual, such as the Sioux City parole officer, who develops and sells the program through the force of his own personality.

It is an understandable tendency. The successful marshaling of a number of volunteers to work in an area of social service that is seldom popular calls for a unique combination of personal gifts. Invariably the leaders of such programs are characterized by ebullient personalities, exceptionally wide acquaintance with useful people in the community, and a knack of getting other people to catch the spark of enthusiasm. This indispensable combination of qualities is at once a boon and a bane. It is important to the successful initiation of a good volunteer program, but it can also mean that the program is so much one man's operation that it may not survive that man's departure or even his continued presence. It may be that this is a condition that is more characteristic now in the field's early experience with volunteer programs and will not be so usual a few years later when we learn to teach community organization methods to more people coming into corrections.

One energetic volunteer program has been created by the judge of Michigan's Royal Oak Municipal Court. On being newly elected in 1959 he started what has become perhaps the most noticed probation volunteer program in the country. A particularly gratifying aspect of this program is that it is conducted in a court dealing with misdemeanants.

Generally the courts at the municipal level represent a vast wasteland of inadequate or nearly nonexistent social services and it is especially heartening to find a major effort in this area such as this court is making.

Royal Oak, a city of 90,000 population, is adjacent to Detroit and is predominantly a middle-class suburb. The new judge found that he had no probation service at all attached to his court and only token service, in effect, available from a county probation office. The judge proceeded to enlist the help of some of his friends who were willing to supervise probationers, and gradually a sizable group of volunteer probation officers was developed.

Inevitably such an effort begins to be strangled by its own success. Administrative chores become demanding and it is found that there is a limit to the number of volunteers that can be enlisted successfully without paid professional direction. The court in Royal Oak, faced with these problems, began to acquire some paid staff although it still operates with a surprising minimum of such.

The essential professional staff consists of nine counselors, each of whom works for the court only about five hours per week. They all have specialized training in various disciplines such as social work, psychology, or guidance counseling, and they all have full-time jobs elsewhere. Most of the defendants who are placed on probation are assigned to these counselors, who carry about twenty-five cases each. However, most of the cases so assigned are then also assigned to volunteers. After six years of development there were about seventy-five volunteers active in the program and it was hoped that this number might be doubled eventually. Each volunteer carries only one case at a time and he is not asked to assume the authoritative role that is usually expected of the probation officer. His role is essentially described in the explanation that he is to be a friend to the probationer. He is to inspire the psychological lift that comes to a probationer who sees a person giving without pay of his time and effort only because of his genuine interest. He may be in a good position to provide help with job finding or with some of the other practical problems that present such frustrations to this kind of clientele. The philosophy which the judge himself holds in regard to this may or may not agree with concepts of volunteer court services elsewhere. "The concern which the judge feels for the probationers must be expressed vicariously. To the vast majority of them, the court purposely remains aloof and punitive. To only a very few can the court speak informally and with compassion. Thus, the volunteer can fulfill a role of a friend and companion of the probationer. It would be a fatal error for the court to try to fulfill this role. It is also wrong for the volunteer to act like a judge. You do not have to be judgmental, you do not have to be authoritative, you do not have to be concerned with punishment. You are relieved of this duty. You must be a friend. Let the court represent authority. You represent acceptance, understanding, affection and concern."

For reasons that are not too clearly advanced, the counselor remains active with the case even though he has enlisted a volunteer to work with it. Both the counselor and the volunteer expect to see the probationer at least once a month. The volunteer is to give the counselor a very brief written report monthly about the number of contacts he has had, but there is little demand for any qualitative reporting of his work. There is no concern on the part of the staff about the dual relationship with the clients, and instead it is supposed that the counselor and the volunteer are carrying somewhat different functions that probably could not be combined in one kind of worker. There has been a trend toward letting the volunteer carry more of the case responsibility by himself, but this is not so much because of a changing concept of technique as it is a matter of yielding to the pressures of increasing caseloads.

The Royal Oak volunteer plan is actually seen to operate with pronounced limitations when scrutinized closely. Not only does the volunteer not carry the authoritative character of a probation officer, but he is restricted in the kinds of cases assigned to him. Volunteers are not given cases of persons over twenty-two years of age and they are not given cases of persons who appear to be emotionally disturbed, or who are sex offenders or alcoholics. Such cases are usually assigned to the counselors only.

To handle the growing administrative demands as the volunteer program built up, the court recruited a retired businessman as administrator of the whole effort. Later two other retired men were added, one as an assistant administrator and one as a presentence investigator. These three are paid from the very limited funds now being furnished by the city of Royal Oak, but they are paid only token salaries. All three are receiving their Social Security retirement benefits and they are paid no more than they are allowed to earn without jeopardizing those payments. They have no clearly required number of hours to work but as a simple matter of interest in what they are doing they are working essentially full time. The administrator and his assistant carry their own caseloads, usually taking the kinds of cases, such as alcoholics, that are not assigned to volunteers. As of the end of 1965 there were about 400 active probation cases. With fewer than 100 of these being carried by volunteers it is evident that the various part-time staff members are still carrying the major burden of work.

A somewhat surprising fact is that there is no paid clerical staff for this program. The administrator has a list of women in the community who are available to give occasional help and these are called upon from time to time to work for a day or so. They get to the job at their own expense and put in a full day with no compensation at all.

One feature of this program that has little to do with volunteers except that it too costs the city no money is a Saturday work program in lieu of conviction. The idea is a simple one and seems to have much to commend it even though there has been no systematic evaluation of it. The philosophy has been that young men with no previous criminal record should be spared the handicap of such a record if they can "learn their lesson" without the adjudication process. It is also felt, however, that in avoiding the criminal record there should not also be avoidance of punishment. So the court has used its "work detail" as a way of imposing a penalty without incurring a record of conviction for the defendant. By arrangement with the Royal Oak Department of Public Works, the court may allow a young defendant to work for the city for a prescribed number of Saturdays while his case is continued on the court calendar. The defendant is told that if he wishes to avoid having a record he may elect to do this weekly work, and for this privilege he must pay $48 per month. If he is interested in knowing what his sentence would otherwise be before he decides which alternative to take, he is told that he must decide without any such information or promises. All he can be assured of is that after completing the prescribed weeks of Saturday work he will have to return to court and if his work has been satisfactory his case may then be dismissed with no court record having been put on the books. If he does not choose this course the court then proceeds to dispose of the case in the conventional manner.

In the usual case the Saturday work is specified to extend for a period from one to three months and occasionally more. The defendant must fill out and submit a formal application for the program and pay his $38 in advance each month. These men work in groups of five to seven under the direction of one of the regular city employees. For this extra Saturday work the work supervisor must be paid time and one half, and this is the principal cost being met by the fee charged to each defendant. After some initial apprehension the unions accepted the plan since it does provide extra employment for a few of the Public Works employees and it is understood that the work done by the court groups is work that otherwise would not be done. Much of it is a matter of cleaning up parks or cleaning park equipment. In most cases these men must accept informal probation supervision along with their work assignments. If they fail to show up or do not work satisfactorily each Saturday they may be returned to court and have their assigned Saturdays extended or else have the plan terminated with the court then making a conventional disposition of the case. The work detail plan is conducted as a truly humane way of dealing with certain misdemeanant cases and has the additional appeal of remarkable economy. The combination of the work detail feature and the volunteer sponsors provides Royal Oak with services which are substantially better than those of most courts serving misdemeanant cases. Furthermore, the enlistment of the volunteers has made many important people in the community aware of and closely acquainted with the court processes for misdemeanants, and this is a unique and valuable accomplishment. Certain values demonstrated by the Royal Oak volunteer program have significance for other courts that might be interested in trying this approach to improvement of services:

1. The idea of building a service composed wholly of volunteers is workable as an initial effort but not as a permanent arrangement. The fact is that a volunteer service needs good administration as much as any other kind of organized activity does. It will survive in its initial stages without professional leadership while it enjoys the fresh energies and enthusiasm of the leader and the early recruits; but as it grows in size and settles down for the long haul there must be strong, skilled, full-time executive direction.
2. A volunteer program can get services started where funds for paid services could never be obtained initially. Particularly at the misdemeanant level it is extremely difficult to get appropriations for adequate probation service, but when a sizable and influential segment of the community is enthusiastic about a program, and when the program's value has thus been demonstrated, the public funds begin to be available to put the work on a properly supported basis.
3. The personality of the leader, usually the judge, is critical as an essential factor in the program's success, and it also has critical potential for later handicapping the program severely. Contributing time, energy, and money to the assistance of criminal offenders is not one of the popular causes. It can seldom compete with

causes that involve the poignant problems of distressed children, for instance. So volunteers are not going to respond spontaneously to the cause of the adult criminal. They will respond to the personality of a leader, however, and the initiation of a volunteer probation service will need such potent leadership in its early stages. The risk is that some leaders do not have the ego strength to give up the spotlight when the initial impetus is gained and the time comes for administrative organization to replace the sole reliance on the personality of the leader. If the leader must keep the controls to himself the program becomes administratively hollow as it gets larger, and if the leader departs for any reason, or if his capacity to lead falters, the program can wither.

Fortunately, the Royal Oak program in its fifth year of operation was beginning to show signs of transition to administrative system. It is a program that deserves permanency and though its existence is a tribute to the leadership of the judge, it will survive and continue to honor the vision of its initiator only if it can eventually become independent of his daily and personal direction.

Leadership Essential to Volunteer Program

The Royal Oak experience points up the fact that a volunteer sponsor program has a better chance when confined to a limited geographical area. When it serves one city or county it gains momentum from the context of local civic pride in which it operates, and the leadership can have greater effect as the person who directs the program can make an immediate and continuing impact on the townspeople who volunteer. By contrast, the federal probation system has for several decades used volunteer parole sponsors, but, with the program spread thinly over a whole country, no leader in Washington, no matter how dynamic, can accomplish any truly infectious influence over volunteers so far removed both from him and from each other. And a volunteer program, lacking, as it does, the motive power of the payroll, must draw its fuel from the ever-fresh enthusiasm of close-at-hand leadership.

This does not mean that a volunteer program can work only at a local level. It means only that efforts of similar quality will show a greater effectiveness at the local level than at a state or federal level. One example of a state-wide volunteer program is found in Connecticut where a private agency, the Connecticut Prison Association, operates a program that provides sponsors within the adult correctional system. Though this volunteer program seems to be working well at the state level, Connecticut is a very compact state in which it would be rare for a sponsor to have to travel more than sixty miles from his home to any institution or to any meeting of sponsors.

This sponsor program, being under a private agency, is, of course, administratively separate from the correctional system and is offered to the latter on a cooperative basis. So in this program the sponsor is not carrying official responsibility for cases; this remains in the hands of the institutional staff or the parole officers. The sponsor supplements the regular services by being available as a friend to the client. The casework staff in any institution may ask the Prison Association to assign a sponsor to any inmate who has no family or whose family is failing to meet the person's emotional need. Or a sponsor may be assigned because there are special practical problems in the case with which a lay person might particularly help. In some instances inmates themselves ask for sponsors, and, of course, their motives are not necessarily pure. But the ulterior motive is not important if the inmate is otherwise a person who is in need of the help that a sponsor can give.

The practice is to get the sponsor assigned six or more months in advance of the inmate's parole date, and the sponsor is then expected to visit his parolee once or twice a month. This period of time provides opportunity to develop a good relationship so that when the inmate leaves the prison and is no longer a "captive case" it is hoped that he will, as a parolee, still make use of the sponsor's friendship. Actually, the client's acceptance of a sponsor is fully voluntary and the arrangement can be terminated any time by either party. Although the program has some of the appearance of a "prison visiting" program it is more concerned with preparation for a successful parole experience in which the sponsor will be even more actively involved. A sponsor is assigned only one case at a time.

The Connecticut Prison Association has directed this program through the services of a social worker from another agency who has been employed to give about twelve hours per week of his extra time to the recruitment, training, and supervision of the sponsors, of whom there were about one hundred active at the end of 1965. Recruitment of sponsors is accomplished largely by stirring up interest through speaking engagements, in addition to the usual word-of-mouth advertising that any such program gets.

As an orientation procedure a number of new sponsors are asked to attend at least three meetings which are set at times convenient to them. These include thorough discussion of parole supervision so that the sponsor will not confuse his role with that of the parole officer. In subsequent meetings discussions are led by prison administrators and criminologists. A final meeting is held at one of the institutions. On a continuing basis there are monthly training meetings for all sponsors.

A program of this kind can expect to meet resistance initially, as the institutional administrators cannot be expected to welcome a radical new idea that someone else thought of. Even though a facade of cooperation may exist there will be need for patience in working out the many little ways in which the institutional world and the volunteer program have to adjust to each other. For instance, the institutions, which restrict each inmate to a limited few visits each month, were inclined to count the visit of the sponsor just as any other. For the success of the program it was essential that the sponsor's visit not be charged against the inmate's monthly quota, and this impediment had to be patiently worked on and eliminated.

At the end of four years of experience with the program the Prison Association is satisfied that the program is worthwhile even though a systematic evaluation has not been done. It is felt that its effectiveness lies in producing greater community awareness of correctional programs and consequent greater support for them.

In Perth, Australia, there is an example of the kind of volunteer program that achieves active community involvement under well-organized professional administration. The Child Welfare Department of Western Australia uses volunteers extensively to help with the supervision of delinquents who are placed on probation to that department by children's courts. Unlike Royal Oak, where the selection and instruction of volunteers is quite informal, the Perth volunteers are recruited systematically, screened, and trained elaborately. Much of the recruiting is done by advertisements in various public information media and then questionnaires are sent to all persons who respond. Detailed information is requested about their life history, education, and work record. An applicant's work history is relied upon as a major indicator of his stability.

Invariably the use of public information media for recruitment of volunteers produces far more responses than are usable, for this brings out persons whose reasons for volunteering are superficial, or suspect in various other ways. A quick and sweeping elimination process is therefore the first step. In one recruiting campaign in Perth 420 persons initially applied. Through scrutiny of the questionnaires these were screened to 80, and subsequent interviews left just 20 persons who were usable. As items of objective criteria it is required that volunteers:

(1) have at least a high school education;

(2) preferably be married -no unmarried man over age 28 is accepted;

(3) be in good health;

(4) show good job stability;

(5) have some hobby interests;

(6) not be involved in too many extra activities.

In the interviews some more subjective criteria can be checked, such as kind and degree of motivation and balanced, healthy quality of religious interest. The volunteer must be willing and available to attend training sessions that are scheduled for twice a week, these usually being held in the mornings for women and in the evenings for the men. Staff persons from the Education Department of Western Australia either give lectures themselves or engage other persons locally to speak to the volunteers on subjects such as child welfare laws, development and use of case histories, preparation of reports, child psychology, causes and treatment of delinquency, human development and behavior. Each session is three hours, with one and one-half hours devoted to each of two subjects.

These training sessions have been supplemented by Saturday afternoon visits to training schools where the volunteers have a chance to help staff members handle groups of boys or girls. These visits provide actual contacts with children; they give more meaning to the content of the training sessions and they keep the volunteers content to stay with the long period of training. Even so, the original six-month period of training was found to be too long, for the volunteers were likely to fret about the delay in getting into actual case handling. The general practice has been to give the volunteers cases at the point that probation supervision begins; they do not do the initial investigations. Originally they were given the more tractable cases, but this was unsatisfactory, for they were bored with them. Consequently, the volunteers now receive more difficult cases, and sometimes even those that need intensive help. They may be assigned up to three cases each. Furthermore, the volunteer carries the case responsibility in a true sense; it is not also carried by one of the professionals.

As would be expected, the Child Welfare Department finds that such a program must include the three basic essentials of careful selection, thorough initial training, continuing supervision. Their sixty or so volunteers are under the full-time supervision of one staff member who allocates cases, reviews case records, and discusses them with the individual volunteers. There are also monthly meetings in which the volunteers as a group can talk over case management and techniques with the staff supervisor.

Ordinarily a volunteer program is assumed to mean that the workers receive no pay at all, but in the Perth experience it has been found desirable to make a small payment that will at least reimburse the volunteers for any of their out-of-pocket expenses. So each is paid about $45 (American) annually, and whether or not this meets the worker's expenses, the department feels that this gives it a much clearer right to require standards of performance and to terminate the service of any unsatisfactory person. There is no assumption that this is a cheap program. It does provide probation supervision at less expense than a fully staffed service, but the cost is not negligible. The selection process includes advertising costs and a considerable amount of expensive staff time in the interviewing and psychological testing. Though the Education Department organizes the training course, it bills the Child Welfare Department for the lecturers' fees. In general, that department is well pleased with the plan as being an economy measure to a limited extent and as being constantly valuable for public relations purposes.

Even though the correctional field seems to have an increasing interest in this use of volunteers, there is some ambivalence about it, with signs that it is even a declining practice in certain areas. Some European observers are tending to give less encouragement to volunteer programs as more people are available who have professional training and as more specialized techniques are developed.

Japan has used volunteers extensively and still is quite reliant on them, but officials there note that with the increased urbanization people have less personal interest in others and the lay citizens consequently do not respond as well to the volunteer probation work. Nevertheless, Japan does still make copious use of volunteers. The Japanese probation system recruits and selects them through its regional Probation-Parole Supervision Offices, where selection committees screen the volunteers for financial stability, motivation, and good standing in the community. The volunteers are formally appointed to two-year terms by the minister of justice and while they receive no salary they are reimbursed for any expenses and are compensated for any accidents incurred in this service. The Japanese government estimates that about 47,000 volunteers were active in adult probation work in 1965 and in regard to their usefulness they make the reasonable comment that "Probation is a treatment method to rehabilitate an offender in his community. Therefore, the understanding and cooperation of the community is indispensable."

For volunteer services to juveniles there is a national coordinating council in Japan that fosters 730 Women's Rehabilitation Aid associations. These are less concerned with direct supervision of individual children than with supplementing state services by operating shelters, supplying medical care, clothing, or money, or arranging employment.

Sweden is another country that has made the use of volunteers an integral part of its probation and parole services. In a major address at the Third United Nations Congress on the Prevention of Crime and the Treatment of Offenders, held in Stockholm in 1965, Sweden's minister of justice spoke of the many advantages of a volunteer program, including its value for good public relations, and mentioned that sometimes budgets for the Swedish correctional system have moved more successfully through Parliament because of the extra sympathetic support of members who themselves have served as volunteers in corrections. This suggests the wide range of kinds of people who respond to the volunteer program in Sweden, and the fact that this service has status enough to attract volunteers of substantial position and ability. Ordinarily a staff person does the pre sentence investigation for the court, and if probation is granted the defendant is placed under supervision of a volunteer already selected by the staff person who investigated. Swedish volunteers are paid a token amount very much the same as the rate used in Perth. And like the experience in Japan, Sweden finds that volunteer probation officers in small towns and rural areas function well enough, but the impersonal bustle of the big cities tends to defeat the interest and the effectiveness of the volunteers.

England has traditionally used volunteers for prison visiting, and in one program, operated out of the Blackfriars Settlement in London, extensive training is given to volunteers, including regular visits to the prisons being served by the aftercare program. The professional staff person in charge of the volunteer program is thus given an opportunity to observe the way the volunteers handle themselves in relation to the prisoners. This provides a testing for the volunteers and gives them an opportunity to begin their acquaintance with the correctional program and the process of helping its clients. No pay is given these volunteers.

In Denmark, where probation and parole services are provided on a national basis by the Danish Welfare Society, the use of volunteers is a well-established practice. Over 800 volunteers are actively supervising probationers or parolees. A few of these carry as many as twenty or thirty cases each, but the majority of the volunteers have only from one to five cases. The practice is for all cases to be the responsibility of the regular professional workers who themselves supervise the more difficult ones, while about three-fourths of the cases on each caseload are assigned to volunteers. These volunteers come from a great variety of professions and are paid a fee of about $3.00 per month for each case they carry. They must provide the professional staff with regular case progress reports and are expected to call on the professional worker for assistance when problems of more than a routine nature arise.

The Committee

There are some potential volunteers who may have little inclination for or skill in working directly with cases, but who can be useful to courts or correctional agencies in other ways. Offering such people committee membership may sound like an unexciting substitute for work with cases, but if it is cleverly conceived, committee work can be both effective and satisfying.

One of the better known practices of this kind is the appointment of an advisory committee, to a juvenile court, for instance. It is usually expected that the committee will advise mainly in respect to the probation services, and it is generally assumed that the creation of such a committee is, categorically, a good thing to do. But it should be recognized that although it can indeed be a good thing to do, it can also be a mistake. Some of the factors which determine which it will be are clear-cut and objective, while others are very subtle.

The subjective feelings with which a judge approaches the concept of an advisory committee may lead him to reject the idea if he is troubled by a sense of insecurity, or he may be led to try the idea for the same reason. That is, his reaction may be that he needs no committee to tell him what to do, for he is the judge and he is the boss. Or he may decide that a committee of townspeople who become, in effect, his claque, will reflect his eminence, and so he looks for ego support in the committee device.

The person with the more secure personality will recognize that an advisory committee is never in a position to usurp or interfere with a judge's prerogatives unless the judge himself is weak and indecisive. He also recognizes that if sensible, responsible townspeople are put on such a committee any action they take will ordinarily be for the same eventual goal that the judge has, the improvement of his court and its services. He will also recognize that these goals are not jeopardized by the possibility of occasional disagreement between him and his committee. If the committee is going to have the prestige to be really helpful to the court it will have to have strong individuals on it, and an inherent feature of such strength is independent thinking.

So it is fairly obvious that the first important factor in the success of an advisory committee is the nature of the motivation of the judge or administrator who chooses to appoint such a committee. It would be too naive to assume that advisory committees are always appointed by people who are truly looking for advice. The appointing authority may see a committee as a practical political move in view of coming elections, for instance. Sometimes the committee is not expected to advise the court on what to do, but only to agree with something the court has already decided on and to help accomplish it. This in itself can be either a worthy or an unworthy motive. If a judge has a specific and subjective goal in mind and asks only that a committee echo his demands for what he has already decided upon, this is not in accord with the usual advisory committee concept and it may lead to disillusionment all around. This does not mean that a citizens' committee must in all instances formulate its own concept of its goal. Sometimes, as a result of a professionally done survey, or because of some amply self-evident condition, there is, properly enough, a predetermined action to be accomplished. In such a case a committee may be appointed and, with no loss of integrity, it may set out to accomplish a goal that has already been objectively determined. But this would be an action committee more than an advisory committee, and if the purpose for its creation has been honestly conceived and honestly presented to the committee it is a fully valid procedure.

However, for a truly advisory committee it is ordinarily essential to give the committee an honest charge to look at a proposal and to recommend or act according to the committee's own independent judgment. Not incompatible with this concept is the situation in which a committee is asked to help accomplish a goal stated in general terms, leaving the committee to determine and act on the specifics. As an illustration of this, one juvenile court judge was handicapped by having to work in quarters which were the shabby and cramped remnants of some city owned facilities provided by the uninterested city council. The judge was unable to get any attention for his protests about the gross unsuitability of the space and nothing was accomplished until he appointed an advisory committee to the court. This is the kind of situation that calls for sensitive handling on the part of the judge, who should have good awareness of his own motives. In this instance the judge did have in mind a general goal for his new committee: to help him improve the working conditions of his court; but he did not dictate the specific form of that goal. He pointed the committee's attention toward the entirely self-evident problem in the court's physical setting and let the committee take it from there in its own way. It was left to the committee members to determine through their own study what was needed and what would be the best way to get it. The result was that these lay people presented to the city council not just a demand, but a plan. They had located a building, developed a design for remodeling, and mustered some broader community interest in and support for the idea. In due time the court moved into its new quarters, an abandoned fire department station which was completely rebuilt to provide probation offices, waiting rooms, courtroom, and judge's chambers, all of it modern, attractively impressive, and spacious. The committee had been used honestly and skillfully, and it did a fine job for the court.

An example of the action type of committee also comes from a juvenile court setting. In one major city there never had been a detention facility for juveniles and the necessity of jailing the children along with adult prisoners was a situation that was clearly bad. It was not necessary to have an advisory committee decide whether or not there should be a separate facility. It was only a matter of having a committee that would get action. To make the matter still more certain, consultants from the National Council on Crime and Delinquency had studied the situation, had recommended strongly that a detention facility be built, and had determined the size it should be. The facility still was not being built because the county board of supervisors was not feeling the necessary urgency about spending public moneys in this way.

At the court's request, the Community Welfare Council appointed a committee that was solely for the purpose of getting this one job done. Fifteen persons were recruited for the committee, and not one of them had any professional connection with social work, courts, or corrections. If they had any real knowledge of the operation of a juvenile court or detention facility it was only incidental. But this reflected the skill in their selection, for their job was not to appraise the need for or the use of such a facility; that had already been done by the professionals. Their job was to mobilize the power structure of the community to get the necessary final action taken. To this end, the members appointed were representatives of several of the biggest businesses in the city, and representatives of various organizations that were prestigious and influential. And in most instances these representatives were not just lower echelon personnel; they were the very top managers.

This central committee, used for its power and prestige, was then given the technical help it needed by the appointment of an auxiliary committee of experts, who became, in effect, an advisory committee to the action committee. Members on this subsidiary committee were social workers, police, agency executives and persons working in various capacities with delinquents. They met with the main committee but sat apart and had no voice or vote in the main committee's deliberations. They were there only to make their knowledge available to the committee members as needed.

The action committee designated subcommittees to explore such questions as the type of building needed, the site to be used, and the best method of financing. It took the committee a relatively short time to formulate its recommendations and to present them with effective publicity to the governing body of the county. When resulting action was taken by that body to go ahead with the project the committee was through.

Even if there is the soundest kind of motivation in the appointment of a committee it may be either a disappointing venture or a successful one depending upon the kind of people appointed and the kinds of assignments they are given. Too often, for instance, such committees have been put to work on a permanent basis when there is not a permanent job to be done; and this is one of the most common and more serious errors. If an advisory committee is intended to be permanent it requires work, imagination, and perseverance on the part of the judge or administrator whom it serves. It also requires skill and devotion on the part of some staff person who works with the committee. It can be a fatal error to suppose that an advisory committee can be appointed and sustained without any continuing investment of staff time. There is both professional and clerical time involved in feeding information and ideas to the committee members, in arranging fact-finding experiences for them, in arranging meetings, keeping records, and dealing with the endless questions and individual problems that a really active and useful committee can produce. The amount of work and the requirements of diplomacy that are involved are nicely suggested by a member of one such committee, writing about the staff members who "either know the answers to our questions or can get them posthaste at the other end of the phone, as well as by mail. Besides, they have genuine political acumen; and they do not have the holier-than-thou attitude that is often encountered in 'trained' social workers who do not realize that most of us are 'trained' in something if only life!"

A committee does not live and function without something to do, and an agency is wise not to set up a continuing advisory committee unless it has a supply of tasks worthy of the committee's attention, and is prepared to provide the staff time necessary. Otherwise, it is likely that after an initial experience of dealing with some specific tasks, and perhaps quite successfully, the committee is called together less and less often, then finally not at all. Or if the agency loses interest and offers less and less real work for the committee to do, the members make little effort to get to the meetings and the committee is then, for all practical purposes, dead. It may never really be recognized as defunct, but is just allowed to wither and cease functioning without any act of termination. This can hardly be called tragic, but it does leave those committee members less satisfied with their experience and so not quite such boosters for the court or agency as they should be.

It is for this reason that there is much argument in favor of the ad hoc committee such as the one described above that gave the final push to the detention home construction. A committee that is formed to give its attention to just one specific problem offers the advantage that committee members can be selected who are peculiarly appropriate to the task at hand; and it is possible to offer them definite release from the committee work as soon as the specific task is completed. This limited term of service also means that it is possible to get particularly high caliber and busy people who would not be able to accept membership on a continuing or permanent committee.

It is fairly natural for an agency to think of appointing an advisory committee and putting on it the educators, clergymen, social workers and others who have the kind of knowledge and concern that is related to the function of the agency they are to advise. This is fully appropriate if the committee is truly to be used for generating professional advice and guidance on some aspect of the agency's program. But when such people are appointed to a committee that may be more of a multi-purpose committee, such as a permanent advisory committee is certain to be, it will be found that the experts have limited usefulness on the committee and may even be a handicap to it.

In one instance a group of high school and junior high principals was deeply concerned about the need for a new facility for delinquent girls and was offering its services to the juvenile court to help get authorization for such a facility. When a study and action committee was appointed to promote the needed facility the principals were disappointed that their proffered help was not being used; no representative from their group was on the committee. The simple reason was that a high school principal, like any other professional who is working close to the problem, is not a suitable person for a committee that eventually has to influence the body of elected officials who must appropriate the money if the hoped-for project is accomplished. The politicians are superbly practical by necessity; they know that such a professional pays an infinitesimal fraction of the taxes that would be involved and he influences no block of votes. A labor union representative might know much less than the school principal about the character of the problem being considered, but if he is briefed on the proposed project and is sold on it he is a far more effective committee member, for his good will is going to be of importance to the members of the appropriating body at the next election. In the same way, the president of a large business concern will be of substantial influence because he represents an important part of the tax source from which the proposed project will be financed.

It becomes obvious that a major part of the art in using citizen committees lies in the sensitive selection of the right people for the right job, and then in giving them only that job to do. Persons of prestige and power in the community are usually gracious about helping an important social service project by accepting a committee assignment. But such people cannot give their time for an indefinite period and they will not be happy or useful if asked to do a job which is beneath their level of ability. This is not snobbery but only the fully practical concern of good use of their time. They are busy people, making important contributions in the business world, and their time should not be drawn upon for committee work unless it is for a task that challenges their capacity and offers them a chance to apply their talents and weight appropriately.

The most noteworthy application of the power-packed study and action committee in corrections is the Citizen Action Program which was developed by the National Probation and Parole Association (now National Council on Crime and Delinquency) in 1955 with an initial grant of $600,000 from the Ford Foundation. The technique was developed in eight states where the program was initially tried and by the end of 1965 there were eighteen states using this device to upgrade correctional services. Some highly satisfying progress had been made in most instances.

The typical procedure is to provide first a professional staff person, and a secretary, and then to start searching for names of suitable council members. This leads to an extremely large number of interviews as suggestions are solicited in conversations with many knowledgeable people. Council members are sought from among the highest level business executives in the state, from presidents of the largest and most influential organizations, or from among outstanding professional persons. As suitable names are acquired and screened the staff proceeds to get appointments to talk with these prospects. This is a crucial step, for it may be almost as much a matter of talking the prospect out of the assignment as of talking him into it. That is, he must be given the sales pitch that will get him interested, but at the same time he must not be oversold. In fact, he must be faced very realistically with the realities of the task, principally the amount of work involved. While it is hoped that he will join the council, he should not agree to do so, nor would he be accepted, if he cannot be a working member. Big-name people are sought for council membership, but no one is wanted just for his name. Each member must be willing and able to get to most of the monthly meetings and must be ready in other ways to help prepare the council's reports or carry its influence to the public or to the legislature. With candid, hardheaded recruitment like this the states have usually been able to put together councils that have great potential for accomplishing concrete improvement in correctional programs. Council members receive no compensation for their time and they pay their own expenses to meetings. This is part of the quality of objectivity and independence that characterizes these councils and that contributes so much to their effectiveness.

In keeping with the initial premise of a truly working council, the members are expected to work from their own knowledge of correctional problems rather than just supporting the views fed to them by professionals. So the first months in the experience of any citizen council are occupied in studying the whole correctional system in the state. In many states council members have visited jails, been locked in cells in reformatories, eaten in prison mess halls, been assigned one by one to spend a day with a parole agent, observed parole board hearings, toured juvenile training schools. From these observations they have been able to assign priorities to the needs of correctional services and have worked energetically to bring to the public more information than it has ever had before about the problems of the state correctional programs. The councils also work directly to influence legislation, but usually they find it essential first to educate the general public, for increased budgets and improved programs can best be accomplished when public concern is aroused.

Some of the significant programs discussed in the preceding chapters were created as a result of Citizen Action Programs. Altogether they have provided a splendid demonstration of the concept that not only can a lay person be highly effective in a professional field, but also the top-level business executive will give his attention, time, and energy to a volunteer effort like this if the effort is intelligently organized and if the issues present a challenge commensurate with the level of executive time and ability being expended.

For the professional agency executive who seeks to influence community attitudes, strengthen correctional resources, or just get larger budgets for his own operation, the skillful enlistment of lay citizens can be a vital factor in progress toward such goals. But he will also need a store of patience, for the public moves ponderously even though the man with the problem yearns for action now. This is true despite the fact that sociological changes are more rapid and profound with every year that comes. We can exploit the climate of change, and should do so whenever it will serve the purpose of local needs, but we must be prepared also for stubborn resistance to change. One author has commented that "Inertia, no less than social change, is a basic characteristic of human society."

This is very true, but the persistence of the inertia we meet will be cracked most effectively by those professionals who learn how to enlist lay persons who, though they start with no technical knowledge of our work, have the energy and influence to generate fresh enthusiasm and perspective. To an increasing extent the significant progress to be made in probation and parole will be accomplished by this combined effort of the interested citizen and the correctional administrator who brings to his job a measure of what we might call practical imagination.

12

Skeleton Guides in the Social Study Case

Introduction

Comprehensive outlines for study of individual cases have been developed in recent years by child guidance clinics, family welfare workers, sociologists, probation departments, and others, as an aid in bringing into focus the essential data to be secured in the study of an individual or family group. A case history outline should be regarded only as an aid to the worker in visualizing the scope of data which are essential in a comprehensive study of a case. These guides should offer an orientation in the subject rather than in the technique. It is needless to stress again that the study in the hands of a competent worker will not become mechanistic or stereotyped if he uses it as a suggestive starting point and as an aid in rounding out the total picture of the case.

It is the experience of executives and of case workers that in many specific instances the worker, with a vision of the objectives to be obtained, develops leads which carry him farther than anything that an outline can suggest abstractly. Outlines are most useful when digested and rearranged by each worker to suit his particular needs. It goes without saying that no outline form should ever be taken into the home of a family, nor should it be in evidence during an office interview.

One of the more comprehensive outlines for the social history is to be found in the volume by Porter R. Lee and Marion E. Kenworthy, Mental Hygiene and Social Work. These authors too desire not only "the concrete factors of family and hereditary forebears but the dynamic and more potent influences of attitudes, interests, prejudices, and personality patterns of all of the family members including the first, second, and third generations."

From a sociological standpoint Clifford Shaw, head of the Department of Research Sociology, Institute for Juvenile Research, Chicago, has demonstrated a successful approach to securing the history of behavior difficulties. His illuminating volume, The Jack-Roller, is a life record of a delinquent's own account of his experiences written as an autobiography and supplemented by a series of searching interviews. Shaw stresses "(1) the point of view of the delinquent; (2) the social and cultural situation to which the delinquent is responsible; and (3) the sequence of past experiences and situations in the life of the delinquent."

History taking in dealing with delinquent and problem children has its beginnings in the work of Drs. William Healy and Augusta Bronner, pioneers in case studies and individualized treatment of children in trouble. A recent outline used by the Judge Baker Foundation Clinic in gathering family and personal history of the offender appears in the volume published by Sheldon and Eleanor Glueck, One Thousand Juvenile Delinquents. This stresses detailed knowledge of the problem; causes for misbehavior from the standpoint of the child, parents, and investigator; the circumstances of the arrest; standards of home and family life, social and cultural background of parents; antenatal, natal, and postnatal history of offender; his habits of eating, sleeping, drinking, smoking, masturbation, enuresis, nervous habits; interests and personality traits as shown at school, work, home, with companions, changes in personality, reactions to various phases of social and physical environment; family and neighborhood resources. Each child studied at the clinic is given a thorough physical examination, several psychological and psychometric tests, as well as a psychiatric examination.

Healy has long ago pointed out that, since nothing happens without a cause, motivation for conduct which is frequently hidden and difficult to unearth must be carefully explored; and since each child is essentially different he must be understood in terms of his own social, mental, and physical surroundings. Such a study requires careful accumulation of a great deal of detailed information.

The White House Conference on Child Health and Protection further stresses the exploration of the basic needs. The old time investigation comprising an inventory of the household and its inhabitants has given way to a study of the nature of relationships of members, their respective feelings and attitudes, the needs of each, their visions, cravings. "To know the delinquent we must know his family, not because it surrounds him, but because the lives of its members germinate, color, and shape his life."

Hans Weiss, in a stimulating article, "The Social Worker's Technique and Probation," concludes that after many sources of information have been tapped the inquiry "should give a comprehensive picture of the individual's own world: of his personality, his relationship to others, his immediate environment as seen in relation to him. We should know something of his likes and dislikes, his desires and hopes, his disappointments and failures, his ambitions and plans, his shortcomings and disabilities, his qualities and assets, and above all, the possibilities of getting him on his feet."

At times views are expressed that social case histories are given an overrated importance, that much of the data gathered are not actually used. One wonders what is meant by "used"? Can we understand the total problematic situation without sufficient data? Is it possible to forecast in advance when a situation will be understood with only a minimum of data at hand? The view is also expressed that if we accept the fact that "in the dynamics of human relationships, as worker or therapist to patient, inheres whatever is of value and of harm for the other person, we no longer need vast quantities of data." This approach assumes that social therapy is based primarily upon a relationship technique. Therapy is too complex a process to be based on one single factor. A satisfactory relationship is indispensable in any form of treatment but it cannot assume the sole role. Clients in trouble, once they discover that the therapist accepts just them, will deliberately seek his advice, relying upon his dispassionate attitude and his experience and training. Whether the task of the therapist is to give advice directly or to reinterpret the situation to the clients, he cannot do so adequately unless he is thoroughly acquainted with their personality traits, their ability to utilize advice, to reconstruct the past, to "reexperience the feeling of past events that have been inadequately assimilated and to which have been attached the anxiety and fear which have created the turmoil of the present." It would follow that a study of comprehensive social history assumes that, while it is possible to establish a satisfactory relationship with the client without becoming thoroughly acquainted with his life, it is doubtful whether such a relation will be of lasting value; furthermore that it is not possible to redirect problematic behavior without an intimate knowledge of a person's life and that it is impossible to release fear and anxiety without sufficient facts as to their origin, their surrounding circumstances, their relation to the life complexes and social setting in which the individual lives and their relation to the personal and social traits of the individual.

A Guide from the Probation Officer's Point of View.—Ralph Hall Ferris, formerly of the Domestic Relations Division, Recorder's Court, Detroit, Michigan, says that in general an adequate social examination will be concerned with the following groups of items, each being developed according to need:

a. The offender's family history, with names, dates, residences, occupations, finances, diseases, etc., of siblings, parents, parental siblings, and grandparents, as well as reactions to them, and reasons for leaving home;

b. Schooling, including age of commencement and termination, studies enjoyed, reactions to school and teachers, reasons for leaving school, and desire for further schooling;

c. Account of offender's migrations, various environments, past and present associates and reactions to them;

d. Work record, including names of employers, dates of employment, reasons for change of employment, kind of employment preferred, wages, nature and periods of unemployment, and ambitions relative to employment;

e. Economic status, past and present, covering income and expenditures, debts, reasons therefore, and plans for liquidation, property (house, car, investments, luxuries), and insurance, and attitude toward these matters;

f. Health, including history of diseases, physical condition, past and present, physical disabilities, and attitude toward health matters such as personal hygiene, etc.;

g. Moral and recreational habits, such as use of tobacco, alcohol, of drugs, resort to prostitutes, homosexual or autoerotic practices, reading, including the type and number of books and magazines read, resort to poolrooms, dancing, bowling, theater attendance, and outdoor sports whether social as baseball or solitary as hunting;

h. Affiliations, fraternal and religious, and attitude toward them;

i. Marital history, if any, and reactions to sex life, marriage and children;

j. Delinquency record, juvenile and adult, and reactions to the same; and

k. In general ambitions, tendencies, aptitudes, hobbies, dislikes and obsessions, as the offender sees them.

It is significant to observe that Mr. Ferris lays considerable stress on reactions, interests, ambitions, attitudes, likes, and dislikes of the offender as well as reasons for his actions. He adds that "the social examination should contain an exact description of the offender's behavior during the interview and his reactions to the interviewer, the interview and the subject matter of the interview any peculiar phraseology or action." Such practice would be highly desirable were it not for the concern of many agencies that "space is too scarce" and that "records cannot become voluminous." No thoroughgoing studies have been made between the relation of inadequate recording and consequent inability to diagnose the case properly and the degree of recidivism. There are students who agree that some attempts to economize on the recording of a single interview tend in many instances to prolong the contacts with a client and thus no space is saved in the long run. Space as such should be of least concern in the record of adjustment of a human life. However, since no studies have been made, it may be argued that the above assumptions are little more than speculation. There are points on both sides.

A Guide from the Sociologist's Point of View.— E. S. Bogardus prepared a social history outline for the study of a problem boy which is equally applicable to a delinquent boy or girl. He limits the social history to conflicts and accommodations within home, school, neighborhood, church, play and occupational activities, in terms of the resulting problems as the individual sees them. This outline is from the standpoint of a social psychologist taking into account one's social world, social relations, and the role one conceives himself to play in a given social group.

1. Heritage.— What was the boy's social heritage? What were the traditions of his parents? Their attitude toward religion, toward racial and national values, toward education, toward industrial activities? What is their type of family life? What was their equipment for training boys, including their handicaps and advantages? What difficulties occurred within the

home in matters of adjustments between parents? What were their hopes and ambitions for this particular boy? What brothers and sisters did he have? What have been their outstanding traits? Their influences upon his life? What musical and artistic tendencies has he? His age, birthplace, race?

2. Early Life.— What was the nature of his earliest distinctive tendencies? The trend of his earliest interests and habits? His earliest conflicts? The first handicaps that he brought on himself? What were the earliest fears that he can recall, and his earliest joys? How were his earliest conflicts settled?
3. Social Contacts.— Which parent seems to understand him best? Which parent is he most like? What routine work does he do at home? How far do he and his parents associate in their amusements? If he lost his parents what would he do? What books, outside of schoolbooks, did he read? What magazines? What did he read that he liked most?

Who are his chums? Describe their likes and dislikes. Has any of them gotten into trouble and in what ways? Does he bring his "pals" into the home?

How often does he go to motion picture shows, to public dance halls, and to pool halls?

What girls has he known well? How intimate has been his friendship with them? What are his parents' attitudes toward the one or ones he likes best? What are their likes and dislikes? What does he do in his leisure time; how much leisure does he have and during what hours of the day? With whom does he come in contact at these times?

To what organizations, such as a boys' club, a gang, a church club or class has he belonged? What was the nature of the activities of each? Has he been a member of a Sunday School, of the Boy Scouts, of any similar organizations? Has he dropped out of any of these? Under what conditions? Does he smoke cigarettes? Why? or why not? His parents' attitude?

In what ways does he get along well at school? In what ways poorly? His parents' attitudes?

Has he been a leader in any of these clubs? In what ways did he lead well, and in what did he fail, and for what reasons?

4. Conflicts and Accommodations.— What difficulties has he had in the home, with either parent, of long-standing nature? What conflicts has he had with other members of his family and what has happened?

What outstanding difficulties has he had with his playmates? Any fights he remembers. Have him describe the history of any boyhood feud that he was a part of for any length of time.

Did he have any difficulties with the older people of the neighborhood? With the parents of other children?

Under what conditions does he remember most distinctly being punished? What activities does he seem to conceal from his parents? Is the home atmosphere one of peace or conflict? Of economic pressure?

What conflicts has he had at school, with any teachers, principals, truant officers, or with other boys at school?

Did he run away ever from home or school? Why and what were the reactions?

Has he a car? Any problems? His parents' attitude toward his use of it? What picture shows does he like best? Least?

Did he ever "swipe" anything, and if so under what conditions? Did he ever get "pinched"? His experiences in this connection? Ever been in jail? Experiences? Ever been on probation, either in school or in connection with the Juvenile Court? Experiences?

Has there been any breaking off of love affairs? What daydreams has he had? Has he had any troublesome dreams? Has he ever had imaginary companions?

In what ways does he feel that he has been treated most unjustly? Has he ever felt hampered, and wanted to upset things generally? What important questions does he decide for himself? How does he get increased independence?

In what ways does he feel that he has been most misunderstood? By whom, and under what conditions? Any disagreements with his parents regarding money, clothes, the automobile, girls, chums? What things does he ask permission to do?

Under what conditions has he experienced "pangs of conscience"? Does he remember feeling distinctly sorry for something?

Has he ever had any religious problems or conflicts or "been converted"?

Has he ever worked for wages? Has he ever wanted money and couldn't get it? Has he ever saved and why? What kinds of work does he like best, and what least?

5. Philosophy of Life.— What was his first or earliest choice of a vocation, and what changes have occurred along this line? What are his greatest ambitions today? His occupational expectations? Does he have any money-making ambitions, and what are his reactions to making money and becoming rich? What is his life aim? Do parents agree with it?

What are his religious beliefs? Does he believe that one political party is better than another? Does he believe in racial equality? Is he interested in more than one race or nation? What does he consider to be the leading public questions of the day? Does he have any ideas of social responsibility and social service and if so, how did they arise?

If he could have one wish above all others granted, what would it be?

While Bogardus seems to lay stress on the child's account of his life experiences from his particular point of view, the data included in the outline take into account the experiences, attitudes, and reactions of other members of the group of which the child is a part. This outline omits specific discussion of health, housing, social-economic, family status, etc., which is included in the previous outline worked out by Ferris. Obviously, the worker could profit by a combination of the two points of view and sets of data, which are highly complementary to each other.

A Guide from the Mental Hygienist's Point of View.— The Louisville Mental Hygiene Clinic (Dr. Spafford Ackerly,

Medical Director) recommends the use of the following outline for the complete study of a child referred by another agency. Attention is called to the fact that complete data are required for a non delinquent member of the family as well as the delinquent.

Outline of Family Tree

Date:

Names, ages. If dead, state same and give age at time of death. Indicate father, mother, delinquent and non delinquent by capitals underlined.

Example

Paternal Grandparents Maternal Grandparents

_____Died 61, _____80 ______70,_________62.

Paternal Uncles and Aunts Maternal Aunts and Uncles.

________died 24________ 34 ________31 ________ 38

Father: Thomas Dole, 36 Mother: Mary Brown Dole, 36 Siblings — 15. Delinquency: John Dole, 13-6. Non delinquency: Joseph Dole, 12. Miscarriage. Names of others in family, relatives, boarders, etc. Part II Identification Data Date:____ Referral date:_____ By whom referred and how delinquent came to be referred: Present court action: Date of court appearance:____ Name of judge presiding and persons present. Brief statement of what took place in courtroom. Final disposition, that is, dismissal, parole, suspended sentence, or commitment. Date of termination of parole or suspended sentence. Name of probation officer and person or persons to whom delinquent is expected to report.____ Where?____ How often?____ Past court action of delinquent and other members of the family. If reports to court or other agencies are requested, dates and nature of reports. Delinquent's reaction to court appearance. Attitude of delinquent and his parents toward the clinic. Why case was accepted. State criteria of acceptance.

Part III Work of Other Agencies

Part IV Sources of Information

Date:____ Description of informants.____ Nature of their interest in the case. Estimation of the reliability of data given, with special emphasis upon personal biases. Number of interviews with each informant. List future sources for investigation Where inconsistent factual material has been obtained or observed from one or more sources state sources or refer to page in the record where source can be verified. Throughout the summary the sources of important data should be stated preferably by a mere name in brackets.

Part V Problems Date:____

Only problems of immediate family will be dealt with in this section; cf. under Personal Histories for problems of grandparents, aunts, uncles, etc.

i. Delinquent: Delinquency as reported by others; as reported by himself. Personality and behavior problems other than delinquencies. Other problems, physical, etc.
ii. Nondelinquent: Personality and behavior problems; other problems, physical, etc.
iii. Family Problems: Delinquency of mother, father, and other siblings. Personality and behavior problems of mother, father, and other siblings. Physical problems. Statement of marital, economic, social problems.

Social History

Date:____ Unless some other scheme is more desirable, entries should begin with the paternal grandparents, finishing up with the father. The same order should be followed for the maternal side. The siblings should come next, putting the delinquent and nondelinquent at the bottom. Under Personal Histories should be placed material ordinarily described under the headings heredity and family background.

Date of birth, place of birth, years in United States, citizenship, general health, occupation, cause of death, age at death. Brief personality studies of grandparents, uncles, and aunts, including outstanding economic, social, educational failure or success, criminal tendencies, mental and physical abnormalities, alcoholism, drug addiction, chronic diseases.

Only the more important facts in the personal histories of the siblings need be mentioned, that is, facts that seem to have a special bearing upon the delinquent or non delinquent.

For delinquent and non delinquent complete prenatal, parturitional, developmental, and health histories should be stated. Dates of illnesses, doctors attending, all diseases and injuries to the central nervous system should be carefully gone into. Actions and attitudes of parents during these illnesses should be noted.

Some estimate of the delinquent and nondelinquent personalities during the preschool period should be made and the interplay of affection with each parent noted.

A year-by-year statement of the important happenings in the lives of the delinquent and nondelinquent from birth to present age is desirable. Such facts as the following could be mentioned along with others—illnesses, accidents, births and deaths in the family, school changes, success or failure in promotion, changes of residence, names of new companions, clubs and gangs joined, play interests, enterprises, travel, camp, all sexual interest, fluctuations of interest from one parent to another, change of policies on part of the parents, severe punishments, etc. On the left-hand side of the page could be listed events given by informants. On the right-hand side the meaning of these events to the subject could be put down or references to the page in the record where such material could be found. The same could be done for the nondelinquent. At any rate, a chronological story of significant events is usually in the record and could be summarized here.

Home Conditions

Date:____ Physical description of home and surroundings. Social ideals, practices of the family; recreations, festivities, atmosphere of the home. Economic status. Estimation of capital in cash or property, past and present holdings, and earnings.

Physical Examinations

Date:____ Family health status. Delinquent, including neurological and psychophysical. [1]_Nondelinquent, including same. Special studies, endocrine, etc. The psychophysical can be carried out in two stages, one before the boy undresses, when he is asked about his health history, that is, operations, injuries, illnesses, and detailed regional questions—head, eyes, etc., the four systems, cardio respiratory, gastrointestinal, genitourinary, and neuromuscular; habits, etc. Leads found during this time can be followed up during the physical examination.

Psychological, Educational, and Vocational

Date:____ General intellectual, educational, and vocational levels of the immediate family, father, mother, and other side.

Delinquent: Psychological tests. School achievement. Vocational: positions held, names of employers, how much earned, and estimate of boy's initiative and resourcefulness in such matters.

Nondelinquent: Same as delinquent.

Family Interrelationships

Date:

Paternal Grandparents: How they react to each other. How they react to the father and mother. How the father and mother react to them. How father and mother react to paternal uncles and aunts.

Maternal Grandparents: How they react to each other. How they react to father and mother. How father and mother react to maternal uncles and aunts. How father and mother react to them.

Parents: How they react to each other, before and after marriage. How they react to their children. How children react to parents.

Delinquent's Reaction to: Grandparents, uncles, and aunts, on both sides, if important. Father—father's reaction to delinquent. Mother—mother's reaction to delinquent. Siblings—Siblings' reaction to delinquent.

Nondelinquent: Same as delinquent.

13

Differential Social Diagnosis for Social Work

Introduction

Some social agencies now have excellent records of both the inner and the outer lives of their clients and of their particular social settings. Almost invariably, however, these records are a mere collection of data invaluable for many purposes as such data are with little or no attempt made to classify and to interpret these data, that is, to diagnose the cases. Under such circumstances social therapy can only be a hit-or-miss and haphazard affair and cannot be based on a systematic plan.

At one time there was a threat to take it [probation] away from us. The reason why probation was attacked was because it was a therapeutic procedure being used without diagnosis. It was often an emotional affair.

The best way to treat a [delinquent], or any other sort of social problem, is first of all to make an adequate diagnosis, such diagnosis depending quite largely upon an adequate case history. This case history should be as complete as it is possible to make it. We must not go ahead with plans for treatment until we have spent more time on the diagnostic side. We must not give way to our tendency to doctor people until we have more data upon which to base our procedure. This is not an easy program to popularize, even though we have had prison riots and fires. The immediate effect of using it would be to cut down the criminal group.

Classification of social data is a difficult process. Medical men have profited greatly by such works as Richard Cabot's Differential Diagnosis. Social workers need similar treatises on differential social diagnosis. The title of Mary Richmond's volume, Social Diagnosis, is from present points of view something of a misnomer, since she deals for the most part with social investigation, devoting more than three-fourths of her book to evidence, sources of information, references, questionnaires of various types, letter writing, and so on. She uses some diagnostic concepts, but in general her book a monumental piece of work which will remain a classic for a long time is of comparatively little use to workers interested in methods of diagnosis, although the material she discusses is essential to diagnosis. Little else of significance has been written on the subject to orient the worker in the problems of social diagnosis. There are several treatises which imply diagnosis but do not treat it at any appreciable length. Certain psychologists have tried their hand at psychological diagnosis but unfortunately they have so far with few exceptions concerned themselves chiefly with a discussion and classification of mental abilities and mental processes of individuals, ignoring for the most part the social-economic and cultural milieu in which the subject lives.

In spite of the fact that it is generally agreed that no sound plan of treatment can be worked out in a particular case without first diagnosing it, social case workers in almost every field of social work often plunge into treatment with little or no actual diagnosis of the social situation.

The subject of social diagnosis in social case work is an uncharted field; therefore, the present attempts to discuss a few factors and considerations bearing on this subject must be regarded as highly tentative. The material is presented with considerable hesitation; one of its purposes is to provoke discussion which may ultimately lead to fruitful contributions to the solution of this problem, from both theorists and practitioners in social work.

An Attempt at a Tentative Definition of Social Diagnosis.— In medicine diagnosis—in its narrowest sense means bestowing a name, from the symptoms presented by the case, upon a certain ill or pathological process. The physician determines from the symptoms described by the patient and those observed during the examination whether the patient is suffering, for instance, from scarlet fever, or tuberculosis, or encephalitis, and so on, or from some combination of ills.

Social diagnosis also in its narrowest sense has come to mean bestowing a name, from the various symptoms described by the client and those observed and studied by the worker, upon the social and personal problems and social pathological processes. These may be named or diagnosed, for instance, as sexual incompatability, marital discord, adolescent tensions, culture conflict, social isolation, amorality, and so on.

In its broader sense social diagnosis means more than naming a problem or a problem complex. It means classification and subclassification of the numerous factors and painstaking individualization of the particular pathological conditions in relation to those social forces, social settings, personality traits, and so on, which produce personal and social unadjustment. These conditions in turn depend upon the nature and the effects of age, occupation, habits, background, heredity, and so on. Thus we at once see that diagnosing a case is a very complex process and furthermore highly tentative since many of these factors may change with greater or less rapidity even during the course of study. A man may get a different job, move into a different environment, lose a member of his family, which may affect his personality as well as the larger social situation.

The Complexity of the Process of Social Diagnosis.—When the social diagnosis of a case is attempted by a worker, it is frequently oversimplified. When he finds, for example, delinquent children whose mothers are employed during the day, or who live in a neighborhood lacking recreational facilities, he concludes the cause of their delinquencies is "a working mother," or "lack of supervision or of proper play facilities." Undoubtedly in many situations these conditions are contributing factors, but it cannot be said with such simple certainty that one is the cause of the other. Social life is seldom so simple as to consist of an isolated situation directly producing an isolated social problem. A worker who makes so simple a diagnosis ignores the fact that he has "isolated but one factor out of a mass of entangled influences and assigned primary importance to that factor." In reality the mother's employment may be only one in a series of highly interwoven factors, such as extreme irritability or even neuroticism which appears when she must attend to disliked household chores, fear of insecurity, overprotection and over solicitation, culture conflicts, personal conflicts between child and parents, and many others, all of which may mean that the mother's absence from the home may be an advantage a stabilizing factor in the child's life. If these conditions do not affect his life adversely a host of others may be held accountable: ill-health, inferiority feelings, school unadjustment, disorganizing community influences, and many others of the tangled skein of social influences.

If the worker by chance or deliberate plan "wisely pulls on the thread he will soon drag other 'causes' into view, and may even find that he got hold of the end or broken middle of the cord instead of the beginning." Furthermore, a classification into problems of ill-health, inferiority feelings, school unadjustment, culture conflicts, and so on, whether viewed one at a time or combined, is highly artificial since these may spring from common or from diverse sources, they may be highly interrelated with each other and with other problems which have not yet come to the surface, and they may highly influence each other, yet classification is only too apt to stress a single aspect of the situation, or at best a combination of a few factors.

The Gestalt psychologists have done much to sensitize us to the "togetherness" of social processes, to the intricate relation between external and inner experiences. "There is something over and above summation of parts which makes up the whole; there is the attachment and integration of parts one with another. By breaking a thing up into elements, one destroys the concepts one is trying to explain.... [An analogy to chemistry may clarify the point.] Potatoes may be made of starch, sugar, water, ash, etc., but put these together in appropriate quantities and you do not get a potato!"

While we fully comprehend the importance of this integration, yet we have no escape from the necessity for classification when we attempt to present a complex, interrelated totality orally, in writing, or even graphically. We simply lack the means to express the Gestalt adequately. Though we must for the time being resort to an artificial isolation of social processes and their component parts, that is, when we are classifying case problems, we need to keep in mind not a series or list of disjointed problems and isolated social conditions, but the inherent interrelated wholeness of a complicated pattern of life, a configuration a Gestalt, which is at one and the same time "a historical and experiential continuum."

Case of Henry Harrison

Henry Harrison, fourteen years of age, was arrested by a police officer for vagrancy. He was found roaming the streets of San Y. late at night. The arresting officer recognized Henry as a previous offender. The record shows that Henry was detained for a few days in Juvenile Hall upon his first offense about six months ago, but, upon being duly admonished, he was returned to his parents and the case was dismissed.

The parents state that the boy has been running away persistently and staying away from home two days to two weeks at a time. He returns home only when he is desperately in need of food or clothing, or when he is ill. The last time, however, when apprehended by the police officer he was in possession of new pants and small change for which the parents could give no account. He has grown thin and appears seriously undernourished. He also suffers from a painful "skin eruption."

Henry states that he ran away the first time because he was afraid of his father who came home drunk, beat up his mother, and kicked his brother. "I was arrested, but why wasn't Pop? They talked to me about staying home but I was afraid of being kicked in the stomach, like Alex was. Why didn't they give him a talking-to?"

The study of the family, made after Henry's first offense, is very brief. Mr. Harrison is thirty-nine years old. Mrs. Harrison is thirty-five. Henry is fourteen, and Alex is twelve years of age. They live in a five-room bungalow, well furnished, in a nice residential section of the city.

Mr. Harrison drinks heavily and is therefore unable to hold a job. When working, as certified public accountant, he earns $75.00 a week. Has been out of steady work for nearly three years, during which time Mrs. Harrison's mother aided. There has been considerable conflict in the home, nagging and quarreling, and displays of temper, since Mr. H.'s loss of employment. Once Mr. H. came home so drunk that Mrs. H. had to run in the middle of the night to her mother's taking Alex with her. Henry had already run away from home.

Both Mr. and Mrs. H. are in good health; both had had two years of college work; they come from "good homes," got along well until "the depression set in." Now they are in constant conflict. The house is illkept and the children are neglected.

Mr. H. was baptized Catholic, but has not attended church for five years. Mrs. H. was born and reared a Baptist, but was married in the Catholic Church. She has no church affiliations. Henry was born in Grand Rapids, Alex in Fresno. The family came to San Y. in 1931, stayed a year, left for M., but after six months returned to San Y.

There are no savings, no negotiable securities, no automobile. The family is in need of food. Two attempts were made to reach Mr. H., but he was not found at home. He has no relatives in San Y.

Though the above presentation of the problems of the Harrison case is more satisfactory than a serial listing of these problems, yet it suffers from several inadequacies. It does not assign relative weights to the different problems which constitute the pathological situation. Undoubtedly some of these problems are not so serious as others in their influence and effect. Furthermore, this presentation does not indicate the order of appearance of some of the discernible elements of the problems. For example, fear and running away appeared first and then the boy started to steal and became ill.

This presentation does not distinguish between symptoms and fundamental underlying causative factors, to say nothing of the lack of consideration of the role of the personal and social traits of the people who present these problems.

Clifford Shaw in his discussion of the "vicious circle" concept indicates the difficulties involved in assigning primacy to any element in the causative complex:

> *X is in prison for burglary. On examination it is found that he is also a "constitutionally inferior psychopathic personality" and an habitual alcoholic. Further inquiry discloses that X and his [parents] have been long in dire poverty and residing in the vilest tenement house in a "delinquency area." Has X's criminality been "caused" by his drunkenness, or have both the alcoholism and the misconduct been "caused" by his constitutional inadequacy, or did X's habitual imbibing of alcohol aggravate his original weak inhibitory capacity? Did X become a drunkard because he couldn't stand his family's miserable economic situation, or was the drunkenness the cause of that unhealthy economic status? All these sequences may have occurred at different times in the life of X, in a series of vicious "action-reaction" mechanisms. But even by close scrutiny of X's developmental history it would be difficult to assign primacy to any of the factors involved.*

The great difficulty lies in determining what is "primary." Some would naturally be inclined to place the constitutional inadequacy first; but it is conceivable that that defect alone would not have caused X to become a criminal, or that without his having lived in a deteriorated neighborhood containing many "speak-easies" X never would have become a chronic alcoholic, or that even if his inebriety preceded his criminality he never would have lapsed into crime, and had economic situation been adequate, etc.

Complexity of Symptoms and Causative Factors in Delinquency. From the definition of diagnosis given above it appears that the diagnosis is made from the symptoms, that is, from the more easily observable, recognizable, and specific evidence upon which is based a judgment of the nature of the underlying problems. The symptoms of marital incompatibility, for example, may appear as abuse, drinking, immorality, nagging, quarreling, jealousy, bad housekeeping, etc. The symptoms of adolescent tensions, as another example, may be spells of weeping, bashfulness, timidity, diffidence, moodiness, daydreaming, over sensitiveness, clash of personalities, etc.

When the symptoms are known and recognizable through empirical knowledge, diagnosis of a certain pathology may be possible. But in cases in which the symptoms are difficult to learn and difficult to recognize, or are missing altogether, diagnosis is exceedingly difficult if not well-nigh impossible. The worker should, therefore, make as thorough an investigation as possible and secure a complete statement as to the manifestations, origin, history, circumstances, sources, etc., of all problematic behavior. He also needs to become acquainted with the symptoms arrived at both theoretically and empirically of as many pathologies as are available to him, allowing, however, for wide deviations in different cases. The test of the diagnostician's power occurs, of course, when two basically different pathologies present similar symptoms.

Dr. Healy's discussion and diagram illustrating at three levels the offense (symptom), the offender (mental status), and the antecedent conditions (underlying causative factors) further show the intricacy of causation in child unadjustment:

We show in this at three levels the delinquency, the offender as a member of some general class, and the causal antecedents back of his tendency to delinquency. The combinations are made from only a few of the ascertained facts and types and could, of course, by the addition of facts, be made definitely more complex. The combining lines represent either sequence or conjunction of the portrayed elements.

We observe from the diagram that classification on any level tells little of what is of practical importance on other levels. For example, petty thieving may be committed by any one of the types of offenders on our diagram, who may in turn have been influenced by any of a number of different remotely antecedent or immediately inciting factors. As an instance, the feebleminded individual, the least difficult of all to group, may be with his deficiency the result of several possible causes, may be directly incited towards crime by inward or outward influences apart from his defect, and may commit any of the diagramed offenses.

Dr. Healy adds a statement to which we wish to call particular attention, since it shows the value and relative advantage of diagnostic diagrams after the disadvantages have been taken account of: "When it comes to the particular case, we find the greatest help from this articulating and viewing the facts. It leads to evaluation of causes by which adjustments become actually possible that otherwise would be blunderingly missed." Cyril Burt, after extensive research in the field of unadjusted youth, observes:

When we glance back through page after page and turn in succession to table after table, one striking fact leaps out in bold relief—the fact of multiple determination. Crime is assignable to no single universal source, nor yet to two or three: it springs from a wide variety, and usually from a multiplicity, of alternative and converging influences. So violent a reaction, as may easily be conceived, is almost everywhere the outcome of a concurrence of subversive factors: it needs many coats of pitch to paint a thing thoroughly black. The natures of these factors and of their varying combinations differ greatly from one individual to another, and juvenile offenders, as is amply clear, are far from constituting a homogenous class.

The foregoing discussion of the complexity of causation will, it is hoped, discourage any tendency to simple, unilateral classification of problems and will result in more deep-searching and painstaking efforts to recognize the multiplicity of the converging influences and forces operating variously in the lives of various individuals.

The assigning of the position of the "cart" or the "horse" to any given factor which is associated with another in the problem complex may be slightly facilitated, though not definitely established, when we trace the problems to their origin and establish their "sequence." Did drinking appear first and then marital in compatability and then unemployment and then running away of the children, etc., or vice versa? It is essential to know whether when drinking is stopped through some alcoholic cure, for instance, marital discord will be softened or eliminated, and whether the children will fear to stay in the home of their father, or whether, on the other hand, we should deal with the juvenile problems directly as basic problems.

The importance of differentiating basic process from symptom is illustrated in the case of Henry H. Apparently in the treatment of this case the running away of Henry was considered by the worker the paramount issue. But upon subsequent study Henry states that "fear of Pop" induced him to run away. When arrested and detained for running away, he developed further fears and he joined forces with a gang to gain a certain security. The gang accorded him some status; he found also thrill and adventure. Running away became a habit. While to begin with running away was only a symptom in a series of problems facing the home, after wrong diagnosis and treatment it became itself a pathological process. That is, running away in the first instance was incidental "first-time-running-away" while later it became "habitual-running-away," an entirely different thing when we examine the motivation. It is of prime importance to distinguish carefully these two varieties of running away. Undoubtedly other factors contributed to Henry's creating a habit of running away, but concentration on the wrong aspects of the problem by the worker gave new force to the disorganizing factors in his life.

A knowledge of the symptoms, their origin, their course, and characteristics which with careful study of the case may be secured will in many instances save much time and aid in preventing further disorganization.

Following are some of the more fundamental sources of child unadjustment, observed notably by the authors of the Child in America, which may help the worker not only in gaining command of certain diagnostic concepts but also in using these in the process of elimination when considering certain types of his own cases.

William I. and Dorthy S. Thomas ascribe the wide variety of unadjustments to conflicts between child and parent, child and social codes, child and society, and to "organic peculiarities of the individual (physical, mental, emotional endowments and deficiencies) and the learning process, the acquisition of habits and attitudes."

Emotional tensions, mental conflicts give rise to reprehensible forms of behavior, fixations, obsessions, incorrigibility, sex delinquency, temper tantrums.

The enumeration of cases of mental disability, emotional instability, mental conflict, post-encephalitic disorders, specifications of stealing, truancy, adolescent flare-ups, family spoilings, etc., give the impression that we have located the sources of misbehavior that it is like a sickness, that "something is the matter" with the child physiologically, mentally or emotionally, or that it is spoiled. But there is in addition a prevalent state of mind in the young a determination to repudiate the way of life of the older generation and the conventional standards. Conformity, moral code, approved behavior, means that there have been established general and usual behavior reactions through definitions of situations. The "don't" of the family and the "shalt not" of the commandments, and the legal code represent such definitions. The family, the school, the church, the court, are representatives of these definitions, of the social, moral and legal codes. But the codes and definitions are themselves at present evolving, vague and unstable. There are rival definitions of situation. Literature and the moving pictures and the show girls may define the situation quite differently from the parent, minister or teacher. The difference in ideals and ways of life between the generations is consequently now very striking. Children may differ from their parents, or at least from their grandparents, in this respect as greatly as races and nationalities differ among themselves. There is thus a disharmony as to ideals and values, connected with the unstabilizing of society.

Frequently children are unable to conform to social patterns of behavior because of mental deficiency; lack of proper distribution of abilities in a way which would enable them to meet the requirements of a school curriculum; failure to form certain important habit patterns because of lack of opportunity to come in contact with such patterns in an intimate and continuous way.

Overpowering desire for adventure, response, and recognition lead to predatory behavior, particularly when associated with gang activities. A sense of social misplacement and personal inadequacy lead to frustrations, inferiority feelings, subterfuges, pathological lying, stealing, running away, sexual promiscuity, and so on.

Frequently children are old enough to respond to and to take on conventional behavior patterns but resist social patterning in a diplomatic manner and carry on amiable conflicts with society.

Poverty is often urged as "a primary cause," but as Mr. Goldstein observes:

> *There are more poor than rich and so it is only natural that the delinquent children brought to the Children's Court should be recruited chiefly from the ranks of the poor.*

With the rich, governesses often take the place of probation officers and military schools substitute for correctional institutions. With the rich, delinquencies of children are often "squared" by parents paying for the damage done and for the injuries inflicted, thus removing the cause that prompts complainants to petition the Children's Court for the arraignment of juvenile delinquents.

Even from this brief discussion we note that there is no general cause of delinquency. While such terms as "cause," "causation," "causal factors," "why," are used frequently it should be realized that it is exceedingly difficult to arrive at a determination of cause or etiologic factors and at an explanation of why a certain situation occurred in such and such form, time, circumstance, and so on. Many thinkers believe that "why" is a purely philosophical question, and even though we know many of the circumstances we are not in a position to trace the result or the effect to its cause.

The case worker is not concerned with ultimate or final causes, as is the philosopher, and does not seek for a final answer to the question "why." On the other hand he is concerned with the immediate causes, the antecedent conditioning viewed as links in a sequence of events which he thinks of as related to each other as cause and effect.

Motive as Causal Factor in Delinquency.— We have so far mentioned only casually the inner life and motives of a delinquent child. Let us refer once more to the case of Henry Harrison and his brother, Alex, who were both subjected to the same treatment at the hands of a drunken father, to conditions following marital incompatability in the home, to conflict and deprivation. Why did not Alex run away? Or examine any of the situations in the cases cited in this volume and question the behavior of the problematic and delinquent child with the contrasting behavior of his or her nondelinquent brother or sister. Why are "bad" environmental influences a stimulus to legitimate, socially acceptable behavior to one person and to illegitimate, socially unacceptable behavior in another? In some cases poverty, or fear, or conflict, etc., as Shaw says, is not only "a situation in the environment but a motive in the life of the individuals involved. Since the situational forces were similar, the difference in outcome in the two cases can only be attributed to the dissimilarity in the persons involved or to accidental factors of an unknown nature." Shaw clarifies this argument by citing the following case:

A, a God-fearing, law abiding bank clerk, has never before even thought of stealing, needs money badly because of the illness of his wife or children, or in the dread of impending unemployment. He embezzles funds. Is the situation necessarily the "cause" of his criminality? The situation is, to be sure, the immediate determining factor; yet if A had been B he would not have stolen, even in the situation described. He would have sought some other solution of his acute and extraordinary situation, such as borrowing funds, or appealing to relatives, or letting his family go without their needs. In other words, the pressing situation would not have become a motive to misconduct. Here we see that, even in cases where the situation is the immediately precipitating stimulus, the make-up of the person (constitutional and conditioned) is still the factor that makes the real difference.

According to Shaw the above illustration suggests two useful concepts in problematic and delinquent behavior-causation studies:

> *(1) A "factor," whether personal or situational, does not become a "cause" unless and until it becomes a "motive" and whether it will become a motive for one form of behavior or another depends upon the constitutional and acquired make-up of the individual. (2) Every person has his individual resistance-limit. It is difficult for all members of any society to lead a socially acceptable existence which involves a submergence of the ego desires to the supposed common weal. But most persons are capable of sufficient resistance and inhibition (natively and through education) to meet the ordinary requirements of the legal standard of the age and place in which they live. If society raises the demands somewhat, or, through social stress, such as continued unemployment, etc., makes it more difficult to adhere to them, more persons will violate the law than before, because it thereby taps the level of those whose resistance-capacity is at present stretched almost to the breaking point. If it raises the social taboos still higher or extends them or renders it more difficult to observe them, it further increases the number of violators of the socio-legal standard by tapping the tier of persons whose resistance-capacity is somewhat stronger than the prior group, etc. The [delinquent] act occurring at any one time is the outcome of constitutional and acquired, personal and situational forces, when the power of resistance has been overbalanced by the strength of the other circumstances. Hence, some men would be [delinquents] (i.e. would violate the social conventions) in almost any society however rudimentary or complex, and in almost any "situation" in life, however ordinary or unique; others would be [delinquents] in extraordinary emergency though not in ordinary situations; still others would be [delinquent] only in an extremely complex society and in an unusually provocative situation. [Delinquency] is thus shown to be relative to the time, place, and occasion on the one hand*

and the constitutional and conditioned make-up of the individual on the other.

Still another question is in order: "Within a given complex social situation, with certain personality traits and critical incidents, why does a person respond by stealing or drinking? Or by any other behavior pattern? It is assumed that he has a tendency or a susceptibility or a habit of body and mind which predisposes him to the adoption of certain behavior patterns and attitudes. This predisposition to problematic behavior is called a pathological diathesis. Pathological diathesis is akin to hereditary transmission but differs in that the characteristics or the condition itself are not transmitted but merely a tendency or a weakness is transmitted.

August Aichhorn's statement throws further light on this matter:

> *This conception of behavior as dynamically determined enables us to correct another common mistake. When I ask parents how they account for the dissocial behaviour of their children, I usually receive the answer that it is a result of bad company and running around on the streets. To a certain extent this is true, but thousands of other children grow up under the same unfavourable circumstances and still are not delinquent. There must be something in the child himself which the environment brings out in the form of delinquency. If for the moment we call this unknown something a predisposition to delinquency, we have the factor without which an unfavourable environment can have no power over the child.*

We like to think that this predisposition is inherited. Psychoanalysis has shown us that heredity cannot explain everything, that the first experiences of childhood are important in determining later development. The predisposition to delinquency is not a finished product at birth but is determined by the emotional relationships, that is, by the first experiences which the environment forces upon the child. This does not mean that every child so predisposed will become delinquent. Bad company, street influences, and the like, factors which are not the underlying causes of delinquency but the direct or indirect provocation, also play a part. When we realize that the provocation to delinquency is confused with its cause, that symptoms are mistaken for the disease, we understand why there are so many false conceptions of what should be done with the delinquent child, and we wonder no longer that treatment often fails. Without the discovery of the deep underlying causes of delinquency, any cure is accidental.

While we do not wish to stress the terms "cause" and "cure" as Aichhorn does, his statements regarding confusion of symptoms with contributing factors are nevertheless quite pertinent and clear.

The Crisis Situation.— There is at least one other aspect of diagnosis which needs emphasis. It should be clear by this time that a child's delinquency may be due to a multiplicity of causative factors, each springing from diverse social and personal situations, that his psychological make-up and social and personal traits effect and are effected by complex processes, but we may ask: "With the same complex processes and the same personality traits yesterday, or last week, drinking, or conflict, or poverty was not associated with misbehavior. Why should it be today?" Undoubtedly there was a long "build-up," but what precipitated the crisis today? Clifford Shaw would say, perhaps, that the "resistance-capacity" was stretched to the breaking point by some sudden pressure or stress, and delinquency emerged. William I. Thomas accounts for unpredictable behavior in terms of crisis a situation in which a decision must be made and which demands focusing of attention. Again we cite from the experience of Cyril Burt:

> *In any given case, amid all the tangle of accessory factors, some single circumstance not infrequently stands out as the most prominent or the most influential. Often, as we have seen, it can be definitely established that the child in question showed no delinquent tendencies until the year of some unfortunate event. An illness, a new demoralizing friendship, the death or the remarriage of a parent, the emergence within the growing child himself of some fresh interest or instinct—some dated crisis of this kind has often ascertainably preceded, and perhaps has plainly precipitated, his first violation of the law.*

The precipitating crisis situation plays an important role both in the diagnosis and in the treatment and should, of course, be related to the total complex problem. At times it may be possible to prevent disorganization by preventing the occurrence of the crisis situation, or by removing the person from the situation.

Assets.— In spite of the intricate network of problems presented by a case, it is possible to list also certain assets. Assets are those positive, organizing factors in the family and individual which aid in reconstruction of the offender and in furthering the plan of treatment. "Nothing, however small, that might serve as an asset in the course of treatment and help to carry out plans toward a successful issue can possibly be insignificant. Whether this be an affection for a small dog, an ambition to play an accordion, or a lost or mislaid loyalty, the social physician must be able to use, and he must be able to recognize in order to use, such tools as these lie ready to his hand."

Each family and each individual has a different set of assets according to its particular circumstances. Assets may include, all other things being equal, such factors as:

Strength of family cohesion. Emotional ties of the family group.

Capacity for further training. Capacity for energetic endeavor, for social development. Intelligence, education, and training, good school record. Health and vigor. Possession of or desire to learn a trade. Steady work of the head of the family. Financial security. Home ownership in a desirable community. Intelligent insight into own problems. Presence of good community resources, etc.

Such stocktaking of the available positive forces, when not undertaken in a purely routine manner, is exceedingly useful not only as clarifying the situation through the use of diagnostic concepts but since it leads the worker and the family to build on a solid foundation of constructive forces and also leads the family and the worker both to realize that they have "something to work with," something to rely on, something to save in their own lives. Thus they acquire a new dignity, new social status, and increased emotional stability, all of which are necessary elements in their readjustment.

Liabilities.— Liabilities are the negative and disorganizing factors which tend to frustrate the efforts of the worker and to hinder the plan of treatment. The number of liabilities is legion and as varied as the life circumstances facing each individual. Liabilities would include such factors as:

Broken home.
Economic insecurity of family.
Poor work habits.
Unfavorable heredity.
Defective mentality.
Poor housekeeping and management.
Poor health.
Lack of training and of ability to become trained.
Lack of education and of ability or opportunity to acquire it.
Emotional instability.
Religious conflicts or lack of capacity for religious training and affiliation, etc.

Prognosis.— Prognosis is the forecasting of the outcome of a case in view of the diagnosis. We have seen that social diagnosis is a difficult and complicated process. It stands to reason that prognosis, forecasting the future, is eminently more difficult.

Even the most careful and experienced workers, whose ability to make a differential diagnosis and whose accumulated knowledge of the outcome of a variety of cases serve them in good stead, often err in the forecast or prognosis of the case.

The worker must view carefully and intelligently the complex of causal factors and the pathological processes in terms of possible amelioration in a given social milieu, with a given set of personal traits, with given assets and liabilities inherent in the given situation. The limiting factors operating against the progress of the case and the positive factors suggesting potentialities for active treatment response which overbalance the liabilities, must, as far as possible, be seen and weighed.

When making a prognosis of a case, the limitations of the particular agency handling the case must be considered. An overburdened staff, or few community facilities, or inadequate equipment and untrained workers cannot contribute much to the favorable outcome of a case, although frequently cases adjust in spite of the activities of the agency rather than because of them. That is, in making a prognosis the worker needs to take full account of the "natural processes" which are operating for or against change in the situation and be careful not to overestimate the effects of treatment in controlling these natural processes.

The Value of Social Diagnosis.— A case carefully diagnosed often means it is more than half treated. If the diagnosis is competently arrived at on the basis of sufficient data secured with a minimum of bias or prejudice, and accurately recorded, it serves to indicate the outstanding or predominating social problems presented by the case. Such a diagnosis tends to eliminate guesswork; it tends to show where attention should be focused; it helps to decide what specialists, if any, should assume responsibility for study and treatment of the problems. Medical problems as soon as discovered are referred to medical authorities, educational problems to the schools, economic problems to the employment agency, social security board, relief agency, etc. The case worker, of course, has to see all these problems in relation to the whole situation and their effect upon personality. He further has to see the effects of the study and treatment of the various problems by specialists upon the person under consideration.

The following is tentatively offered as a summary of elements which enter into a social diagnosis of a case:

Presenting situation (the situation as it appears; behavior viewed as symptomatic): running away; quarreling; drinking; etc.

The complex of basic problems: ill-health; marital discord; culture conflicts; etc.

Contributing underlying factors: to ill-health as determined by a physician; to marital discord; unemployment; sex incompatibility; mother-in law-ism; drinking; etc.

Personality and social traits.
Precipitating incident or crisis.
Assets upon which to build.
Liabilities to overcome.
Prognosis.

Tentative Social Diagnosis

Presenting situations: running away, truancy, emotional attachment to a man nearly twice her age.

The complex of basic problems and their contributing factors: social isolation of and lack of common interests between parents and girl. Girl craves companionship and response but both parents are preoccupied with own interests. Lack of parents' participation in girl's recreation. High degree of native intelligence, wide reading, and numerous social contacts contribute to girl's maturity, which is not recognized by parents. Parental protection and overindulgence in girl as a young child and later inconsistent discipline which provoked confusion and impulsive behavior. Lack of girl's participation in family affairs causes further estrangement and social isolation. Lack of ethical standards of conduct of friends and relatives, also

Religious hybridism and lack of religious affiliation.
Lack of challenging activities in school.
Unwholesome employment.

Precipitating incidents or crises: newly found economic freedom. Meeting a man who showed interest and attachment.

Assets upon which to build.

Girl's craving for affection.
Devotion of parents to girl and to each other as well as to the entire family.
Intelligence and good health of entire family.
Girl's wholesome interests and desire for career.
Girl's cautious attitude toward sex matters.
Parents' high ambitions for girl.
Four well-adjusted and devoted sons.
A feeling of accomplishment and success in ability to raise the sons.
Happy and harmonious home background of both parents.

Liabilities operating against successful plan of treatment: parent child conflicts are of long standing and are deeply colored emotionally and extend into many phases of their relationships.

14

Juvenile Court Hearing for Criminals

Introduction

The citation has been served or the summons or the warrants issued, and after an informal adjustment seemed inadvisable or impossible, the case is formally heard in juvenile court. At this time the petition together with the probation officer's report and all other findings, including clinic reports, are considered by the court. In some cases the probation officer reviews or supplements orally this report just before or during the hearing. We present two transcripts of juvenile court hearings and one of a hearing in municipal court (a preliminary hearing) for comparisons:

IN THE JUVENILE COURT OF THE COUNTY OF LOS ANGELES,
STATE OF CALIFORNIA

TO THE HONORABLE JUVENILE COURT OF THE COUNTY OF LOS ANGLES, STATE OF CALIFORNIA:

YOUR PETITIONER A. L. D. respectfully represents that the above named person is residing within said county and is a person under the age of twenty-one years, to-wit, of the age of sixteen years, on or about the 3rd day of September, 1935, and is a person defined in subdivisions 2 and 11 of Section One, within the meaning of the Act of the Legislature of said State, known as the "Juvenile Court Law," approved June 5th, 1915, and Acts amendatory thereto. In that said person Amy Stewart, who has no parent or guardian; or who has no parent or guardian willing to exercise or capable of exercising proper parental control; or who has no parent or guardian actually exercising such proper parental control and who is in need of such control, in that the parents have been unable to keep this girl from associating with undesirable companions. In that said person, Amy Stewart who is leading, or from cause is in danger of leading an idle, dissolute, lewd or immoral life in that for the past year and a half this girl has been associating with one, John McFarland, 19 years of age (Oriental). Girl admits being pregnant and admits having sexual relations with John McFarland.

Juvenile Court Law, the Probation Officer of Los Angeles County has made an investigation of the facts herein alleged and has approved the filing of this petition.

That the said person is now in the custody and control of Juvenile Hall That your petitioner is the Policewoman of said person, and is entitled to the custody thereof. That the names and residences of the relatives of said person living in the said County are as follows: Parents: That in order to secure the attendance of said person at the hearing of said matter, it will not be necessary that a warrant be issued for the arrest of said person, Amy Stewart.

Wherefore, your petitioner prays that this Honorable Court inquire into such matter and declare said person a ward of the Juvenile Court and deal with said person as provided in the above entitled Act of the Legislature, and make such order in the premises as to this Honorable Court may seem meet and proper, to which order your petitioner now consents.

A. L. D.

Petitioner.

Address____________

A. L. D., the petitioner above named, being duly sworn, says that she has read the foregoing petition, and knows the contents thereof, and that the same is true of her own knowledge, except as to the matters which are therein stated on information or belief, and as to those matters that she believes it to be true.

A. L. D.

Subscribed and sworn to before me this 5th day of November, 1935 L. E. LAMPTON, County Clerk.

by__________________ , Deputy.

Hearing in the Juvenile Court

This matter coming on regularly to be heard on Friday, this fifteenth day of November, 1935,at 10 A.M.

Amy was present together with the following witnesses and parties: Mr. and Mrs. Paul Stewart, parents; Mrs. H., probation officer.

The following proceeding was had:

Court. Will you all stand and raise your right hands to be sworn? (Witnesses sworn, including Amy Stewart.)

Court. What is your name? Girl. Amy Stewart.

Q. How old are you? A. Sixteen, on Sept. 3. Born in 1919.

Q. Where were you born? A. Los Angeles.

Q. What grade are you in school? A. B-12.

Q. Do you go to church or Sunday school? A. Not very regularly; once in a while.

Q. What is your name? Mother. Florentia Stewart.

Q. Mother of Amy, are you? A. Yes.

Court. Your name? Father. Paul Stewart.

Q. Father of Amy? A. Yes, ma'am.

Q. What is your occupation, Mr. Stewart? A. Electrician.

Q. Where are you employed? A. WPA.

Q. Where were you employed before you had to get work through that agency? A. B. Department Store.

Q. Where? B.? Were you employed there a long time? A. Well, I was there off and on for the last seven years as an extra.

Q. Are you employed? Mother. No.

Q. Do you stay at home and take care of your children? A. I do.

Q. Amy, will you tell me what brings you to Juvenile Court? Amy. I am pregnant.

Q. Are you married? A. No.

Q. And who is responsible for your pregnancy? A. John McFarland.

Q. Who is John McFarland? A. A boy I have been going with.

Q. With your mother's permission? A. No.

Q. With your father's permission? A. No.

Q. And why are you going with any boys without your parents' permission? A. (No answer.)

Q. Amy? A. Because I knew they wouldn't give it if they knew.

Q. Did you expect to marry this young man? A. I did when I was old enough.

Q. You did. Whether your parents would give permission or not? A. Yes, ma'am.

Q. Mrs. H., will you tell us what the situation is in this case?

Mrs. H, This petition was filed by the [Police] Juvenile Bureau. I never have got just exactly clear how it came to their attention. It says an anonymous report. Amy—it had become known at school that she was pregnant and she had been going with this John McFarland, who is part Oriental, a senior at high school. Amy was also a senior. The boy is nineteen. Amy is sixteen. She, Amy, told me that she has been permitted to go to the library and to a show, slipping out and going with him, meeting him in the park nights where these acts took place. She says that she started this affair through chumming with another girl; they used to hang around when the boys were playing tennis and practiced their athletics and that the other girl made this boy fond of her and then she threw him over and treated him very badly, and Amy felt sorry for him.

Q. Was the other girl an Oriental girl? Amy. No.

Mrs. H. A white girl. The father, I think, feels that the school has failed in not reporting the matter to them, and of course, I think it should have been. However, as I see it from the school angle, it was not a particular problem in the case of these two young people, but a group of young people.

Q. I still agree with the father that the parents were the first ones who should have been advised of the situation. A. I think so too.

Q. Did you have sexual relations with any other boys than the Oriental boy? Amy. One other about two years ago.

Q. How many times within the past year? A. None.

Court. Amy, you may wait in the other room. (Exit.)

Q. Mr. Stewart, are you making any effort to secure regular employment? Father. Yes, ma'am.

Q. What is your opinion about this situation? A. Well, of course, it is a very serious situation and the way I look at it, of course I don't know—in what way do you mean?

Q. Well, your sixteen-year-old daughter having these ideas about her friendships. A. Well of course if we had had any idea at all that there was anything of that kind going on, why we would have prevented it, but not knowing of course, I had no idea such a thing—now as to her going to the library and so on and into the park, I had told her that she could only go to the library in the daytime. Well the situation is that we get sixteen-year old girls who get an idea that parents and other adults are old-fashioned, and old fogies in their ideas and that the young people are modern, have different ideas and only their ideas are right and I presume Amy thinks that they have outlived the age of white people feeling as they have toward other races. As far as—

this is the first time we knew—she couldn't get our consent to go with him and she promised me and her mother both she would never go with any boy until he came and met us first. I told her if she wants to go out with a boy if he would come to the house and let me meet him and have a talk with him, then if I saw fit, I would let her go with him.

Q. Mrs. Stewart, what do you think about it? Mother. It is just too big a problem for me. I don't know.

Q. You have been a good mother to Amy, have you? A. Well you can ask Amy as to that.

Q. I say do you think you have? A. I think I have.

Q. Have you tried to teach her to be self-respecting and a good citizen? A. Yes.

Q. Have you? A. I have. (Pause.)

Court. Let's have Amy again. (Entrance.)

Q. Amy, you have a sister. Does she associate with boys as you have? Amy. No, she doesn't.

Q. Do you think she should? A. No.

Q. Then why did you think it is right for you? A. I don't say that it is right.

Q. Did you tell your parents that you wanted to marry this young man? A. Yes.

Q. Where do you think you could go to get married? A. Mexico, for one place.

Q. You know that isn't recognized as legal in this state. The law and the courts have the opinion that people who go out of the state to evade the laws of the state are not legally married when they go to another country for the sole purpose of evading the laws.... Well, Mr. and Mrs. Stewart, of course you will have to begin to think of this responsibility that you will have to assume. The care of your daughter and your little grandchild that she is bringing into the world. It will need care for many years. Children are minors until they are twenty-one in this state. Under the circumstances, there won't be anything else except for the family to take care of this little baby.

Mother. Well, we understood that this boy's mother would adopt the baby.

Q. That won't be considered. This is Amy's baby. We will have to wait until after it is born and begin to see what is best for it later on.... Mrs. H., will you ask for a psychiatric examination? Mrs. H. All right.

Q. What is your recommendation for Amy? A. I recommend that she go to A.B. Maternity Home for maternity care.

Q. Is this man in jail? A. Yes. I recommend that she remain in Juvenile Hall until after the District Attorney is through. The day the preliminary hearing was set, Amy was unable to attend as she was in quarantine here in the Hall and I don't know when the next hearing of his will be.

Q. Who is investigating this situation in that school? Mrs. H. Well, the police were investigating the case of the other girls. I don't know what they found out. Of course, I myself had a long talk with the principal and she feels terribly about it and I think they really have met the problem there.

Q. Well, I want to know what is being done about it. A. All right.

Q. I want it followed up. Bring us a report from the Police Department. Father. I want—what I would like is, won't there be something done why they don't notify the parents. They admit it has been going on for about a year and a half. They didn't see fit to notify us at all.

Q. They knew Amy had been associating with this boy for a year and a half? A. Yes.

Mother. They said she quit for a while.

Father. They said she quit for a while and started in again. I asked the vice-principal why I had not been notified and she said Amy asked them not to notify us. That would have been all the more reason why they should notify us and at that time we were living there within less than a block of the school and there was no reason that I can see whatsoever why we weren't notified.

Recommendation.— I recommend that Amy Stewart be declared a ward of the Juvenile Court under subdivisions 2 and 11, and be placed in the custody of and under supervision of the probation officer, to remain in Juvenile Hall until no longer needed as a witness by the District Attorney's Office in the case of John McFarland, and that she be placed in the care of A.B. Maternity Home . . . that a county order at the rate of $25.00 a month be made in favor of the A.B. Maternity Home from date of placement ... and this matter be continued four weeks on the oral calendar for further report. These findings and recommendations to be presented to the Judge of the Juvenile Court in not more than ten days, nor less than five days from this date, to wit, Nov. 25, 1935, at 2 P.M. ...

Amy. I thought that I would be allowed to go to my cousin.

Q. You need hospital care, Amy, and you need protection and you need to be away from everybody for a while. A. Don't you think it would be better for me to be happy and contented?

Q. You are going to be very happy in A.B. Home. It is very quiet and a very beautiful place to be and your mother and father will be very happy to know it is possible for you to be there and have hospital care and nursing care which you need. It means much to know that you are going to get through this and have good health afterwards.

Mother. You don't think it would be advisable then to take her home for a few months?

Q. No. A. If we move away?

Q. She wants to get away from everything that would remind her of this experience. A. We would move out of the neighborhood.

Q. I want the psychiatric examination to be finished first so we know, if anybody can tell us, what the trouble is; and she has to stay here anyway until the District Attorney has completed his case against this man. That may take some time, and by that time it will be nearer the time for her confinement; and you can go to A.B. Home today if you want to and see it for yourselves and know just exactly why we are placing her there. We are doing it for her welfare.

Father. Sure, well, I think so myself. I think it is the best thing for her care.

Q. I think, to get away from any chance of neighbors' reminding her of this situation, is best. We are going to ask for an investigation of the situation in the school and it would be better for her to be away.

A. I think there should be something done in that school. If what I found out is true....

Court. Amy, I know you feel badly, but I am telling you that we are doing the thing we think will make you happiest in the end. You are going to enjoy A.B. Home. Wait until you get over there.

Girl. It wouldn't make me happy to be away from my mother.

Q. What can we do about it now? A. Nothing, I guess.

The Petition.— As far as the petition which initiates the court hearing is concerned we are at once struck with several outstanding features in this case which are not common to the apprehension, arrest, and detention of adults. We note that a petition was filed, giving name, age, residence of the girl and parents and stating briefly the facts which brought the girl within the provisions of the law. This petition is not an indictment or accusation of criminal behavior, and therefore no formal prosecution is in order. The filing of the petition is a means of informing the court of the problematic situation which the police officer (or probation officer, or parent, or any interested person) alleges to exist regarding the offender. The filing of the petition is essential to establish legal jurisdiction.

Amy Stewart was detained in a juvenile detention home which provides temporary institutional care, clinical and hospital facilities, and a school for girls under eighteen years of age. This home is an observation agency for minors and is in no way to be regarded as a punitive institution.

The Hearing.— Amy, as a delinquent girl, was regarded by the court as misdirected and misguided and needing aid, encouragement, and assistance, as it has been expressed in many statutes. In accordance with the best practices of juvenile courts, the case of Amy was heard separately from adults and in a small courtroom, simply furnished and devoid of any formal symbols with the exception of the court reporter and the clerk. The offender and the parents and the probation officer sat closely together as if in personal conference. In accordance with established practice, the public and newspaper reporters, had they tried to gain admittance, would have been excluded from the room. The publication of court proceedings in the newspapers is not allowed, and the court record is withheld from indiscriminate public inspection.

The court proceedings under chancery or equity practice were informal, though dignified, devoid of technicalities and of strict legal formalities, though not arbitrary and irregular in character.

The parents and the witnesses were sworn in by the clerk of the court. Generally a minor is not sworn in, but since Amy had to give testimony regarding the man implicated in her delinquency she was also asked to be sworn in. The court had the complete social history, including the results of the physical and of the brief psychiatric examinations given to Amy by the clinical staff of the detention home. Before the court was also the petition alleging that Amy came within the definition of the juvenile court law. The probation officer substantiated that the girl did violate a law of the state. The offender admitted in court the alleged offense. Therefore, the necessity of asking the question by the referee: What brings the girl to juvenile court? No charge was read to her and no entering of plea of guilty or not guilty was required of her, as was the case of her cooffender in the municipal court. While Amy's delinquency was established according to the rules of evidence no strict application as that which is in order in criminal proceedings was adhered to in this case. Had it been a matter of establishing facts by evidence, only a preponderance of evidence would have been required.

The offender's interests were represented by the probation officer and not by an attorney. The court, filled with the spirit and welfare of parents patriae, is regarded as defender as well as protector. Though the child is entitled to representation by counsel his appearance is discouraged in the child's interests. The court acts as the "medium of the State's performance of its sovereign duties as parens patriae and promoter of its general welfare," to use the words of Judge Edward F. Waite.

The primary function of the court was not to prove that Amy was guilty of an offense but to secure sufficient social data to enable it to decide on an intelligent plan of treatment. The hearing was held in a sincere friendly manner, conversing briefly with the minor about personal details and gradually leading up to the offense. There was not the slightest cross-examination, intimidation, or embarrassment. The procedure was intended to approximate the conduct of a wise and tender parent dealing with a wayward child. When the court questioned the parents or outlined the responsibilities to them the girl was excused from the courtroom and allowed to sit in the general waiting room, which is under supervision of a matron. However, the court did not get a chance to get acquainted with Amy on that first day, to learn of her motives, interests, and attitudes. There were many other cases waiting to be heard that day. The court had to rely on the social history prepared by the probation officer for a study of the delinquent girl. At no time, however, does a party in the juvenile court become merely a number on the court calendar. He or she is a human being and is not lost sight of when reduced to the common denominator of "defendant" and "respondent," as Jonah J. Goldstein puts it.

The hearing in Amy's case can be considered more than a socio legal procedure. The court had initiated a plan of treatment, and some attempts were made to create insight in the girl into her own problems. The questions regarding the associations of Amy's younger sister were particularly appropriate. Also, Amy was led to see that the court's plan of sending her to a maternity home was for her best interests. Thus, when the girl arrives there she will have fewer inhibitions and defenses to break down.

The court did not consider Amy's case an individual problem. A special investigation of the school was ordered. Throughout the hearing the court was concerned with the social implications of Amy's delinquencies: the social control and discipline by the parents, their attitudes and ability to understand and cope with modern youth, Amy's confidence in them, the bonds of solidarity existing between parents and girl; the economic status of the home, the influence of the church in the life of Amy. Since the home had actually little to offer to Amy it was deemed best to send her to a maternity home for care and "to get away from everything for a while." While both parents and Amy were impressed with their degree of responsibility, there was no scolding, no antagonism, and no ordering-and-forbidding. The case was continued two weeks for further report. Amy appeared in court once before she was transferred to the A.B. Home, once after the clinical reports were completed, and once after the birth of her baby. Space forbids in this chapter to present more than a summary of this hearing. Amy was eager to keep her baby but her father refused to allow her to return home with it. Amy felt that under those circumstances she was being forced to give up her baby, but the court ordered her placed in a foster home until she as well as her parents could have more time to decide on a plan under lesser tensions. In August, 1936, the parents moved from the neighborhood, and Amy and baby returned home. Amy hopes to marry the father of the child when he leaves the Industrial School, provided the court gives permission. Thus the court continues to hear these cases until some satisfactory plan is made, considering the circumstances, or until the "probationer makes good and the petition can be dismissed."

The Hearing in the Criminal Court.— While the following is a transcript of a preliminary hearing in the Municipal Court— which in the State of California may hear the preliminary examination of a defendant and of witnesses in a criminal case—and while there was no jury trial, no counsel for the defendant, and no contest of charges, we observe that the hearing is much more formal than in the juvenile court.

CASE OF JOHN MCFARLAND

Los Angeles, California, Nov. 18, 1935.

At 10 o'clock A.M., this case was called for preliminary examination before the Hon. J. R., Judge of the Municipal Court, City of Los Angeles, County of Los Angeles, State of California. The defendant appeared in court in person, without counsel. The People being represented by Mr. B., Deputy District Attorney of Los Angeles County.

The defendant had previously appeared, at which time he was duly arraigned, the complaint was read to him, and he was informed of his legal rights, viz., the right to a speedy preliminary examination, to have the presence of counsel at his own expense at all stages of the proceedings, to have the process of the court issue to compel the attendance of any witnesses he may desire to appear and testify in his behalf, to be confronted by the witnesses testifying against him in the presence of the court, and to admission to bail, at which time said defendant gave his true name to be John McFarland. With the consent of the defendant his preliminary examination was set down for Dec. 11, at the hour of 10 A.M., thereof.E. E. was appointed as shorthand reporter to report the testimony and proceedings in this case in shorthand and to transcribe the same if the court should so order. At this 10 o'clock A.M., the foregoing parties to the case duly appearing and announcing themselves ready to proceed, the following proceedings were had, to-wit: The Court. People v. John McFarland. Is that your name? The Defendant. Yes. The Court. Are you ready for examination now? The Defendant. What examination? The Court. The proceedings in this court is a preliminary examination. It is not a trial. Are you ready to proceed with the examination? The Defendant. Yes. Mr. B. Dr. White. Flora White, called as a witness on behalf of the People, being first duly sworn, was examined and testified as follows. The Clerk. Please state your name. The Witness. Flora White.

Direct Examination

By Mr. B.

Q. You are a physician and surgeon, licensed to practice in the State of California? A. I am.

Q. You are the examining physician for Juvenile Detention Home in this city? A. I am.

Q. Did you examine Amy Stewart? A. Yes, I did. I examined her on the twenty-first day of October, 1935.

Q. Tell us the result of your examination. A. I found the hymen ruptured and relaxed, which was not recent. The womb was the size of a three and a half to four months' pregnancy. There was no disease.

Mr. B. That is all.

The Court. Do you want to ask the witness any questions? The Defendant. No, sir.

Amy Stewart, called as a witness on behalf of the People, being first duly sworn testified as follows:

The Clerk. Please state your name. The Witness. Amy Stewart.

The Court. Speak loud enough so the defendant can hear you.

Direct Examination

By Mr. B.

Q. Where do you live? A. 0042 James Street.

Q. Have you a telephone there? A. No, we have none.

Q. Do you go to school? A. No.

Q. Are you the Amy Stewart who was examined by Dr. Flora White, the witness just off the witness stand? A. Yes, sir.

Q. Do you know the defendant, this man over here? A. Yes.

Q. Is he your husband? A. No.

Q. How old are you? A. Sixteen.

Q. When were you sixteen? A. September 3d.

Q. Have you ever had sexual intercourse with the defendant, John McFarland? A. Yes.

Q. Did you have sexual intercourse with him on or about the fifth day of March? A. Yes.

Q. His private parts penetrated your private parts? A. Yes.

Q. Did you have intercourse with him on or about March 10? A. I don't know for sure.

Q. When was the next time after the fifth of March when you did have intercourse with him? A. I couldn't say for sure.

The Court.

Q. Can you give us approximately the date? A. No, I can't.

Q. Did you have intercourse with him again? A. Yes.

Q. Approximately how many days was it after March 5? A. I don't know, it might have been a week or two weeks.

By Mr. B.

Q. Did you have intercourse with him about the middle of July? A. Yes.

Q. This happened in the County of Los Angeles? A. Yes.

Mr. B. That is all.

The Court. Do you want to ask this witness any questions? The Defendant. No.

Florentia Stewart, called as a witness on behalf of the People, being first duly sworn, was examined and testified as follows:

The Clerk. Please state your name. The Witness. Florentia Stewart.

Direct Examination

By Mr. B.

Q. Where do you live, Mrs. Stewart? A. At 0042 James St.

Q. Do you have a telephone there? A. No, sir.

Q. What is your occupation? A. A housewife.

Q. Amy Stewart, the girl who was just on the stand, is your daughter?

A. She is.

Q. How old is she? A. Sixteen.

Q. When was she sixteen? A. September 3d.

Mr. B. That is all.

The Court. Do you want to ask the witness any questions? The Defendant. No, sir.

A. D., called as a witness on behalf of the People, being first duly sworn, was examined and testified as follows:

The Clerk. Please state your name. The Witness. A. D.

Direct Examination

By Mr. B.

Q. You are a policewoman of the City of Los Angeles? A. Yes, sir.

Q. Attached to what station? A. 032d Street.

Q. That is, the Juvenile Prevention Bureau? A. Yes, sir.

Q. Did you have a conversation with the defendant? A. Yes, sir.

Q. When did that take place? A. On the twenty-eighth of last month.

Q. Where did it take place? A. In the office of the Juvenile Bureau.

Q. Who was present besides you and him? A. Amy Stewart, and another officer, I don't remember just who.

Q. What time did it take place? A. I don't know, sometime on the twenty-eighth or twenty-ninth.

Q. Did you or any other officer use any force or threat of force against this defendant? A. No.

Q. Or offer him any reward or promise him immunity? A. No, sir.

Q. Relate the conversation. A. I asked him if he had had any sexual relations with the girl, and he said he had; and I asked him how many times, and he indicated he didn't remember. Mr. B. That is all.

The Court. Do you want to ask this witness any questions? The Defendant. No, sir.

Mr. B. That is the People's case.

The Court. Do you want to offer any testimony at this time?

The Defendant. No, sir.

Mr. B. The officer who is in charge of the case expresses the opinion now that $3,000 bail or a lesser bail than the amount recommended would be sufficient to hold the defendant, although we have no evidence that he can make any bail—we don't know.

The Court. It appearing to me that the offenses charged in the complaint herein, to-wit: rape, a felony, charged in Counts 1, 2, and 3, have been committed, and there is sufficient cause to believe the defendant, John McFarland, guilty thereof, I order that he be held to answer to the same, and that he be admitted to bail in the sum of $3,000, and be committed to the custody of the Sheriff of Los Angeles County until he give such bail. The defendant will be required to appear for arraignment in Department 04 of the Superior Court at 9:30 A.M. on the second day of December. Witnesses will not be required to appear at that time unless further notified.

In this court the case is considered as a matter of the state which becomes the plaintiff versus defendant who is charged with a crime. There is a formal direct examination of witnesses in order to establish positive proof of guilt. There is no inquiry into the social, economic, educational, religious, or other factors which might have influenced the offender. There is no inquiry into the reasons for the offense nor into the plans to be made for the offender. The court is concerned with the offense and not with the offender. There is no attempt made at individualization of justice. If the defendant is proved guilty the nature and degree of punishment will be prescribed according to statutory provisions. There are other and more sharp distinctions in the procedure and the philosophy between the juvenile and the municipal and criminal courts which will be considered later. Here we wish to point out that the judge and the referee of the juvenile court follow a socialized procedure, which is a greater aid to the minor and to the work of the probation officer.

However, not all juvenile court cases are dealt with in the manner and spirit displayed in the case of Amy Stewart. The following transcript of a court hearing in the Juvenile Court of S. County presents a sharp contrast and serves as an illustration of the need of a more socialized point of view, more training on the part of the judge in psychology, sociology, and social work, and also serves as an illustration of the problems such a judge presents to the probation officer when the offender and his family are compromised, insulted, and antagonized.

CASE OF NORA NORMAN (Continued)

This matter coming on regularly to be heard on Wednesday, this fourth day of March, 1936, at 2:00 P.M.

Nora was present with the following witnesses and parties: Mr. A., the store detective, Mr. B., a store clerk, Miss C., the saleslady who waited on Nora, Police Officer Riley, Tom and Dick Dickson, Mr. and Mrs. Dickson, Mr. and Mrs. Norman, Mrs. Alden, the "aunt," and the probation officer. The following procedure was had.

Court. Will you all stand, except the boys, and raise your right hands to be sworn? (Witnesses sworn, including Nora.)

Court. What is your name? A. Nora Norman.

Q. How old are you? A. I was sixteen on Aug. 3. I was born in 1919 in —.

Summary of Hearing.— The probation officer briefly reviewed the facts regarding Nora's act of petty theft. The court was chiefly concerned with the degree of loss or damage of goods. Since no loss or damage was incurred the store witnesses were excused. Arrangements were made to hear the case of the boys later, and they and their parents were asked to wait in the lobby.

Court. Nora, what else brings you here today? (No reply.) (Question repeated twice, no reply.)

Q. Nora, why should you come up before a Juvenile Court? (Nora swiftly glanced at two rows of witnesses but did not reply.)

Q. Who is responsible for your pregnancy? A. John.

Q. John who? A. I won't give his name. It is as much my fault as it is his. I don't want to make any trouble for him. He left the state.

Court (To Mr. Norman). Are you the father of this girl? A. Yes, sir.

Q. And you are unable to control her? A. No, sir.

Q. Have you tried? A. Yes, sir.

Q. What's the matter? Are you afraid of her? A. No.

Q. How much do you try to really control her? A. I had tried everything I know.

Q. Parents should never bring children into this world if they can't train them. A. She was the first baby. I didn't know then . . . Well, what am I going to do?

Q. What can you do? A. I can't do anything with her. We live in a small town. She has no mother. I have remarried. Why can't she go where there are people who know how to handle her?

Court. Are you the stepmother? A. (Nod.)

Q. Can't you take care of her? A. I have troubles of my own. He drinks himself silly. I wouldn't stay with him if I didn't have to.

Q. The situation is this: the girl is not a public charge nor a public responsibility. She is yours. How much are you making a month, Mr. Norman?

A. Don't know exactly. Just started to work last week. Will probably make ninety dollars a month. (Wife interrupting: If he stays sober long enough.)

Q. How many are there in the family? Three, without Nora? A. Yes, sir. I don't like to have her gone, but I can't wreck the other girl's life. Decent girls won't have much to do with her.

Q. Well, that is not the court's concern in the matter. We cannot change her companionship very much. Is there any reason why you can't pay $20 per month for her support in a maternity home, if there are only three of you? A. It will be hard.

Q. You brought this girl into the world and she is a burden on somebody. It is up to you to make a sacrifice and to do your duty in this matter as long as you are unable to do your duties of parenthood; you will have to handle the financial end of it. The responsibility rests where nature put it. A. I was gassed in the war. I fought for this country and lost my health and soul. I am not the same man that I was a few years ago. I don't know what you mean by responsibility rests where nature placed it?

Q. I can't go into that here. But you are not doing your duty. A. (Nod.)

Court. Well, Nora will be declared a ward of the court and placed in the custody of the probation officer, to be maintained in a home of her choosing. It will be further ordered that the parents of the girl pay the sum of $20 a month for her support and maintenance in said home, and that the County of S. supplement not more than $10 a month. The parents are to make a payment to the probation officer on the first of each month, beginning Apr. 1, 1936, and to continue until the further order of the court. The girl is to remain in Juvenile Detention Home until no longer needed by the District Attorney's office. Now, Nora, you may wait outside.

Court. Nora won't talk here, although her report does not sound like it. Who is responsible for her pregnancy? Father. She won't tell.

Probation Officer. I can't find out. She is afraid that it will spoil her chances of marriage if she gives the name.

Court. You learn his name. Use the right approach. We can't let the man go free. What will she do with the baby? A. Has not decided.

Court. You get the name of that man. A. I'll try your honor, but I don't know if . . . Court. You try.

Social Value of the Court Hearing

Nora's case, a case of sex delinquency and pregnancy, was heard before a male judge. Such a situation is inevitable in counties not large enough to maintain a referee, who generally is a woman. Undoubtedly Nora was embarrassed and hesitated to tell a man the circumstances that brought her into court. But, since the juvenile court is a court of record, facts must be established and recorded, particularly when adults contributing to the delinquency of minors are involved. Otherwise it would have been advisable to talk to Nora privately.

While the hearing in Nora's case was informal in character it was in some respects held from the legalistic point of view. No inquiry was made into the social, educational, religious, and other aspects of the case which were considered in the case of Amy Stewart. The court did not initiate a course of treatment, and Nora was not enabled to place her confidence in the court and to share her plans and thoughts with it. Legally Nora is under the jurisdiction of this court, but personally she did not accept it, and she virtually remained without natural parents and without parens patriae, which is the chief function of the juvenile court. Thus Nora's case was disposed of. Courts frequently assume that a girl is "sufficiently jolted" by arrest, detention, court hearing, commitment, pregnancy, facing the parents, and an empty future "to keep away from trouble." But does a young girl, if the sex experience has been satisfying to her, find "the jolt" a substitution for sex expression? The probation officer needs to remember that these young girls need absorbing work, physical exercise, congenial home atmosphere, sex instruction, religious affiliation, and whatever idealization and sublimation processes are suited to the circumstances and temperament of the girl.

It is apparent that there is considerable dissension in Nora's home, that there are no bonds of affection, of sympathy, or of common interests. Nora senses her homelessness and realizes that John is her only escape.

Yet John is guilty of statutory rape, and he might involve other girls in pregnancy. The court's concern must, of course, be the welfare of the many instead of that of the single individual.

Under the present juvenile court organization the probation officer has little control over the nature of the court hearing in a particular case. He should, however, note all turns of the hearing, the effects on the offender and the family, and decide accordingly in what manner to follow up the case. He needs to be sensitive to the reactions and interactions resulting from the examination. He should not feel that the court is doing the work and that he can sit back and rest. The court hearing is one of the crucial moments upon which the officer can build his plan of treatment. Frequently he may have to undo much, particularly after such an encounter with a judge as was exemplified in Nora's case.

Tom and Dick and their parents appeared in court on the same day as Nora. The boys were remonstrated with, were ordered to "go directly home after school," and "to mind their parents." Both of them vociferously promised "to be good." Suddenly the judge asked the question: "And what made you do these things?" The boys looked at each other in confusion. The question was repeated. One boy mumbled in utter bewilderment: "I dunno." "But you must have a mind of your own and not allow others to mislead you." Again the boys promised, but somewhat less emphatically. And there the matter ended in court. The boys and parents were dismissed. Now the question may be raised: How can the court expect these little boys to keep their pledge, no matter how emphatically made, when so little is known about their ability to avoid future temptations or to resist them when encountered? Cyril Burt advocates to the child adviser to "draw from his young client what aims he has in view, how he thinks he can still satisfy his strongest interests without running counter to the law, and, with some well-framed policy of life will induce him to fortify himself against failure in the future."

The judge, however, will make an outcry against this obvious real truth. He works overtime as it is. He is obliged to hear and to pass on ten, fifteen, twenty, and more cases daily. When can he follow this wise counsel? And after all is it his duty to assume the long process of reeducation of the wrongdoer? The probation officer, however, may be depending on the rascal getting his "jolt" in court to "reawaken him to his right senses." The appearance in court and the hearing are calculated, in some subtle way or otherwise, to be at one and the same time a critical and impressive moment in the offender's life. Only too frequently, however, does the child leave the courtroom bewildered and unable to carry out the promise which he made in all sincerity, since no practical ways and means were pointed out to him which would actually enable him to keep the promise.

Juvenile court authorities would agree that the procedure involving children's cases needs to be much more socialized than has hitherto been attained in most juvenile courts. On the other hand, we should not forget the real progress made in handling children's cases. Flexner, Oppenheimer, and Lenroot cite two typical hypothetical cases, before and after the establishment of juvenile courts, which indicate the far-reaching nature of the change due to the new procedure:

In the middle of the nineteenth century a boy thirteen or fourteen years old set fire to a stable. He was indicted by the grand jury, and because he could not give bail he was sent to jail until he was tried before a petit jury in a crowded courtroom. The State's attorney presented his evidence, consisting of proof that the boy committed the act with which he was charged and that he was old enough to know what he was doing. The boy's attorney offered evidence to the contrary. The judge ruled on questions of evidence. Hearsay evidence was not admissible. No one thought of offering testimony as to the boy's surroundings. He was convicted and sent to the penitentiary in which he served his sentence in the company of the usual hardened convicts in a penal institution.

That boy's grandson to-day sets fire to a garage in a jurisdiction that has a modern juvenile court. Complaint is made. The boy is brought in and sent to a juvenile detention home in which are no adults except the persons in charge. There he is examined physically and mentally. In the meantime a court probation officer investigates the boy and his environment. He finds that the boy's grandfather was sent to prison, that his family is poor, that they have moved from state to state, that he has had little schooling, and that he has been associating with vicious companions. A plan is made for the boy's care and training. His case is heard in a room informally arranged in which there are no spectators except those immediately concerned in the case and no lawyer except the judge. The judge hears the complaint and reads the reports of the physician, the psychiatrist and the probation officer. The boy admits the act complained of. (If he had not admitted it the judge would have heard the testimony and decided the question of fact.) The judge talks to the boy and to his parents and places him on probation. The cooperation of social agencies is enlisted and a better job is found for the boy's father. The probation officer consults the school authorities and arranges for the boy to have school work that will hold his interest. He puts the boy in touch with recreational activities that will occupy his spare time in a wholesome way. The boy comes to the probation officer regularly to report progress and to talk over his problems. The probation officer visits the boy and his family at frequent intervals and endeavors to bring the mother and father to a better understanding of their son and his needs. Finally, the boy is discharged from probation, or, if he continues in his old ways, he may be committed to a training school for boys.

In the second case cited we note that the probation officer enlists the cooperation of the social agencies in finding a better job for the father; the interests of the school and of the recreational authorities are secured in behalf of the boy. Undoubtedly much more was done for the boy and his family than this brief report indicates. It is apparent, however, that the executive and routine phases of social treatment predominated. Chiefly external aspects of the boy's behavior were considered. Motives, attitudes, emotional reactions, and the whole complex of the inner life of the child are not mentioned. This hypothetical case is typical, as the authors maintain, of a large number of cases handled by many probation departments. If one may be allowed to read into a case, it may be stated that the recorder of this case had the premonition that not all was well with the handling of this boy when he indicates that "if he continues in his old way, he may be committed to a training school for boys," as, indeed, a large proportion of delinquents do persist in their old delinquent patterns, if treated in the above manner.

As the procedure is being carried on at present, what is the law doing in the hearing of children's cases? To cite again the authorities on juvenile court law Flexner, Oppenheimer, and Lenroot the situation may be summarized as follows:

> *First, generally, as in cases of contract and property, it [the law] is determining an event. It determines whether or not the boy set fire to the garage, as it might determine whether a deed was actually signed or whether a seller failed to deliver an order. Second, it is determining a condition the boy's health, mentality and environment again the factual question. Third, it is treating the event in the light of the condition, just as it may weigh considerations of public policy against considerations of individual interest in deciding whether a noise from a factory constitutes a public nuisance and should be enjoined. Fourth, it gives the case continued treatment, as it continues to supervise the administration of a trust in equity.*

The court hearing, ideally conceived, is in effect a conference at which all interested parties are able to secure an interpretation of the facts of the given case as well as the bearing of public policy, morals, and customs upon them. At such a conference issues are clarified and a decision is reached. The delinquent and his parents are thus able to get new definitions of the social situation, even though these may not be explicitly stated at the hearing. New conceptions of communal relations, of social controls, and of the role the offender plays in the group are bound to come out if the court hearing is planned to reorient him socially.

15

Techniques of Recording Treatment: Processes and Plans

Introduction

The Department of Probation of the County of Westchester provides the following outline to aid probation officers in their summary or block recording of case treatment.

Underlining is most efficiently used when used most sparingly. Devote separate paragraph to family support and restitution status preferably at end of summary.

This outline is merely suggestive of the scope of material to be included in the record. Each worker must use discretion in using any outline and not attempt to fit unique experiences and particular situations into a definite mold. Ethel N. Cherry, Supervisor of Case Work of the Probation Department of the County of Westchester, writes:

A committee of the probation officers representing each type of education, worked on an outline for summary or block recording. We have used it now for a period of over a year and with few exceptions find that it keeps the work up to date, that it is simpler for the probation officer but far more important in that he puts some diagnostic thinking into his work in addition

> *to simply factual recording. In order to combine a month's work and put in all the important things, the probation officer finds that he must think through exactly what has happened and this calls to his attention what still needs to be done for the case.*

Summaries can be arranged under appropriate headings, suggested in the foregoing outline, or any other headings suited to the particular character of the case. Miss Cherry supplies the following sample of block recording.

During this period the family moved to a new six-room apartment at 6 Blank Street, White Plains. Mrs. Esposito with the help of Mrs. J., a more Americanized neighbor, has put up new curtains, and there is now a room which may be used for a common family meeting place. The bedrooms are lighter and airier and the house was in much better order. The mother's whole morale has been helped by this change and was very much pleased by P. O.'s approval. They pay $30 a month rent, which is partially paid by the Public Welfare Department, who are supplementing the earnings of Mr. Esposito and the two oldest boys. The location of the home is nearer the clubhouse and the mother with great pride told the P. O. that she would be able sometime now to go over "and straighten up the club."

Tony's health continues to be a matter of concern although the mother states that he is taking his cod-liver oil and eating better at meals. She is concerned about the father, feeling that he is growing thinner and coughs some at night. The father was interviewed on the second home visit. He is still opposed to having a physician examine him, but is not so belligerent and accepts the suggestion with better feeling.

The school reports show the boy's effort has improved. Copies of these are filed. Vito's promptness at school has improved. At a recent meeting of the club, when the school reports were discussed, Vito told this with a great deal of pride.

The boy has continued to go swimming at the Y.M.C.A. each night. There was only one thing of concern that happened during this period.

arrangement:

HV :	**Nov. 20**	
	Dec. 12	
SV:	**Dec. 3**	
OC:	**Dec. 3**	**(Report should follow.)**
L:	**Dec. 3**	
R:	**Nov. 15**	
	Nov. 29	
	Dec. 6	**[P.V.Y.]**

Both boys failed to appear at home one night until eleven o'clock, when they were supposed to have been attending a workshop. The mother was quite terrified. The P. O. had learned from the instructor that a substitute had been placed on that night and because of the boys' intense interest had neglected to close the class at the 9:30 hour. It took a great deal of time on the part of the P. O. to convince the mother that the boys were not hanging around the streets. The old-world attitude of distrust of any deviation, while commendatory in checking on the boys' whereabouts, caused some difficulty. The boys have gotten to the place where they both resented the fact that their story was not believed. The family's attitude was interpreted to the boys, which they finally accepted. Both tried to understand each other's view points in the future.

Tony and Vito are planning with the other club members for the Christmas celebration. A Christmas basket of food which is to be paid for by their two cents a week dues is to be given to some needy family. The boys earn this money by running errands on Saturday.

AWT:eg

This form of recording may be compared with the diary or chronological entries. Perhaps the record on Sam Fineberg's case would have lent itself more readily to block recording. It is agreed that chronological entries are useful when the case is known only a short time, when the worker does not think in diagnostic terms, or when he is extremely busy and carries an excessive case load and cannot remember the clients sufficiently to summarize the case work processes in these particular cases. (Note that the case of Marilyn Smith is purposely recorded in diary form since this record is reproduced primarily to indicate in detail the thinking behind the worker's procedure and not as a model for case recording.) The following case progress record, which is in reality a case work organizer, is found by many to be of great service in keeping up with the mechanical details incidental in all case work procedure. Erle F. Young, who designed the case progress record sheet, writes as follows:

Certainty and speed of action are two prime considerations in efficient social case work. The case worker must be at once a leader able to discover and develop the hidden resources of family and community and a skilled case work mechanician. The mechanics of case work are a sore burden to many case workers; frequently they require so much energy that the quality of the work is impaired. With a heavy case load there is constant danger that decisions will be forgotten, promises unfulfilled, letter-writing needlessly delayed, and many important treatment details lost sight of. The usual hastily scribbled notations which the supervisor attaches to case records are lost or forgotten, and there is no regular method for checking up on the performance of operations agreed upon in case conferences or in consultation with the individual case worker. Oral instructions are even more apt to result in failure to perform or in misunderstandings. During the early stages of intensive work on a case the first interviews, verifications, and so on when special attention is focused upon the case there is relatively little likelihood of serious oversights. The trouble begins after the first diagnosis has been made and a plan determined upon. Then attention is apt to shift to the investigation of new cases which require intensive work. A natural result is that the investigational and diagnostic phases of case work frequently secure relatively more attention than case strategy (planning) and case administration (the execution of the plan). Needless delays in the execution of plans result in a too low case turnover and a consequent piling up of the case load. The drain on the financial and personnel resources of the agency becomes excessive and the quality of work drops. This situation causes loss of public confidence in the agency and makes adequate financing difficult. Many devices have been developed to set standards of performance and insure thorough investigation and proper social diagnosis. However, there are few facilitating devices to assure workers and executives that action will be certainly and speedily taken. The Case Progress Record is a simple device which is designed to reduce to a minimum delays in treatment and follow-up and to make certain that instructions, decisions, promises, and so on, are not unnecessarily overlooked or delayed. The Case Progress Record is designed to supplement rather than displace existing record-keeping devices. Well organized records are already provided with face sheets, budget sheets, case diagnostic sheets, treatment-plan sheets, and so on. In using the Case Progress Record the executive will find it advantageous to follow certain procedures:

1. The form should be presented and explained fully in staff conference. Be certain that everyone understands how to use it.
2. Emphasize the help which this device affords the individual worker. Do not present it as an executive control device, though from the executive's point of view it serves that purpose also. The wholehearted cooperation of case workers is best secured when they appreciate fully its usefulness to themselves in doing good work particularly when under a heavy burden.
3. Note the method suggested for dealing with letters.
4. Entries should be made in the first six columns at the time each decision is made. The last two columns are used to check results.
5. Supervisors should not be encouraged to forego necessary individual conferences with workers by using this as an instruction sheet. Rather they should

use it to make notations of instructions given during such conferences.

A treatment evaluation summary, particularly in cases extending over a long period of time, would be useful if recorded in brief summary form periodically (and not only when closing the case), indicating what has been attempted but failed of results, what has been successfully accomplished (for teaching purposes it would be valuable to know the method of such accomplishment and the reasons for success or failure), and further plan of treatment by client, by agency, through the use of community resources, etc. Miss Hamilton shows some of the wider implications and complexities of recording in the following statement:

> The notion of recording a plan is particularly relevant if "executive treatment," or service, is contemplated or if environmental factors are to be manipulated or if habit training or other similar education is to be attempted. Planning is less easy to state if methods of progressive education are to be employed and the client is to learn from experience in a dynamic situation. A formal plan seems less relevant in so-called relationship treatment or attitude therapy. The ideas of treatability, planning, controls and outcome instead of plan are, however, inherent in all methods of treatment and not the least in relationship therapy. If the worker has a definite plan it is probably wise to state it; if the plan is one offered by the client and agreed upon with the agency, it is wise to state it; if no plan is contemplated, it is impossible to state it. Workers of certain training and approach would prefer to think of "movement" rather than activity, and when the stress is on the client's use of the worker, rather than on the leadership of the worker, the planning process is fluid and difficult to formalize in any ordinary sense.
>
> Evaluation lies close to diagnosis, but we think of it more in connection with treatment. What has proved better or worse, more or less constructive in the progressive handling? The norms in evaluation are social and personal. Mores shift from generation to generation and from country to country, and people may differ or deviate markedly from

the mores without necessarily feeling unadjusted. The case worker has to resist alike the temptation to arbitrary over-simplification and useless qualification. "This seems apparently, in a manner of speaking, to be approximately something or other." All diagnostic effort or treatment evaluation is extraordinarily complicated, tentative, and flexible, and is understood as such by the well-trained reader or writer of records. The difficulty is not in recording clearly but in learning to think clearly, and no record can be said to be professional until our fragmentary and imperfect diagnostic thinking is included. The patient exposed to the full battery of scientific method was right in complaining that he wished just for once he could be treated for what ailed him.

The closing entry should stress the outstanding problems at the time the case was referred, those developed subsequently, the course of treatment followed successfully, and of that attempted without success, the results of treatment obtained, and the reason for closing.

"A closing entry need not in simple cases be longer than a paragraph or so, and a narrative style ... seems to be the most satisfactory."

Attention is called to the final petition in the case of Sam Fineberg, which is illustrative of a concise summary report on a case active in the agency for eighteen months. Undoubtedly this summary could be abbreviated, but it shows the essential points to be included in the summary.

For Bibliography See Chapter VI (p. 112) Suggestions for Further Study

1. Read Ralph Hall Ferris, "The Case History in Probation Service," in Sheldon Glueck (Editor), Probation and Criminal Justice, pp. 153-159. What constitutes a supervision record? a treatment record? How should such a record be kept? How should all the subtle phases of probation supervision be recorded? of child welfare work in general? How can a record serve as a "map of the road" to another probation officer or judge? or other worker? Should the treatment record be written in the first person? Why, or why not?

2. Read Ada E. Sheffield, "The Social Case History", pp. 60-69, "The Summary." What does Mrs. Sheffield include in the summary of a social case history of a family? What should be included in the summary of a probation case? of a problem child case?
3. Read Gordon Hamilton, Social Case Recording, and indicate her method of recording case summaries, transfer summaries, closing summaries. 4. What does Erle F. Young mean by a case work organizer?

16

Coordinating Council Movement and Social Work Development

Introduction

A large number of public and semipublic, private and semiprivate agencies have launched various programs and have developed independent organizations, societies, clubs, republics, leagues, councils, orders, plans, codes, committees, brotherhoods, federations, associations, ideas, agencies, settlements and so on. To this motley array the schools, the churches, and some national and language groups add their welter of organizations. The lack of coordination of efforts, of policies, of procedures, of services of these various organizations is appalling and disconcerting. Erle F. Young writes:

> *It is little wonder that conflicts of interest have developed, and that unhealthy competition between organizations is rife in the struggle for available funds, public attention, and exclusive responsibility for certain desirable classes or special programs of action. Only too frequently in the resulting chaos the interests of the juvenile have been well-nigh lost sight of by the very agencies whose special guardians they were presumed to be. In-coordination of*

> *effort is not merely a matter of wastage of effort and funds but a certain proportion of juvenile disorganization can probably be directly charged to the resulting inefficiency of the institutions concerned. Many students now insist that one of the first necessary steps in social advance is the integration of the efforts of all responsible agencies.*

The Origin of the Movement for Coordination.— The first pioneer plan for coordinating the work of local departments interested in the welfare of youth and their communities was started when the Chief of Police, August Vollmer, in Berkeley and the Assistant Superintendent of Schools, Dr. Virgil Dickson, realized that their departments were dealing with some of the same problems of children. At first they met once a week for luncheon to discuss these problems and as time went on they gradually included other officials and social workers who could help in working out a plan of adjustment for individual children. This group adopted the name "coordinating council," writes Kenneth Beam. This council was formed in 1919 in Berkeley, California. The Berkeley experiment was recommended by the State Commission for the Study of Problem Children in 1929 for adoption elsewhere.

Robert H. Scott, Judge of the Juvenile Court, Los Angeles County, defines the Coordinating Council as "a clearing house where sincere, devoted, intelligent individuals and organizations discuss mutual problems of child, family, and community welfare; while the [coordinating council] can be inspiring success we naturally should not rely upon that or any similar movement to be a power-house to supply energy to all its related organizations."

Los Angeles County, under the leadership of Kenyon J. Scudder and Kenneth S. Beam, of the Probation Department, and Judge Samuel Blake of the Juvenile Court, followed the lead and organized in 1932 the Los Angeles Coordinating Council, adapting the plan of the Berkeley Council to local needs. This council is a voluntary organization including within its membership such persons as court officials, probation officers, school attendance officers, police juvenile officers, representatives of service clubs, civic organizations, group workers and case workers from private and public agencies, and lay persons.

As early as 1928 Judge Robert H. Scott organized an extensive Juvenile Court Committee with some 800 citizens from the general community as members participating in learning and disseminating the facts, functions, and the work of the Juvenile Court. This large body of citizens soon became aware that the sources of delinquency were embedded in the disorganizing forces of the community. Many of the leaders of this community became community-conscious, and when the coordinating council movement germinated in Los Angeles the social soil was ready for it. Undoubtedly much of the success which this movement has achieved in Southern California is due to a large extent to the early work of the Juvenile Court Committee.

Its underlying philosophy is based on the fact that mobilization of resources and coordination of effort are essential for effective work and that the causes of delinquency are too diverse and too complex to be dealt with by any one group working alone. The philosophy is embodied in the definition of a coordinating council formulated by Francis H. Hiller, in a "Report of a Brief Study of the Coordinating Councils." He says:

> *A coordinating council may be described as an association of public and private welfare agencies and civic bodies to coordinate their work, to discover and estimate more accurately than heretofore the demoralizing influences in their community and neighborhood, and to plan and act jointly for the betterment of conditions, most frequently with special reference to the prevention of juvenile delinquency.*

In July, 1936, there were 110 councils in California, 60 of which were organized in Los Angeles County. An additional 104 councils are scattered in eighteen other states in the Union, ranging from one council each in New Jersey, New Hampshire, North Carolina, Oklahoma, to 24 councils in Pennsylvania, 21 in Michigan, 10 in Illinois, while the rest of the states have 2, 4, 6, 8, or 9 councils each. In Los Angeles County there is a central executive board with representatives from the local committees and from the various county and city departments and other special groups interested in children's behavior problems. It is evident that the movement is spreading comparatively rapidly in some localities, particularly in Southern California. At the Attorney General's Conference on Crime, held in 1934, a resolution was adopted recognizing the work of the coordinating councils and urging state and national sponsorship of them.

The Program of the Coordinating Councils. — The first councils, according to Beam, were interested solely in the adjustment of individual behavior problems of particular children, and representatives of various schools, health and welfare agencies of the police and probation departments formed an adjustment committee. To this committee behavior problems of children were presented in sufficient detail to enable it to make a referral to the appropriate agency for treatment. The committee itself did no case work. It operated on the belief that through the consideration of cases and plans and of the programs of the suitable agencies the various members of the committee will become familiar with the programs, equipment, administrative setup, and points of view of the representing agencies and will, therefore, be in a position for more effective cooperative effort. Mr. Hiller observes:

The question arises why these cases should not be referred directly by the police or schools to the appropriate agency. The answer is that participation in the council has created a situation with a spirit of mutual understanding and confidence, which has resulted in the referral of more cases than previously and what is more important, earlier than they otherwise would have been. When police officers, for example, find boys on the streets late at night or in undesirable places or engaged in some minor misconduct, the procedure in the past was usually to warn them or at most to take them to the station house and send for their parents. Probably from a quarter to a third of all cases of boys coming to the attention of the police are of this character. Previously nothing more was done about them.

Such indifference gave rise to the question, " Does a kid have to break into jail before the community will give him a lift?" These cases, through the adjustment committees, now come to the attention of some social agency which may render a helpful service in time to prevent the development of more serious delinquency.

Later the interests of the councils embraced the development of constructive play and leisure-time facilities for youth and elimination of unwholesome community conditions which have a direct bearing on delinquency problems. With the development of these wider interests representatives of many of the so-called character-building agencies were invited to join the councils, and a character-building committee was formed; and with the inclusion of representatives of civic organizations, such as men's and women's clubs, parent-teacher associations, the American Legion, an environment committee was formed and was assigned the specific task of improving both home and community environments. However, there is a great diversity in the matter of committees, observes Kenneth Beam. Some council has no committees at all but do all their work in one general meeting.

The programs, nature of meeting, efficiency, and procedures vary widely from council to council and committee to committee, depending largely upon the quality of the local leadership, professional standards and attitudes of the members, personal interests in publicity of certain members who have been termed "publicity hounds," as well as on the amount and quality of provision for leisure time of youth and the degree of local community organization and support. Equally varied are the objectives and purposes of the various councils. The following fundamental principles concerning coordinating councils grew out of the discussion at the San Diego meeting, 1934, of the California Conference of Social Work.

a. The Council should provide a careful study of the various areas in the community in order to determine the problems and needs of the community in dealing with juvenile delinquency.

b. The Council should coordinate into one plan the various services offered by all the social agencies in the area, to combat juvenile delinquency. This is the task of the Adjustment Committee of the Council.

c. The Council should provide all the agencies in its area with the facts by which they can evaluate their program and by which they can be directed in their efforts and plans for expansion.

These fundamental principles indicate the uniqueness of the coordinating councils and distinguish them from the Council of Social Agencies, which is furthermore organized on a city-wide rather than on a neighborhood basis, and which gives immediate consideration to problems of agency organization and relationships rather than to community conditions.

Erle F. Young states:

> *The widest possible latitude has been given each local council. The simplicity of the council organization has made possible whatever activity special conditions and local interests have suggested. Certain problems, for example, the sale of liquor to minors, are county-wide, if not state-wide. A plan has therefore developed to devote at least a portion of the work of all councils to these wider interests, following a schedule of topics agreed upon at a meeting of officers of all councils. Topics listed for discussion in the immediate future include such matters as social legislation, liquor and youth, the summer camp program, church and youth, and home life of modern youth.*

Annual conferences give further opportunity for securing united effort and developing a common point of view. By these means the weaker councils, which have had difficulty in developing concrete activities, are provided with a minimum program and are stimulated to action.

The activities of the central committee have led to a number of city-wide and county-wide projects. The State Employment Relief Administration has provided a high-grade personnel including many unemployed professionals. A group of such persons was organized and assigned to the playgrounds to supplement the work of the professional personnel. Some were assigned to help the individual councils and the probation department. Various survey projects were set on foot. A careful study of delinquency by elementary school districts has provided for the first time useable local statistical pictures of the delinquency situation in the city. A directory of all recreational and character building facilities was also prepared.

The leadership of the movement in Los Angeles County is in the Juvenile Probation Department and the Juvenile Court. However, probation officers do not act as officers in the local councils. A high degree of local autonomy and local control is thus assured while at the same time providing the necessary intimate contact of the local community with the juvenile court; this easy access to the court frequently results at first in "dumping" the local difficult children on the court. Through the adjustment committee this tendency is soon sharply counteracted and local community resources are called into play. The net result has been a sharp reduction in the number of cases referred by many communities to the court.

The above comments, though relating to the Los Angeles Council, are equally applicable to the plan of many other councils.

What Do the Councils Accomplish?— Mr. Beam reports that many groups and individuals ask the above question. The present writer had made a preliminary study of the activities and opinions in connection with the article by Erle F. Young of various councils members who are in executive positions both in their own agencies and in the councils with which they are intimately connected. Some saw specific advantages, which may be quoted in part.

The council makes the juvenile delinquency problem a community problem rather than that of some one agency. Social workers moreover are discovering that it is not simply a matter of "cases"; it is a matter also of the "community."

It provides a sympathetic approach to the child and a better understanding of his problems. Successful treatment depends largely on that type of approach. In particular we are humanizing the approach of the police, the sheriff, and the probation officer.

The council arouses an interest in prevention and induces officials to think in such terms.

We have now a suitable technique for referring cases to the right agency. It is showing community leaders the value of case studies.

The surveys sponsored by the council have given us real information on community situations with which we have been struggling. Furthermore, it is now good form to pool our information rather than utilize it simply for self-promotion.

The council puts every agency "on the spot." We are all coming to know each other's affairs and a failure on the part of one is soon common knowledge. We are all challenged therefore to put forth our best effort in order to maintain our status. We no longer operate in the dark or go our own way unheeding of the opinion and plans of other workers.

Most of us have not changed our procedures very much as yet but the Police Department is a notable exception. They have instructed their officers to give full cooperation and have begun referring certain cases to the adjustment committee which heretofore received no special attention. That includes about 25 per cent of the cases coming to the attention of the Police Department. It is a great step forward in organization.

To these statements may be added one by Mr. Hiller:

> *The carrying out of the council's programs has been greatly facilitated by work relief projects in many areas under the state emergency relief administration. Hundreds of workers have been so employed in Los Angeles County, chiefly on the making of surveys of social conditions under the direction of the central executive and research committee but these workers have also been assigned to aid many of the neighborhood councils in carrying out some of their projects.*

Scudder and Beam have stated that they "do not expect the full effect of the councils to be felt for another generation." It is clear that a satisfactory evaluation of the council plan cannot be made when it has been operating only four years and a half. Erle F. Young believes that such an evaluation can be accomplished only after the institution has been tried under more varying conditions and over a longer period of time. "That it has been successful in certain communities and in dealing with certain problems is a well established fact. Whether these successes can be repeated in other communities and with other types of problems" is just now being learned. Excerpts from interviews with some of the members referred to before will illustrate not only certain problems which these members in Los Angeles have found to be at times very disconcerting, but also the fact that the agencies need far greater integration than has been achieved to date.

It is very true that to a large degree the social and civic workers have learned to get along better together and to discuss their problems with each other, but each then goes back to his own organization and continues his work in his accustomed routine way. As yet there has been no real reorganization of any agency. This is a very difficult matter.

One of the greatest difficulties has been that, from the point of view of the local agency, the program has been developed and sponsored outside of the community and independently of the agencies concerned. It is, in fact, a child of the probation department, turned over to us for foster care. We have had very little to do with the planning and those who have imagination and organizational ability have had little chance to make any original contributions, while those who are unimaginative and lack organizational ability consider it an abstraction, or as something of a routine procedure which they work out faithfully but frequently ineffectually. However, there is considerable leeway in the local councils.

Another serious difficulty of a similar nature is the relation of the agencies to delinquent children. In some communities the children are now being over-importuned to join organizations and participate in activities. Many things are offered them. They are invited to pageants, programs, picnics, and so on in large numbers where everything is arranged for them. Children and parents are impressed by such affairs and come to the conclusion that it is not necessary to earn the privilege of belonging to clubs or to earn the pleasures provided them.

At present these communities are frequently over-run with schools, playgrounds, character-building agencies and community affairs. A very unhealthy competition has developed between social agencies for the available juvenile clientele. That seems paradoxical in view of the principles of the council and of the large number of unchurched and unorganized boys and girls, but it is the actual situation in some few communities.

We social workers are a very busy people at our own tasks. An additional committee to attend is a real burden for most of us.

Most of us have had little experience at organization work and little ability for it while most of the work of the council calls for just that.

We have few of the leading people on our councils. We do have the responsible social workers but they cannot accomplish the tasks they have set for themselves without the active help of the real leaders in the community. Hence we have failed to clear the neighborhoods of disorganizing forces, low grade movies, dance halls, saloons, and the like.

It is true that we social workers, through council activities, have come to know our problems better, to work together more harmoniously and have drawn into our groups many lay persons but our difficulty is that as yet no real technique for adjusting juvenile problems is known. All of the good-will in the world and all possible cooperation will not remedy many situations. We simply do not know what to do or how to do it. Conferences, committee meetings, paper plans are no solution for these situations. Much further real research is needed.

We are quite innocent of any formulated social philosophy. Since organization is itself presumed to be a good thing we have apparently assumed that that is what is needed in this case. There is a good reason to think so, of course, but we do not have any carefully formulated point of view such as the juvenile court movement had. That makes us almost wholly empirical in our approach but gives us a very confused picture of what it is all about.

The number of people making the above observations are comparatively few. Mr. Beam, while making an extensive study of the coordinating councils in several states for the National Probation Association in 1936, reports various activities which are a direct result of the council's discovery of need, backing, planning, and selecting the agency to carry the plan into effect. The council serves as a medium but some agency actually does the work. Among the major activities may be listed some ten:

(1) sociological studies of neighborhoods made by graduate students in certain universities;
(2) education of the public regarding the work of the councils, through published booklets, articles in local papers, radio programs, forums, and lectures;
(3) closer coordination of the work of member agencies;
(4) development of recreational and library facilities;
(5) service for individual children through the adjustment committees;
(6) development of a public-school behavior clinic (in Berkeley);
(7) special attention to young people from sixteen to twenty-five years of age;
(8) promotion of better films;
(9) agitation against child labor and sale of liquor and salacious literature to minors;
(10) referral of problem cases to the schools or child welfare agencies without recourse to the juvenile court.

The councils have been able to keep out of court many children whose problems were, at least momentarily, adjusted by more informal and noncourt procedure. Also, social workers have become more "community-minded" and less "agency-minded"; communities have awakened to the needs of children; and unification of forces and concerted action is a very helpful procedure to all concerned. Then there are what Mr. Hiller calls "intangible values."

Most participants in the work of the councils feel that their most valuable contribution is in the fostering of inter-agency cooperation, acquaintance and understanding, in the stimulus to better and more extensive work, and in community education in problems of child welfare and delinquency. Some testify to their astonishment at discovering how little known to each other were some of the most active agencies. Organizations have been stimulated and challenged by facing together serious community problems. The presence of representatives of religious and civic organizations creates a psychological situation in which each agency is more eager to do its best. The head of a police department, for example, admitted that his department probably acted much more promptly and thoroughly in getting evidence upon which they abolished gambling places near a high school, by reason of the fact that the problem was presented by school officials and two or three citizens at a meeting of the coordinating council of which a police officer was also a member. Of course the schools could have referred the problem to the police without the intervention of a council but the reference was facilitated by the acquaintance of the school and police representatives and action was encouraged by the knowledge of the police department that representative citizens and organizations in the neighborhood wanted this thing done and would applaud them for doing it.

The educational value of the council movement is undoubtedly considerable. The activities of civic groups in child welfare work have been directed through participation in the councils into channels mapped out with reference to a study of community needs, whereas formerly each group was left to choose more or less at random whatever activity had the strongest emotional appeal. The results of surveys and news of activities of the member organizations are taken back to the various organizations by delegates. In many neighborhoods the councils have organized educational courses for the public, particularly for parents, combining with the educational addresses some entertainment feature to increase the attendance. As a result, instead of the usual rather select group who attend a parent-teacher meeting, as many as 2,000 parents have been brought out for the "community nights" in some districts.

Electrical transcriptions for use in informing organizations of the work being done in delinquency prevention, are an exceedingly effective educational device. The transcriptions give the audience a vivid sense of being actually on the scene of action.

Suggestions Concerning the Coordinating Council Movement. The intelligent and farseeing leaders in the movement realize that the young councils, because of the immensity of the problem, have made but a modest beginning in the planning for child welfare and in community reorganization. It is suggested that the councils concentrate more on the real fundamental issues in our complex American life, and that they engage the interests not only of social workers, public officials, and laymen but also of a larger number of the more experienced of the social scientists and the social engineers.

It is suggested that the councils learn the modern trends in social group work and promote and stimulate organizations which are youth's own choice, born of creative ability under intelligent guidance rather than organizations for youth created and handed down to them by adults and maintained under varying adult policies and motives. The prewar German Youth Movement will well repay study on this point, as well as the boys' brotherhood republics in this country.

It is suggested that the councils learn the more modern trends in community organization and stimulate and develop indigenous leadership and promote self-direction of groups and support whatever values there may be in native institutions.

Another point of view could be taken on this subject and the question raised as to whether or not the local communities can supply the indigenous leadership now supplied from the outside, and in general whether such a procedure is workable and expedient? We see some disheartening examples of the misuse and ineffectiveness of democratic government. The principles underlying democratic government, on the other hand, are unimpeachable and they should be utilized to their fullest extent in every energetic enterprise involving the lives and destinies of other individuals and groups. There are representatives of successful merchants, of the professions, of the lay group of the communities in which these councils function, but as yet, not a single member is a representative of the very folks whose lives are being "planned," "guided," or "adjusted." May we assume that the "common people," the "clientele," cannot supply intelligent representatives who can be educated, if necessary, in social ethics and in discreet relations with their neighbors? Many experiments by social workers in "client participation" have proved too valuable to be disregarded in this field without trial.

Alida Bowler writes that many people expressed great satisfaction in seeing community after community face their responsibility to youth and childhood and settle down to an organized effort to meet that responsibility. They report that when these communities now have to file petitions in juvenile court, it is no longer with a "good riddance of bad rubbish" attitude. It is much more likely to be with expressions of regret that the community has been unable to solve the problems of this child without the aid of outside agencies. There is a real recognition of the fact that he is definitely a product of things his community has done, or permitted to be done, to him and of things it has failed to do for him.

Miss Bowler is undoubtedly using the term "community" to mean a constellation of secondary organizations, such as the schools, the police, the welfare agency. As such, the community is performing a valuable service through concerted action and unified forces, but the primary group organizations, the family, the church, the mutual aid groups, the labor union, and others are not considered as possible assets in working out a plan of action, and therefore such procedure neglects fundamental principles of sound community planning.

Certain social workers and public officials may object to extensive participation and representation of the people whose destinies are under consideration in council plans and meetings. Undoubtedly tact and discretion are needed in this work just as much as in any other line. But it cannot be said that the council committee members know the wishes, goals, policies, and culture of many of the very groups they attempt to serve. This is particularly true of the large number of immigrant groups and communities with which the councils are concerned. They are not truly in contact with the life of these groups and can, therefore, have no true power over them. In these situations there is little insight and little social imagination, to use Cooley's terms. Individual teachers and social workers may at times seek the views and consult the leaders of immigrant groups regarding the problems encountered with their children, but intimate views are difficult to grasp by one who does not "think and feel immigrant"; the minds of these leaders seem impenetrable and remain largely untouched. One young Russian leader asks:

Why do the Americans always want to make us over and to run things their way? If our way works with Russians, why change and borrow trouble? It takes a Russian to run things for Russians. But we are not given a chance.... We can Americanize ourselves in our own way. We can be good Russians and good American citizens at the same time.

Again it may be argued that American social agencies which are secondary group organizations have attempted to fulfill the functions which should be left to the local native and indigenous institutions to fulfill only because the latter had failed to do so. We can only point out that modern social case work as well as modern social group work and community organization have vindicated the policy that under no circumstances should anything be done for individuals or for groups which they can be stimulated to do for themselves. Numerous groups have demonstrated remarkable ability for leadership and community organization, according to Allen T. Burns, a profound student of community problems. As to the other groups we do not know. They have never been sufficiently stimulated nor given the opportunity and intelligent backing. Under such circumstances the functions assumed by outsiders are rarely more than an imposition and an artificial and ineffectual substitute for those institutions which are "freely developed by initiative and cooperation of the people themselves." Under such circumstances outside leadership can never be anything but a foreign power dedicated to proselyting or "uplift" work among people who would attain greater efficiency if stimulated to work out their own plans.

There are many communities which can supply indigenous leadership, which should be exploited to its fullest extent. Native leaders know how far and how rapidly they can go in the adjustment process. They know the emotions which this process calls into play, they can feel the pulse of the community, so to speak, and can recognize the danger signs by the frank and constant personal reactions of their fellow members. As one intelligent Mexican leader said, "Our children are not losing faith in us.

They feel that our means for social control are sanctioned by the Americans." We shall repeat what has already been stated in connection with case work with individuals: "There are leaders and there are runners." The group and social institutions which have become the concern of the councils need leaders drafted from their own midst as well as supplied from the outside, but they do not need "runners" of any kind to run their lives. Everyone wishes to have a decent chance to guide his own life, under intelligent native leadership. To adopt the words of Donald Young , author of American Minority Peoples, these groups will become adjusted automatically, if given a chance without oppression and exploitation.

It is suggested that the councils concern themselves with the far-reaching effects of social and economic disorganization and what the Gluecks call "the mountain of deleterious urban social conditions" and become more active in the promotion of appropriate social security acts and needed social legislation in general.

Undoubtedly the coordinating council movement will in the near future direct its efforts toward social legislation in favor of the establishment of minimum wages, of abolition of child labor, development of socialized medicine, of slum clearance, of health and food protective measures, of broader and more effective principles of public education and vocational guidance, and a host of other needed developments which retard the advancement of child welfare.

It is suggested that the councils learn more of the pressing need for parental education and concern themselves with the establishment in every community of permanent parent-guidance clinics conducted by experts.

It is possible to give full assent to various points of view and policies in dealing with the problems of child and community welfare yet to face an impasse in dealing effectively with these problems. The great barrier to early success lies in almost total lack of tested ways and means. Of course, we must recognize our problems first in order to plan effectively a positive course of action. Experimental programs are urgently needed. This field awaits the appearance of social technicians thoroughly conversant with the culture and the intimate life of the various neighborhood groups, endowed with creative imagination, and backed by thoroughgoing research before attempting any solution of problems. So far the situation has been complicated by the fact that agencies have attempted to "solve" problems without adequate knowledge of "what works" and "what does not work" in the adjustment of the serious life problems of individuals, communities, and groups.

On the basis of the expressed problems which the social agencies are facing, the following suggestions might be offered:

It is suggested that the agencies work in closer cooperation with the central executive committee among whose various functions is to plan with individual agencies as to how to adapt their work to the unique needs of the whole community. The central executive council having a broad view of the entire community is in a position to supply the perspective of the total situation which might be difficult to attain by any one agency.

It is suggested that since the council itself does no social or community work, which is properly left to be carried on by the social agency the social agency take more initiative in effective cooperative planning and in reorganizing their communities. When the social agencies complain of ineffective work it reminds one of the constant cry that democracy is failing, yet the very people who complain are the last ones to participate in public affairs or even to vote.

It is suggested that the social agencies interpret to the children in the community the advantages of the various activities organized for their benefit. There is no reason why the children should not be offered the same "opportunities to earn the privilege of belonging" to a new club if that has proved to be a desirable procedure as were offered in the old clubs.

It is suggested that the social agencies disregard the possibilities for immediate gains for a particular agency but view the coordinating council movement in its broader ramifications and realize that by becoming "community-minded" rather than "agency-minded" the individual agency will make its biggest strides.

The coordinating council movement, however, has already assumed far-reaching significance because of its aims of coordination of effort of members and agencies, of programs of wide variety of organization in the field of child welfare. If the councils have accomplished nothing else than coordination of work of public and private agencies legal, educational, recreational, and welfare it has accomplished its goal. For this reason we may agree with Hiller, that "the councils will undoubtedly change as to methods and policies but not as to fundamental purpose." "It is now a lusty movement well worth the attention of students of social organization and worthy of development and experimentation in other communities under good leadership."

Mr. Kenyon J. Scudder, who has been closely associated with the work and organization of the Coordinating Council movement in California, writes as follows with regard to the coordinating councils and crime prevention and community organization.

Community Action and Crime Prevention.— Crime and delinquency will never be reduced until the community decides to do something about it. More than half the youngsters coming into the Juvenile Courts of America are ordinary children who quickly adjust themselves when given an opportunity. The other half are less fortunately endowed with a mental capacity somewhat below normal, and these unfortunate youngsters are entitled to better care and attention than the community has seen fit to give. If we would keep these youngsters out of trouble we must make available to all children the fine facilities in the community which are now restricted to a select few. Too often these select few are the ones who need it the least. If this program is good for these certainly it should be expanded for those who are underprivileged and who now cannot afford to join.

A recent study of some 14,000 Juvenile Court cases in Los Angeles County during the years 1929, '30, and '31, indicated that less than 14 per cent of these children belonged to any kind of a character building organization. Eighty-six per cent found their comrades in the street. Is it any wonder that they found themselves in trouble? It is natural for youth to organize in gangs. The Boy Scout troop is a gang; the Hi-Y group is a gang; but these are gangs under trained leadership with a constructive purpose. A gang of delinquents is organized but it lacks decent leadership and purpose. Yet, these destructive gangs can be turned into fields of usefulness and good citizenship. And this is what the Coordinating Council program is trying to do.

When a child is in trouble in a neighborhood, the easiest thing to do is to take him out. Too often the community clamors for this kind of service from public agencies. They are afraid that one child will contaminate the others and yet they assume no responsibility for conditions over which this child has no control, and which have contributed definitely to his delinquency. It has been said that the Juvenile Court was never designed to prevent delinquency; it was planned as a better method of combating delinquency after its occurrence, and as such it has amply fulfilled the expectations of those who sponsored its beginning. Its function was, and still is, diagnostic and not prophylactic. With the last statement we agree. However, that was yesterday. Now the Juvenile Court has a new function. We now stand upon the threshold of a new era. New forces are at work. The community is beginning to organize. It is looking around. It is shaking itself out of its lethargy. It is anxious to clean up unsatisfactory conditions which affect youth.

Juvenile Courts and Probation Departments have in their possessions vital information about local conditions. Too often this is withheld. Public and private agencies, officials and lay pcople must be drawn closer together. Sheldon Glueck tells us: "In many communities most of the facilities for effective coping with pre-delinquency, delinquency and crime already exist; they require effective integration."

The Juvenile Court and Probation Department of Los Angeles County became very much incensed over the old policy of dropping cases into the Court. The community shed these cases like an old skin. It didn't want them; neither did it want them returned. And yet, when these cases were returned to the community often the agencies and organizations got together and rendered very valuable service and made many splendid adjustments.

But these agencies and organizations were in the community before the child got into trouble. The facilities did exist but they required effective integration. For this reason the Juvenile Court and Probation Department sponsored the Coordinating Councils.

When this movement started many agencies and organizations became very much concerned. Was this a new child which was to be dumped on the community, this organization known as the Coordinating Councils? Was somebody going to have to feed it and nurse it? Or was it going to be able eventually to stand on its own feet?

It is always easy to find people who will criticize a new movement. People do not like change. They have been so long embedded in their individual ruts that they glance with suspicion upon anything new. "We didn't do things that way in the past." "We question the advisability of this program." "Isn't this a fifth wheel?" "Don't we attend enough meetings now?" "We are very busy people and we have our own programs to consider." "Then, after all, how do we know that the bringing in of lay people is going to help our program. In fact, they'll muddy up the water."

Mr. Justin Miller refers to these people as the "Prima Donnas" of social work. They do not want to do any community planning, neither do they wish to be disturbed in the regular routine of their work.

Fortunately these are but a few of the fine people who are interested in the Coordinating Council work. These complaining drones have very little interest outside of their own social agency. They fear lay people. On the other hand, Professor Lindeman, of the New York School of Social Work, in speaking to the Coordinating Councils in Los Angeles, recently said, "We must learn how to work out means and methods of collaboration between laymen and professionals. These Councils ought to be the places where the best trained professional people will find themselves strengthened and their efforts enlivened by the presence and experience of lay citizens."

As we review the chronological histories of each of the sixty-four Councils, we find that in some instances action has been slow, in others rapid, but in practically every

Council a fundamental change has come about—the awakening of a new social consciousness.

Throughout the organization process we have all frowned upon undue publicity. Council meetings rarely reach the papers until the group have become well established. We cannot afford to have these Councils looked upon as "purity squads" or "cure all" groups, where the community can dump all of its problems. When we do that, the councils are through. The Coordinating Council is not another social agency. Rather, it is an opportunity for all groups interested in community and child welfare to get together and to coordinate their efforts.

These Councils have actually reduced delinquency in certain areas. In others they have started many worth while projects and have enlisted community support for the fine programs offered by its members. In January, 1935, the Los Angeles Crime prevention Bureau reports:

"There were 3,013 boy arrests in 1934 as compared with 3,552 in 1933. This means a reduction of 509. This large decrease of approximately 13 per cent cannot be attributed to any change in the policy of the Police Department affecting juvenile arrests. There are now many more Police Officers assigned to juvenile work than ever before, and for this reason fewer cases should escape their attention. We must, therefore, attribute this marked decrease in delinquency to other influences of which the Coordinating Councils would seem to deserve the lion's share. Their work with 'First Offenders' and pre-delinquents has been undeniably effective, as shown by this unbiased Annual Report."

Community Projects Encouraged by the Councils. —Only a few community projects encouraged by the Councils can be listed here. They include:

a. Summer Camping.—Forty-two Councils are actively participating and more than 3,200 children will be given camping experience this summer. This represents an increase of 35 per cent over any previous year.

b. Vacation Church Schools.—Last year there were 110 such schools. This summer 214, over 100 per cent increase. The churches are working together for the first time. Most of these new schools were in neglected areas. The results have been very satisfactory.

c. Toy Loan Libraries.—Eleven toy libraries located in neglected areas receive their supply from a central shop. These libraries circulate more than 5,000 toys each month.

d. Prevention of Sale of Liquor to Minors.—Fifty-four Councils are definitely active in curbing the sale of alcohol to minors. They have cleaned up many acute situations.

e. Community Dances.—Eleven Councils are most active in sponsoring or backing community dances in their council areas.

f. Special Trips.—Many special trips are planned for children in certain areas through a "Youth Activity Committee." Thousands of children have visited new scenes, attended ball games, races, parks and museums. These children could not afford to go themselves. Many lay groups have been called upon to make these trips possible.

g. Censorship of Salacious Literature.—A case study was made of thirty questionable magazines under the direction of Dr. Martin H. Neumeyer, Sociology Department, University of Southern California. Ten were finally selected and were removed from the news stands by means of Court action.

h. Leadership Training Courses have been sponsored by character building organizations in districts participating. This has resulted in several new groups being formed in neglected areas.

i. Motion Picture Estimate Service has been established in the Los Angeles Public Library. Anyone can call the library and ask about any motion picture, particularly as to its desirability for children.

These are but a few of the accomplishments of the Councils in Los Angeles County.

In December, 1935, Miss Katharine Lenroot, Chief of the United States Children's Bureau, addressed representatives of the Coordinating Councils of Los Angeles. She had been preceded by Miss Hester B. Crutcher, Director of the Delinquency Unit of the Children's Bureau, who was in Los Angeles making a study of Coordinating Councils. Miss Lenroot prefaced her remarks by referring to Miss Crutcher's study, and also that she had followed the Coordinating Council program very carefully through the Coordinating Council Bulletin and other publications. She then proceeded to point out five outstanding accomplishments which could be credited to the Coordinating Council program.

1. Changed Public Attitude toward Delinquency.— The first thing of importance is a change in the public's attitude toward delinquency. This question of attitude has been, perhaps, the most difficult problem with which those interested in providing for adequate methods of dealing with juvenile delinquency have been confronted.
2. A Positive Approach to Community Problems.— The Councils I visited this morning were considering such things as the liquor problem, salacious literature, health problems, and all those things which are involved in community housekeeping and which can definitely help to set your neighborhood in order, so as to eliminate some of the things which are most detrimental to the development of youth.
3. Better Understanding of Agencies for Community Service.— It is quite apparent that in coming together in Adjustment Committees, Character Building Committees and Environment Committees you are dealing at first hand with the resources of the community for service to the family and for group activities of various kinds, obtaining a knowledge of their functions, methods and programs.

4. Preparation of the Community to Attack New and Difficult Problems.— Community organization on a neighborhood basis brings all the agencies together and should help to make the community able to attack new and difficult problems. I was interested at the Downtown Council this morning in certain studies that are being made there which ought to lay a basis for a constructive program of this kind.
5. Broader Understanding of Economic, Political and Social Problems.— This type of organization is of significance because it affords an opportunity for many people to work together for community service in ways that cannot help but broaden our understanding and appreciation of great underlying economic political and social problems. I think that you have special opportunity here in Los Angeles to forward this ideal for American society and I want you to feel that in doing this you will be making a contribution of significance to the State and to the Nation, and perhaps to mankind as a whole.

It is of great significance that while Miss Lenroot was in Los Angeles only two days she found time to attend two Coordinating Councils and to address the Officers of the Councils at an evening meeting.

Sanford Bates, Director of Federal Prisons, in addressing the California Coordinating Councils at the California Conference of Social Work which met in Los Angeles in April, 1936, said:

> *"We know what's right; we know what's wrong with our community; we have enough knowledge and so on; we have schools enough, usually playgrounds enough; we have doctors who are skillful enough to treat the individual child; we have child clinics if we know where to find them; we have the tools and the materials. The thing we lack is the organized, dynamic conscience of the community that brings these forces to bear upon the conditions that need remedying. I think that's what makes the Coordinating Council Movement so significant, so prophetic." At the National Conference of Social Work which met in Atlantic City in May, 1936, the first Annual Conference of Coordinating Councils was held. This was attended by more than four hundred delegates from all over the United States.*

Evaluation of the Coordinating Councils.— The Council of Social Agencies of Los Angeles, through its Character Building Division, prepared the following evaluation of the local Coordinating Council movement. This was done to clarify for the Council of Social Agencies many questions concerning the place of the Coordinating Council movement in the community. In preparing this evaluation for the approval of the Executive Committee and the Council of Social Agencies due consideration was given to the fact that the local Coordinating Councils were still in a formative period. The statement follows:

Constructive Achievements

1. The Coordinating Councils have developed closer cooperative effort among professional and lay workers, as related to the field of social work, in local committees.
2. The work of the Coordinating Councils has offered each agency an opportunity for self-evaluation and criticism, and makes possible comparison of its work with the work of other agencies in similar fields.
3. A consciousness of community responsibility and community planning has been engendered by the Coordinating Councils within the local areas involved among professional and lay people, as related to the field of social work, especially in relation to the problems of delinquency prevention.
4. Much valuable information concerning neighborhood resources and local problems has been secured through surveys conducted by the local Coordinating Councils under the supervision of a central research committee.
5. The Coordinating Councils have assisted in the enrichment of community recreational and character-building activities by the assignment of workers of the S.E.R.A. and other governmental projects.
6. Commendable freedom from arbitrary central control has tended to develop in each community local leadership and responsibility. In the course of such

developments, constructive direction from a central advisory board should be continued in matters of organization, policy and program in order that mistakes may be avoided.

7. In particular, the Coordinating Councils have fostered community movements beneficial to youth, among which are: Suppression of salacious literature; referral of cases of pre delinquent children to specific agencies best equipped to meet their needs; dissemination of accurate information regarding liquor control laws, etc., in relation to minors.

Dangers to be Guarded Against

1. There is danger of local Coordinating Councils proceeding too hastily in dealing with problems of individuals and in planning new activities to meet community needs. This is observed most frequently in groups where adequate skilled leadership with experience in community planning is not available.
2. There is an ever-present danger that local Coordinating Councils will set themselves up as new agencies.
3. In metropolitan areas where a Council of Social Agencies exists the discovery and reporting of needs, problems and resources are considered to be responsibilities of the Coordinating Council, but in the development of a community program, clearance, guidance and direction should be given by the Council of Social Agencies.
4. In organizing such a movement on a state or national basis, serious consideration should be given to adequate representation of the collective organizations—private and public—and of civic and service organizations.

At the first Conference of Coordinating Councils of California in San Francisco in May, 1935, eighty-six Councils were represented. In reporting on the accomplishments of the Coordinating Councils at this meeting, Dr. Norman Fenton, Director of the California

Bureau of Juvenile Research, made several important statements based upon the returns to a questionnaire sent out to all Coordinating Councils in California.

"Let us pause to examine how the Coordinating Council may be of help in community betterment. In the field of juvenile delinquency, for example, there has seemed to be no fundamental organized Community consciousness. Each agency of government has laid the problem of delinquency on the doorstep of some other agency. All public officials have, with unanimous voice, blamed the situation upon the home and the parent. The community itself has decried the inefficiency of the public service, thinking perhaps by this criticism of its public officials, to absolve itself of responsibility for error. Instead of voicing recriminations and rationalization, the Coordinating Council accepts the challenge of delinquency, faces the problem and studies it thoughtfully. Practical recommendations are made. The community consciousness is strongly behind their accomplishment. No wonder that where Councils exist the everyday life of children has already been improved, and incidentally the community life of adults."

The Coordinating Councils of Los Angeles County are hardly under way. It will be many years before the real accomplishments of this movement can be measured with any degree of accuracy. Committees, organizations and lay people, however, are being drawn together as never before. There now is evidence of a community consciousness which is taking hold with firm hand upon unsatisfactory community conditions affecting youth. Coordinating Councils are merely one method of approaching the problem of delinquency and crime. Social facilities must be coordinated and made available to all children rather than to a select few. The Coordinating Council plan brings all of these groups together. Its primary object, however, is not limited to a reduction of delinquency and crime, but a sincere determination to make the community a better place in which to live.

The Child and the Community. — The philosophy upon which the work of the delinquent child in relation to the community should be based is well expressed by Jessie Binford in her article "Understanding the Delinquent," from which we quote in part:

> *The child's needs for security and development can never be fully met by his home, his school, his church or industry. He needs group life, widening interests; he craves the adventure and the opportunities to act as an independent human being which are to be found in what we call "the community." All children, privileged and underprivileged, take what the community has to offer. Adults make it what it is and when it does not satisfy the needs of the children or thwarts and exploits them, then the responsibility is theirs, and no clinics or juvenile courts or reformatory institutions can very fully adjust them.*

If a child's earlier and most intimate group fail him, he will, while still very young go forth into his community to satisfy his longing for affection, appreciation, companionship, adventure and will respond to what he finds there with an immature evaluation. What attracts and satisfies him the most may be the very thing that will make him socially unadjusted, delinquent or criminal.

However, under any circumstances, the child will eventually seek the community because of his need for it. His family may try to delay having him meet complete experience and adventure, but it is more and more difficult to do so, because families live so much more outside their homes. Apartments, hotels, clubs, with all their ready-made, mechanical devices, and without yards for play, are chosen to live in partly for economic reasons, and are preferred by many. Crowded city areas for both the rich and the poor mean that all the children are in the community for their leisure time. To meet this situation, community groups and agencies are consciously attempting to attract children and to draw them into what they have to offer, although they may have little conception of their part in completing the life of the child, or that he must be especially safeguarded because he is too immature for all experiences. The community has not yet realized that it is responsible for building to satisfy the fundamental needs of the child, and that it must not only offer opportunity for creative play, companionship and adventure, but must also protect children and young people from negative, demoralizing recreation. This new, most modern situation is being met to a certain extent by conscious planning on the part of certain private, municipal and commercial groups. They make it easy for parents who wish to evade responsibility, and it is only those that are least constructive that are taking in all children. There are also those less concrete and obvious community agencies and influences the press, the spirit of the neighborhood, the lawlessness of the present day. Through these, patterns are formed in the early years, of childhood and youth, which symbolize our morality, our integrity, our philosophy of life. Apartment life and its consequences, the restriction of the physical area of family life, the easy access of outside influences through the news, the automobile and the radio; perhaps never before have community influences had a larger part in the life of the individual. The great commercialization of recreation, the national organization of character building agencies, the syndication of news and opinion, the wholesale standardized recreation of municipalities perhaps never before have community influences been so utterly beyond the control of the individual. We can better understand and help the delinquent child only when we evaluate and analyze community groups and influences in relation to individual behavior, and make a basic attack on them in communities where "traditions teach delinquency, and where crime is the most interesting play of children." Recommendations were made by the various sub-committees considering the child in relation to these social institutions. Sometimes present steps are in the wrong direction we considered it even more disturbing that we often so thrill over them as to forget that they have validity only as they lead on to other steps. There are three implications in the entire delinquency report that transcend all others representing those goals which we are always to keep before us. Generations that have gone before have primarily stressed the clear duty that environment has for the child, and this we reaffirmed, and in doing so, emphasized that in all social relationships adults who have the guardianship of a child have:

1. A duty to develop in him regular and correct habits of living.
2. A duty to provide such richness of wholesome ideas and interests as will answer his ideational needs. It is not sufficient to use casual amounts of constructive and healthy material as coloring matter for the great masses of sensationalism and artificial stimulation to which the child is subjected.
3. That the guardians of the child have the duty to present in their own living such patterns of honesty, sincerity and courage as shall challenge the child's emulation. In an age when mechanical devices bring distant wonders and the spread of wealth provides ease and comfort beyond our wildest dreams, it is of the greatest importance that all adults realize that by no such trickery is wholesome life produced. It is only in the examples of sincere living that the child finds the dynamic impulse for his own wholesome development.

We affirmed the recognition of delinquent conduct as one of the natural outcomes of those clashes of interest, prerogative and need that are inherent in the matter of living as a social group. Finding fault, laying blame that most paralyzing and childish of all our human interests in the past has largely invaded our philosophy as to delinquency. The point in hand is not so much that delinquency is inevitable as that we appreciate the naturalness and ubiquity of those processes which lead up to it. This is fundamentally a matter of recognizing that the stresses which bend the delinquent are of precisely the same character as those which bend our own lives. The needs which have been pictured are those which are of the lives of all of us. All of us, too, have to meet the most unyielding moulds of the various institutions which surround us. As we see the delinquent as a part of this natural and inevitable clash we naturally bring into our concepts a dispassionate attitude which (perhaps for the first time) will allow us to consider the problem of delinquency in a way that leads to some real solution. Thus can we place ourselves in a position to test out our work with the child, whether we focus on the treatment of the child's problem in relation to himself, his family, the state, the school, industry, the church or community forces.

17

Role of Recreation in the Adjustment of Social Work

Introduction

The recreation leader of the newer school of thought recognizes the fact that any conditions in family life or in the social group which promote repression and handicap the child directly or indirectly promote conflicts in the child which cannot be removed merely by supplying "proper recreational activities."

Recreation and leisure-time activities are regarded by many as important factors in the program for crime prevention and not from the narrower point of view as benefits to individual persons or families. Frederick Thrasher, as can be judged from his discussion of the Lower West Side New York Leisure Time Conference, looks upon these leisure-time activities largely as programs in crime prevention.

The principle of district recreational planning with a view to crime prevention was applied in the spring of 1934 with the organization of the Lower West Side Leisure Time Conference as a permanent department of the Council of

Lower West Side Social Agencies. This Conference, which is composed of representatives of all the recreational groups and interests of the community, has as its general purpose to develop an integrated program of leisure time activities for all children and adolescents of the Lower West Side irrespective of race, creed, or economic level. It has stated its immediate objectives as follows:

Fact Finding.— To provide a scientific basis for a community leisure time program through furnishing all agencies with useful facts and information.

Conference and Co-operation.— Increased co-operation and better understanding among all agencies dealing with leisure time problems.

Outdoor Play Facilities.— (a) Utilization of vacant land, play streets, and roofs to provide additional facilities and reduce traffic hazards; (b) co-operation with Park Department and playgrounds.

Summer Activities and Camps.— To study vacation activities and to promote wider opportunities for camping.

Co-operation with Public Housing Authority.— For the development of recreational facilities as an integral part of slum clearance projects.

Prevention of Delinquency.— Co-operation with Juvenile Aid Bureau of the Police Department for a better organization of leisure time facilities for preventing delinquency.

Leisure Time Adjustment of Problem Children.— Co-operation with Public Schools of area, Bureau of Attendance, and Children's Court to make available more adequate leisure time activities for problem children.

Circulation of Toys.— To co-operate with the Toyery in promotion of more adequate facilities for this work.

Wider Use of School Plant.— Promotion of wider use of school buildings and grounds for leisure time activities after school hours and in vacations.

Wider Use of Church Plant.— Promotion of wider use of church facilities for wholesome leisure time activities.

Better Films Council.— Development of a Lower West Side Motion Picture Council to improve public taste in pictures and provide more opportunities for children to see suitable films.

Radio Committee.— To study the role and possibilities of the radio in relation to the use of leisure time.

Reading and Exhibits.— Promotion of more extensive use of libraries and museums.

Volunteer Workers.— Fuller utilization of local leadership for recreation: (a) Fuller co-operation with parents and parents' organizations; (b) fuller utilization of Big Brothers as recreational advisors.

Parent Education.— Promotion of parent education and organization to facilitate more adequate leisure time activities for children.

Experimental Block Program.— To develop experimentally and evaluate programs of leisure time activities for all children of given blocks where recreational problems are acute.

Recreational Advisement.— Development of specialized personnel to organize leisure time programs for individual children referred by agencies.

Leisure Time Information Bureau.— Development of a clearing house for all information as to local leisure time activities and resources.

Recreation for Handicapped Children.— Development of special facilities for children who are hard-of-hearing, cardiac, etc.

Education of the Public.— As to importance of wholesome leisure time activities for children and adolescents and stimulation of increased support of existing leisure time activities.

New Facilities.— Study of leisure time resources of community and development of more adequate or needed new facilities.

While the above objectives were formulated for purposes of educating the community, rather than to achieve academic precision, they are based upon local researches and they embody an application of sociological principles essential to effective community planning. Definite, though uneven, progress has been made in the realization of each of these objectives. A few examples may be cited. About 50 per cent of the children of this area are unreached by an organized recreational agency. The growing recognition of the failure of supervised recreation to reach the boys on the local block led the Leisure Time Conference to develop its play street program, which was designed to occupy the leisure time of children not reached by other agencies. Seven play streets were set aside by action of the Board of Aldermen, and a director and staff of emergency workers were provided by the city. During the summer of 1934 a daily average of about 1,000 children enjoyed a variety of games and leisure time activities on these play streets. Seven hundred boys participated in stick-ball tournaments and 900 boys were taken to big league baseball games at the Yankee Stadium. At the end of the summer the program was continued after school hours and on week-ends and some indoor facilities were made available for use of the children in inclement weather. This program is being guided by a Steering Committee (of the Leisure Time Conference), which is composed of representatives of the recreational agencies of the community. This committee has frequent meetings to discuss policies and plans for the development of the program.

It should be noted that the Leisure Time Conference makes contacts with numerous agencies such as the church, the school, the library, the radio, committee, and others engaged in the interests of the parents, educational agencies, housing authorities, the police department, and others. But the efforts of the conference in relation to these agencies are directed only toward the promotion of wholesome leisure-time activities. Of course, it is a Leisure Time Conference and should undoubtedly not concern itself with the other numerous needs of the underprivileged child. But the question may be raised as to how a community planning program can be organized effectively and economically when the other needs social-economic, mental hygiene, educational, medical, religious, and others not met by leisure-time activities are not taken into account by a conference carrying on a program on such a wide scale as indicated above?

Is it wise to isolate "leisure-time needs" by one conference and allow other conferences and agencies to make contacts again with the schools, churches, police, housing authorities, the parents, and others in order to deal with the wider and often more pressing needs, mentioned above? Surely, the schools, the homes, the churches, and others can offer more than just recreational facilities. Is not the conference undertaking too much unilateral specialization along activities which have not been conclusively proved to be the "lifesaver" in delinquency? There must be a large number of children on the Lower West Side of New York who do not avail themselves of these activities but who are not delinquent. At least a study with a control group by the writer in Russian Town yielded such results. Every intelligent person will agree that wholesome play and recreation are indispensable in the lives of all persons, but other things must be taken into account in the intricate life pattern of families, persons, and communities, living in a changing social economic and moral order.

The Relation of Group Work to Case Work.— Robert C. Taber, Boys' Club and Settlement Representative, Council of Social Agencies, Philadelphia, raises the pertinent question in a paper read before the Pennsylvania Conference on Social Welfare, Group Work Division—"Will Increased Wholesome Leisure Time Activities Alone Prevent Juvenile Delinquency? If not, What Will?" We quote him in part:

Leisure time activities alone, no matter how wholesome or how extended, cannot prevent juvenile delinquency. Leisure time activities have an important role to play in a prevention program but there are definite limitations as to what can be accomplished through this medium. A full recognition of this fact is necessary at the very beginning if we are to give recreation an importance which is not out of all proportion to its actual effectiveness.

What is there in the very nature of delinquency which makes it a problem that recreation alone cannot meet? It would seem to me that there are certain generalizations concerning delinquency which can be made without treading upon dangerous ground.

In the first place, there is no one cause of delinquency and, consequently, there can be no one solution. Every delinquent child presents his own unique problem. As human beings, we are not only born with different physical, mental and emotional equipment but the forces which have gone into our life experiences are dissimilar. How could a recreational agency be expected to give the time necessary to know any great number of its members on such an intensive basis?

Secondly, a goodly portion of delinquent behavior is symptomatic, just as certain physical maladies are symptoms of an underlying disorder. In other words, there is seldom a direct cause and effect which can be simply traced. Causal factors frequently lie far beneath the surface and require deep insight on the part of the worker if they are to be reached. The fact that delinquent behavior is so frequently symptomatic makes it an unwise practice to refer juvenile delinquents to recreation centers in a wholesale fashion. It is not that leisure time activities have nothing constructive to offer, but that such a practice would mean that we would be blind to other phases of the problem which cannot be met by the recreation center.

A third consideration has to do with the difference in our ways of solving difficulties. How could leisure time activities alone prevent delinquency when we choose different methods of achieving a satisfactory adjustment? They could not possibly meet the needs of all individuals. It would seem to me that this point warrants further consideration inasmuch as it represents a stumbling block for many of us as group workers when we set about to plan a preventive program.

The child who is unusually fearful is overwhelmed by a group. The strange faces and the new experience of sharing with others makes him feel that he is in a foreign land. He finds it so difficult to make a place for himself within the group that he drops out after one or two visits. Unless he receives personal help or unless some fortuitous circumstance brings about a change in him, he may never become affiliated with an organized group. He will keep to himself as much as possible. Often- times this same person feels comfortable in an individual relationship with a case worker and can work through some of his fear.

On the other hand, there are children who find more freedom within a group than in a relationship with a case worker. For them, the meeting with a worker alone is a terrifying experience because they feel caught, whereas their meeting with a group gives them the comforting support of the other members. The attention of the leader is not concentrated on one person but on the group as a whole, and therefore, the relationship is not so intensive.

Again, the recreation center is limited in what it can offer the child whose problem has reached the acute state. I recall the case of a boy who found out for the first time at the age of sixteen that he had been adopted. He became infuriated with his foster mother and his usual quiet behavior suddenly changed to deliberate and intentional revengeful acts against her. She had been an unusually good mother to him but that did not make the shock any easier for him to bear. He ended up by running away for nearly a year during which time all efforts to locate him were unsuccessful. I think that you will agree that if anyone had been able to reach him during his depressing period and had invited him to attend a recreation center, he would have been completely indifferent toward the invitation. His indifference would not be due to any failure on the part of the recreation center but to the fact that recreation was not the thing that was most concerning him at the moment. The very idea of mingling with other boys who were enjoying themselves might be repulsive to him. He needed to go away from people where he could think his problem through for himself.

In Philadelphia we have been engaged for nearly three years in an experiment with boys who have been discharged by the Juvenile Court. Each boy is referred to a center in his own neighborhood and visits are made to his home for a period of several months. A survey was made of 1,600 cases and some interesting figures resulted. Out of the total, we found that 18 per cent were active members of some organized group when the initial visit was made; that 58 per cent had never been affiliated with a recreation center despite the fact that facilities were available within ten blocks of their homes; and that the remaining 24 per cent had been members at one time but were inactive at the time of our first interview. A goodly portion represented boys who were definitely opposed to participation in supervised play. They preferred the adventure and freedom of the street where they were practically a law unto themselves. They could not adjust to authority of any kind with perhaps one exception. They could tolerate the authority necessary to hold their group together but they could not accept the simplest of rules which must, of necessity, be set up by any recreation center if its work is to be anything but chaos. In other words, an individual must have already achieved a certain sense of adjustment if he is to find organized group experience attractive. If those figures and illustrations have any validity, we cannot infer that the provision of recreation facilities will assure good use of leisure time. On the contrary, we must recognize that the poor use of leisure time on the part of many delinquents, is just another indication of their lack of capacity to make a satisfactory adjustment.

To be sure we have not done all that we can as group workers in meeting this wide range of problems, and yet I feel certain there are limits as to what we can do. Perhaps this process of defining limits will be helpful to us in that we need to know what we cannot accomplish before we are free to concentrate our efforts upon that area in which we can be effective. If we continue to feel responsible for the whole program of juvenile delinquency, we shall be overwhelmed by it and become lost in the struggle. On the other hand, if we can see recreation in its proper relationship to other services, we can be more helpful.

The boy who is busily occupied is less apt to be exposed to undesirable influences and, therefore, runs less risk of getting into trouble. More important, however, than the amount of time he spends at the center is what the time he does spend there means to him. It can be satisfying experience in that it provides for the expression of the fundamental urges within him. He can achieve power in a constructive way by becoming a leader and by taking certain responsibility for phases of the program. He may find satisfaction in becoming a respected member of a group.

The group experience gives him an opportunity to learn the all important lesson of sharing and cooperating with others. The importance of human relationships in living cannot be over-emphasized. So much of importance hinges on our capacity to get along with other people our economic, social, and personal security. Inasmuch as supervised play does provide another group experience in addition to the group experience in family and school relationships, it becomes an exceedingly important contribution to the development of a child.

The recreation centers also meet a day by day need. It goes along with the child over a period of time in contrast to a case work service, which usually involves a temporary relationship in which help is found for a specific problem. It represents an element of stability, something which acts as a hitching post in the important process of finding one's self.

The Case of Frank Ryder.— A concrete illustration will clarify the point: Frank Ryder's case shows that a recreation center could not be of direct help with his specific problem because of the pressing nature of his difficulty. He is fifteen years old, born of an Irish family who have always lived in a small house in bad repair within a block from the waterfront. He is one of six children with only one child younger than himself. He has a twin brother by the name of Thomas. Mr. Ryder has a very soft quality as a person but has become embittered toward his neighbors. He feels that they are all against him because of his effort to keep Frank on the right track. He has finally washed his hands of any responsibility toward Frank, in fact he has not spoken to Frank for one whole year. Mrs. Ryder is an exceedingly emotional and dramatic person who gets highly wrought up on the slightest provocation. Her own mother died of epilepsy. She is very dictatorial and domineering over the father. She herself is given to having frequent spells and it is obvious that she lives in mortal terror of having her own condition diagnosed as epilepsy. She shields all of the children against the father. Her husband has become resigned to his position of providing for the family and no longer attempts to play a part as head of the family. He seems to have set himself apart from his family as he has from his neighbors. He keeps to himself entireiy with one exception. He is exceedingly fond of his one-year-old granddaughter. All of his affection seems to center about her.

Frank, himself, is an ungainly boy whose one outstanding characteristic is antagonism toward everything and anything. He speaks of himself as the black sheep in the family. He is physically handicapped as the result of a trolley accident in which he lost part of his foot.

A goodly portion of the tension which existed in this family could be traced back to this accident. It had taken place when he was eight years old, and during the seven years that followed Frank had become very demanding and antagonistic until he arrived at the point where his own parents turned to the court in desperation because he had gotten beyond their control. They had him arrested with the hope that it would scare him. He was placed on probation by the court and at the same time referred to our agency. Upon inquiring from the settlement house in his neighborhood, we found that he had been a member of their center since he had been a youngster. He was known as a general trouble maker, as a decided misfit. He deliberately went out of his way to antagonize the different members of the staff. He intentionally disrupted the activities program in any way that he could. Occasionally the workers had been obliged to suspend him from attending but each time he would return and very rapidly slip back into his old ways.

It was obvious that the recreation center alone could not help him in making an adjustment. It required individual attention of a case worker as well.

As we came to know Frank and his family, we found that his mother made a pet of him after the accident. She would be seen sitting on the doorstep with Frank's head in her lap. She would stroke his head and meanwhile complain to the neighbors of his injury, saying that he had been the "sheik" of the family and now his good looks had been marred forever. In her sympathy for Frank she spoiled him by doing anything he wanted. She shielded him from his father so that Frank missed the ordinary firmness which any father must exercise in bringing up his children. He quite naturally expected everyone to bow to his demands and to have his battles fought for him. As he began to enter into the period of adolescence he missed the protection of his mother. She could not extend her control into his school and neighborhood life. He found that his new associates ignored his demands. He got no special consideration from them and became very antagonistic toward them. It was the only weapon he could fall back upon. He did not know how to win a place among his associates through a constructive kind of behavior, and he, therefore, turned to this destructive channel which he found effective.

Added to this was an incident which occurred between him and his father. A year before Mr. Ryder had caught Frank entering the house by climbing over the roof. He had punished Frank and a group of older boys learned of it. On New Year's eve, when they had been celebrating with liquor, they encountered Mr. Ryder and told him he was discriminating against Frank. He became infuriated and the boys finally attacked him. He escaped and ran into his home. As he did so, a shot was fired which barely missed him. He was certain that Frank had gotten these boys to "gang up on him" and from that point on he positively refused to speak to his son. Needless to say, a tremendous amount of ill-feeling existed in that home. They didn't trust each other and were continually taking out their feelings on each other in some subtle way.

The case worker enabled the father to express a tremendous amount of his resentment and he finally arrived at the point where he would speak to Frank and take some responsibility for him. However, Mr. Ryder can never fully forgive Frank even though he now knows that his son did not get the boys "to gang up" on him. He cannot give Frank what he might otherwise have given him in his relationship as a father. Mrs. Ryder now enjoys a freer relationship with her husband and has taken over the responsibility for Frank with Mr. Ryder in lieu of sharing nothing with him. Frank has made a better adjustment in that his antagonistic attitude has diminished as the tension of the family has lessened. Through his regular interviews with the case worker he learned to take some responsibility for his own actions. He is no longer entirely irresponsible. However, he has a long way to go.

Frank had attended a settlement house regularly for many years, but as previously stated, he had been very antagonistic and disruptive. As the result of his relationship with the case worker, he had expressed and was relieved of a tremendous amount of resentment and came to feel more comfortable in his home relationship. This partial adjustment carried over into his settlement activities. He helped the staff by doing little things for them. The workers gradually gave him more responsibility as he was ready, and he took great pride in giving assistance. He worked in harmony with them for the most part. The settlement activities provided a medium for self-expression which brought him a sense of "power with," instead of "power over" people. The recreation center carried along with Frank long after the case worker ceased his visiting. In fact, it will continue to serve Frank in his need for the expression of his positive self. In this instance case work and group work have worked together in his behalf.

Harry M. Shulman, formerly of the New York State Crime Commission, brings out similar points in connection with his studies of delinquency in Brooklyn and Manhattan.

National and local recreational agencies operate on several diverse theories. The more conservative seem to feel that recreation is a substitute program for delinquent activities, and that the extension of recreational facilities to fill in the entire free time for the child will combat delinquency by affording him no opportunity for delinquent behavior. Other recreational agencies have faith in the transfer of attitudes acquired in supervised recreation, and feel that children trained in ideals of sportsmanship will communicate these ideals to other children who have not had direct contact with recreational programs. Certain agencies are primarily concerned with the overcoming of physical and mental disabilities or the utilization of special aptitudes, on the theory that the problem child has developed conflict around an inferiority which must be compensated for by giving him opportunity for success. Many of the older child guidance agencies, dominated by the psychological point of view, have worked on this principle. Problem children do not adapt themselves well to normal groups. They are not merely normal children who steal, or stay out late, or play truant. These behavior manifestations are symptomatic of deeper underlying conflicts with their families and society. These children often have distorted personalities. They have deep feelings of inferiority, are oversensitive, and crave response and security. They are frightened by the size of the average community center or club. They are awed by the complexity of its system and irked by the inflexibility of its rules.

These excerpts clearly indicate that perhaps too much reliance is placed on group recreation and play groups in the adjustment process of problem youth. It has been frequently assumed that "group play can do no harm but will do some good," like sunshine and fresh air for any physically ill patient. While that is undoubtedly true in many instances, it may be distinctly harmful in others, as was shown by Shulman and Taber. Therefore, the worker needs to use care and discretion as to when to rely on mass recreational opportunities as a major factor in the adjustment process and when to use them in conjunction with other resources.

Frederick M. Thrasher made an exhaustive study "of a Boys' Club, newly opened in a crime-breeding area of New York City. The Club was established [for boys of seven to eighteen years and older] because delinquency was prevalent in this area. The Study measured the influence of this Club during its initial four years from 1927-1931, utilizing the descriptive, ecological, statistical, and case study methods." The conclusions drawn from these case studies are of importance:

> The case-studies made by the Study revealed that the Club had a negligible influence upon its problem members during the Study period. The acute behavior problems in these cases precipitated by various combinations of family disorganization, dire poverty, school maladjustments, gang activities, association with older hoodlums and underworld characters, demoralizing experiences on the streets and in institutions of commercialized amusement and neighborhood hangouts these influences for the most part were beyond the power of the Boys' Club to neutralize, particularly in the limited time each week which the average Boys' Club member spent in club activities involving as they did, little real guidance from the Club personnel.

Five years have elapsed since Thrasher made certain recommendations, one of which might be quoted in full.

> Surely an institution organized so definitely with the avowed purpose of preventing delinquency should have at least one full-time specialist on the staff with psychological, psychiatric, and sociological training who could apply the recognized methods of scientific study and treatment to the very numerous problem boys, both potential and actual, who become a direct responsibility of the Boys' Club.

The extent to which Thrasher's recommendations have been adopted by the club in question can be judged from the following statement:

> *Record-keeping has been made more efficient. Attendance has been improved and turnover reduced. A staff-member with psychiatric training has been added to the Club's personnel to handle difficult cases. The attitudes of the boys of the neighborhood have become more cordial. The program has been enriched by the addition of handicrafts and shop-work.*

The boys have given more time in the gymnasium by the later scheduling of tournament events. A representative of the Bureau of Attendance of the Public Schools has been added to the staff to route all known truants in the area into the Club. This man, whose function is not known to the boys, provides the means of reaching an important class of known potential delinquents, namely, truants.

A social stocktaking, so to speak, is of importance in keeping up to date with modern and scientific methods in the adjustment of individual cases or in the whole program of crime prevention. The progressive recreation departments frequently review their activities and change their program and approach to meet the changing conditions of the times and of the particular community. These departments are also using the case work approach more and more to problems which cannot be adjusted by mass recreation.

It should be noted that in the cases of James R. and Peter Smith recreational activities were planned and directed from the standpoint of the family and social situation of the boys, and from the standpoint of their particular interests. Furthermore, the probation officer knew that Peter Smith had several boy friends, alliance with whom did not seem perilous. However, he sought to combat the influence of an unorganized group and to supplant it with the silent supervision of an organized club whose specialty it is to provide legitimate pastimes. He recognized that since clubs differ greatly as to their nature, activities, fees, government, and general atmosphere, it was essential to choose the organization keeping in mind the requirements and the circumstances of Peter's case. Cooley's experience in his former connection with his work at the Court of General Sessions is of significance.

Activities of Delinquent and Problem Youth

Directing and superintending the delinquent's spare-time activities was a far harder task than that of placing him in a fitting occupation. Once more the best approach was that of discovering the probationer's own tastes and inclinations through consultation and repeated contact.

Changes of recreation involved, first of all, a new outlook on life, changes of associates and friends, the making of new contacts, and the breaking up of cherished habits of conduct.

The probationer, bent upon indulging himself in various amusements, could be induced to relinquish them only after he had been convinced of their disadvantages and of the existence of more absorbing and constructive types of recreation. In most cases, discussion or argument produced but little result. It was generally possible, however, through the use of repeated suggestion and through arousing the curiosity and interest of the probationer, to induce him to experiment with new types of recreation. Experience with these new forms often engaged his permanent interest and assured his continued participation therein.

In each case the probation officer sought to discover some particular hobby that would fire the enthusiasm of the young delinquent. Usually this device was found successful, and the new found interest often proved a safe and sufficient substitute for previous disorderly habits.

Probationers preferring sports and outdoor recreation were encouraged to join athletic clubs and gymnasia, while others, who were interested in less strenuous activities, were induced to become members of settlements, clubs, and civic organizations located in their neighborhood. More serious individuals, often of the introvert type, who shunned contact with their neighbors, were interested in hobbies and attractions which provided them with wholesome diversions during their spare moments.

Recreation ideation and habits, however, were extremely difficult to change. It was soon found that the delinquent's concept of recreation was in many instances very limited and in some cases scarcely extended beyond the crude interests of alcohol, sex, and gambling. To materially change this situation, to broaden and elevate concepts of recreation, to eliminate the misdirected leisure time so frequently attendant upon delinquency, and to direct basal instincts and energies into channels of sublimation represented one of the most difficult problems of work with delinquents. In many cases, it was only after slow, painstaking effort that an improvement in leisure time pursuits, could be effected.

Cyril Burt is of the opinion that the adolescent girl is in far greater need of supervised and special recreation than the adolescent boy. Hard work, physical exercise, even strenuous bodily activity "have always been counseled as a means of chastening the instincts of the flesh." Club activities, supervised dances and parties, avoiding isolated pairs, should be encouraged.

Recreational Facilities.— Every large city and many towns in America have developed suitable recreational activities and amusements to appeal to varied tastes and moods. Indoor and outdoor sports, swimming, organized games, hikes, dancing, art galleries, concerts, museums, motion pictures intelligently chosen are among the facilities which at least the large cities contribute to wholesome entertainment which "fire the enthusiasm of the young defaulter." Elizabeth Pendry and Hugh Hartshorne devote a large book, Organizations for Youth, to a comprehensive discussion of the resources in a community program of recreation and education through recreation for adults and youth. These authors list every conceivable type of formal organization, discuss its history, growth, philosophy, method, program, administration, methods of motivation, and evidences of success. It should prove of value to every worker in the recreational field. The problems are: Which of these varied organizations are the most suitable for the particular offender, and how shall he be put in contact with them to his best advantage?

In most large cities the Council of Social Agencies has an up-to date inventory of agencies for leisure-time activities. The Los Angeles County Probation Department has compiled a useful handbook for its workers and all leaders of youth, Youth's New Day, which provides a classified list of social agencies. This handbook lists not only playgrounds, schools with playgrounds open after school hours, settlements and social centers, and preventive "character-building" agencies, but divisions of welfare relief, health agencies, hospitals, clinics, churches, family welfare agencies, employment agencies, etc. These various agencies are listed by district with a brief characterization of the general conditions in the district, the juvenile population, and the juvenile delinquent population.

Handbooks of this type are useful to a worker for purposes of reference; they are useful to the community leaders in knowing the presence or absence of facilities for youth; and they are useful for general research purposes and studies correlating the number and kind of agencies for youth and the rate of delinquency in a given district.

The White House Conference on Child Health and Protection makes some very pertinent remarks with regard to recreational agencies and their activities:

During the last thirty or forty years settlement and neighborhood agencies, boys' and girls' clubs, community centers, Boy Scouts, Girl Scouts, Campfire groups, and the recreation movement have developed to meet the needs of thousands of young people and have made notable contributions to our civic life. We are now, however, at a period when an intensive study of the general influence of all these agencies should be made, not only from the point of view of what they accomplish in terms of their own membership, but also from the point of view of their general effectiveness in clearing away from childhood those handicapping influences within the individual which spread from child to child like a contagion. The individual must be studied more in relation to his group association, or in relation to his friend or friends, than has been done in the past. Daily, the full force of group influences is being borne in upon us. The challenge before community agencies is to reach out into the districts they are serving by providing leadership of a quality which can win the children on the wing. Intensive knowledge of the neighborhood is required, knowledge of local personalities and of local thought. Cooperation of the adults of the districts must be won in meeting the needs of the child on the basis of the child's free choice of associations. The agency should pay as much attention to those who do not come to it as to those who do.

Moreover, back of the effort with individuals must be the constant effort to strengthen home life and conditions of living.

Organized Municipal Recreation Groups. — Privately organized groups have reached comparatively few children and as the need and appreciation for community recreation have grown, our municipalities have extended their functions to support and supervise recreational centers, playgrounds, beaches, forest preserves, camps. As these become larger, and take children in cities far from their homes and neighborhoods, they have many of the dangers of commercial centers, since children and young people meet in them without the safeguards of any other association and cannot know whether they are finding good or bad companionship. The time has come when these municipal groups need evaluation. Without this evaluation we must not be content to extend what would seem in themselves to be good institutions. Are these great, highly organized recreational groups making patterns for our children and deadening individual tastes, abilities, creative powers, just as modern industry and business methods do?

Do these planned, regulated, supervised activities surpass the simpler, but more creative outlets for which all children should be given an opportunity?

Are we depending too much on large group activities to the exclusion of the development of neighborhood workers who could foster and develop small groups?

Are these municipal groups adapting their work to the delinquent? Must we not consider their dangers, political domination, lack of leadership and educational programs, failures to meet individual needs?

Playgrounds.— In considering juvenile delinquency the query constantly arises, to what degree will a well organized recreation program lessen delinquency? In 1929 Andrew G. Truxal, reviewing figures which claimed to show the reduction of delinquency after the establishment of playgrounds, came to the conclusion that there seemed to exist a significant correlation between the absence of juvenile delinquency and the presence of play areas. He maintains, however, that too much emphasis has been placed upon recreation as a single factor and too much claimed for the effect of playgrounds. Mr. Truxal is undoubtedly right in being conservative. Nevertheless, the evidence that comes from many sections of the country indicates that playgrounds are a leverage in prevention. This appears logical, since playgrounds provide for boys and girls outlets for action meeting their natural impulses for physical and mental activity. Certainly, there is nothing more dangerous than pent-up vitality and mental energy not focused on constructive interests.

Leadership.— The playground not only provides open space for activities, but leadership, the influence of one, or more men and women to stimulate children's participation in a program. The personalities of leaders should be such that they will know, and be known by, the individual child. The day for squad work on the playground is over. The present demand is for a high degree of individualization. No longer is the activity the keynote, but the person in relation to the activity. Further, the playground official of the future will be rather a community agent than a playground director, because full responsibility will be placed upon him for reaching children where they are, which seems, in most cities, to be the city streets. The background of child life must be known as it is seen, not only on the playground but on the streets and in the alleys.

Most important, too, is the fact that children cannot be dissociated from adults. This means a wide and inclusive program participated in by the older folks as well as by the younger.

Individual children must be reached in the home setting, and known in relation to their playmates, and a fine analysis must be made of the tastes, abilities and interests of the given boy or girl. The playground leader, then, is responsible for the individual and to a high degree for the social setting of which that individual is a part.

The importance of the recreation leader is brought out by this quotation from Clifford R. Shaw's Delinquency Areas: "The play group is a spontaneous form of primary relationship which reflects community life and is very significant in determining attitudes, habits, and standards of conduct in the juvenile ... the behavior of the members. Some gangs become so powerful in their hold on members that the patterns persist and actually dominate the community."

Clearly, if this be true, every effort should be made to fill our city streets with influences that establish elements of right conduct rather than wrong. This cannot be done, however, if leaders are tied to given playgrounds their entire time. Every playground should have certain workers-at-large in a neighborhood. It is surprising and startling to walk through the congested sections of almost any city and to see the streets swarming with children and a nearby playground comparatively empty. And the city street! Listen to the language. No control of conduct there. Watch the aimless and enervating action. Notice the pathetic acceptance of leadership from an older boy or girl and listen to the often ribald suggestions of a corner gangster. The challenge to the playground is the city street. Playgrounds can no longer wait for children to come to them, but their personnel must find children where they are, mingle with them, and win them to those elements of the playground program which meet their inclinations, and which give free rein to their desires for spontaneity. We are just at the beginning of the development of method in this respect. Cincinnati, through so-called Play Street has made a national demonstration. The results of the efforts of the Playgrounds Association of Philadelphia and of Community Service, Inc., of Boston in increasing the patronage of the public recreation facilities in those two cities, by discovering the naturally organized groups and giving them something to do which leads them to the playgrounds and athletic fields, point the way to major developments in the next few years.

Many years ago Jane Addams wrote in her book, The Spirit of Youth and the City Streets, that the object of settlement work was not to take children off the streets but to make the streets safe for children. It is advocated that every playground should have certain workers-at-large[1] in neighborhoods where children tend to congregate and play on the streets.

An Experiment in the Use of Recreation in Treating Delinquents. — M. L. Pettit, formerly Probation Officer, Juvenile Court, South Bend, Indiana, now Professor of Sociology, University of Notre Dame, reports on "An Experiment in the Use of Recreation in Treating Delinquents." The excerpts are self-explanatory.

Some four years ago, in tabulating data concerning the social causes of maladjustment among boys, it appeared to the investigators that in about 75 per cent of the cases, inadequate recreation or antisocial companionship depending upon recreation were among the contributing causes. In some instances, it was the boy and his gang, in other instances it was the individual boy and chance associates. In some cases, the whole social background of the boy was excellent; in other cases, the reverse of this situation was true. The question naturally arose as to what means were available, and as to what methods were used in dealing with these problems. Were these isolated problems of the boy, or the boy and his gang; or were they problems of certain geographical or delinquency areas?

It was ascertained that the "repressive method of rehabilitation" was generally used in the attempted solution of these cases. If the anti- social activity or offense, as many of our courts still call it, was a gang activity, it seemed as though the main direction of the rehabilitative processes centered around the break-up of the gang. Gangs were presumed to be vicious breeders of crime and detriments to the community. One of the probation rules most frequently used was: "The probationer shall not associate with boys who have violated any law or who have not a good reputation in the community."

It was comparatively easy for the probation worker to "order" his charge to discontinue association with his gang or to discontinue some type of antisocial recreation. But it was extremely difficult for the boy to sever these bonds of loyalty, good fellowship, and perhaps his only opportunity for recreation, which "quitting the gang" implied. The strange and phenomenal part of the situation, so far as the probation officer was concerned, was that if the boy's relation with the gang was other than merely nominal, he rarely severed this relationship. Penalties might follow, but the gang remained intact. Probation reports showed that the cultural level of the boy or the degree of his social experience, particularly so far as home training was concerned, made little or no difference. The leader of the gang was the master of the boy's destiny.

Another feature of the problem presenting itself was the question of the delinquent boy whose maladjustment seemed to be primarily coupled with his inability to find the proper type of recreation or the proper associates, the introvert who suddenly tried to shift himself out of his social rut and to join the normal activities of his psychosocial age level. Numerous cases were found where this situation had resulted in a social misstep and the adventure had ended in the juvenile court.

These investigators reasoned that a new philosophy and a new plan were needed in dealing with boys before the court. Repressive rehabilitation is not rehabilitation. It was felt that the pertinent question in regard to the boy's activities is not what has he done, but, why has he done it in this particular manner rather than in a socially normal manner? We decided that these boys whose chief deficiency seemed to be a lack of means of expressing the normal social activities of adolescence, or else a socially abnormal method of expressing them, should be given an opportunity of doing something instead of "don't doing" something.

The philosophy of our experiment became, "Any boy who is within the range of normalcy, that is, not noticeably deficient mentally or physically, and who is delinquent because of lack of proper leisure time guidance in his program or because of improper associates, will be given the proper program to meet these determined needs." It was felt that if diagnostic accuracy could be reasonably expected, normal programs could be substituted for socially abnormal programs and boys would be rehabilitated through their own volition.

Furthermore, it was felt that all cases before the court regardless of causation should be determined as to a definite leisure time program and if it were found that such programs were insufficient to meet the needs of the boy, they should be strengthened as a matter of juvenile court responsibility. The gang, for instance, is not fundamentally antisocial in nature. It is a natural phenomenon of the gregarious tendencies of adolescence. The difficulty lies not in the gang but in the gang's lack of a supervised program. It is the community organizations who fail to reach the boy and not the boy who should shoulder the responsibility. The general conclusions suggested by our experiment are:

1. The problem of the delinquent gang may be independent of, but generally is a problem of delinquency area. Delinquent gangs may be rehabilitated under their own leadership through the use of recreational programs fitted to their needs. Both the Boy Scouts and the Y.M.C.A., if they can be induced to see this phase of their work, are effective. Scouting is probably more effective than the Y.M.C.A., however, as its program may be brought into the district where it is needed. It is a part of the work of the probation staff to convince these organizations that they should undertake this type of work.
2. Delinquency areas may be controlled and often eliminated through the proper recreational set-up.

3. In dealing with the individual boy, success depends upon accurate psychological and sociological groupings; a wise choice of program, and placement with boys who will accept the newcomer as a member of the group. Both the Y.M.C.A. and the Scouts were successful in this type of work, although the Y.M.C.A. had the larger percentage of success due to the number of types of work possible in a centralized building program.
4. Approximately 60 per cent of all individual cases supplied with proper recreation were rehabilitated. Where it was found impossible to supply recreational adequacy, the reverse was true. All gangs supplied with recreational programs were rehabilitated while our one attempt to break up a gang resulted in failure.
5. The Boy Scouts and the Y.M.C.A. without changing their programs are equipped to deal with the delinquent boy. Such changes as are necessary to meet the need of the individual boy and gang are not deviations from the regular program but merely a shifting of emphasis.

What Constitutes Wholesome Recreation in Particular Cases? When the worker suggests employment in leisure-time activities he should ask himself: What do these activities have to offer to the youth which would appeal to youth as worth while and stimulating? Would he receive adequate and intelligent supervision? Would he have a chance to develop potential leadership qualities? Would these activities tend to overbalance the excitement and thrill of commercialized recreation or the values to him of the gang? Would these activities tend to keep the child away from a home where he is needed or whose norms are in conflict with the particular recreational program? "The family that plays together stays together," is a slogan adopted from National Recreation Association by many cities for their campaigns to promote home play. Do the activities advocated promote such play? These and other questions need to be carefully considered before "ordering" an offender "to choose only wholesome recreation."

The worker needs also to remember the powerful and alluring appeals made by the motion pictures, by gambling houses, road houses, obscene literature and a crime-gorged press, gangsters, and others. Youth lacks discretion in choosing the proper play groups and forms of recreation. The facilities must be sought out, explained, and checked upon with regard to providing the adventure, security, and response which a child seeks from play activities and groups.

A group of public-spirited women, alumnae of the University of Chicago and members of the Mortar Board, have launched upon a plan under the intelligent leadership of their president, Mrs. Marion Farley, and in cooperation with and guidance of the Juvenile Court of Cook County, Chicago, which promises fruitful results. These women, working in very small groups, three to every eight or ten children, have undertaken to familiarize young wards of the Juvenile Court with what may be termed the better types of recreational facilities available in their own neighborhoods and in the city at large.

Irene Kawin, Chief Deputy Probation Officer of the Juvenile Court of Cook County, found that their wards knew only the cheapest forms of recreation, which frequently added to their delinquency patterns. The probation officers dealing with these cases cannot devote the time and the court cannot afford the money necessary for conducting outings and visits to public recreational and educational institutions. The members of the Mortar Board volunteered their services in February, 1934, and have continued since that date.

A brief summary of one letter from Mrs. Marion Farley, their president, indicates that a trip has been taken practically every month since the above date for a group, or groups, of children. The number of children varies from five to thirty, depending on the nature of the trip. Only in two or three instances has a child shown lack of interest, and very few of the original group of women have discontinued their services. The volunteers do not attempt to do any professional work or to learn the facts surrounding the cases. Their primary concern is to provide fun and educative recreation to a group of children designated by the probation department as having ability to profit by the opportunities and able to get along in a group.

The trips included visits with guide service to the Merchandise Mart, Field Museum, Lincoln Park Zoo, Industrial Museum, the World's Fair, Cook County Forest Preserves, the coal mine and cotton exhibit at the Field Museum, motion pictures of various habitat groups at museums, picnics during the summer months at the public parks, Valentine, Easter, and Christmas parties at some park field house, at which time the children made the decorations, cards, and arranged for the program.

Mrs. Farley further reports:

> *The most outstanding change which we have noted in the children since our first contacts with them is the apparent desire of each of them to participate whole heartedly in the activities of the group. This has seemed significant to us because we have both boys and girls and their ages vary considerably. We were at first in doubt as to whether the more sophisticated girl would retain a rather sullen and bored attitude. This attitude disappeared in the course of time because of the delegation of authority to them in recognition of their seniority and because they became friendly with the Mortar Boards who are older and who played all the games and enjoyed them. Probably at first these girls thought the group's fun beneath their dignity, but in time they found enjoyment in joining in with the rest. Also the boys, who are very lively, found they had a good time making Valentines with the group as well as playing baseball. The way in which these youngsters have adjusted themselves in such a mixed group has been a very interesting process.*

We have noted an attitude on the part of the older children that they must watch out for the little ones, that is, to see that they don't get lost and that they always have their full share of refreshments. There has been a similar lack of the selfishness which is so often apparent when children play together. This responsibility that the older ones assumed of their own accord was not at all apparent at first.

We have endeavored to give this group a series of trips which they could repeat, if they wished, with their families or other friends. For the most part, we have made use of community resources of various types and we have made a point of explaining that no tickets were needed and the arrangements could be made by following certain procedures. Although the children have learned a lot in their various trips, we have not tried to impress that fact. We have rather sought to give these children good and genuine fun. We have spent as much time as possible out of doors and in places where there was room to run and chase without being told to "get off the grass." In other words, our philosophy has been that just plain fun, in a group, is of itself highly beneficial to children. We are all trying to show these youngsters how they can find good times for themselves and their families.

The experiment of the Mortar Board is interesting and promising, particularly in view of the fact that throughout Mrs. Farley's report are evidences of sympathetic insight and genuine ability on the part of these members to deal with a group of children as well as with individual situations which with other people might prove compromising. Here are a few instances in point.

Jane Jones appeared for the afternoon outing in a long black dress, a chiffon velvet wrap, and high heeled slippers. There was only one thing to do to prevent her from feeling completely out of place and so we delegated the important functions of the afternoon to her. She purchased the pop corn balls and peanuts and decided on the place and time to eat them, and when the time came, she distributed the food.

Two of the girls told the Mortar Board members of the experiences they had had in "homes" and discussed quite seriously and in an interested manner, how many babies one could carry about at one time, and how many times a day a baby had to be changed. We have been pleased to note that the older girls who at first seemed indifferent to the activities of the group have accepted the friendship of the Mortar Boards and have concerned themselves with helping the younger ones to have a good time and not get lost.

Only those children who expressed a desire to join the outings participated. There was no persuasion, no pressure, no reward, no punishment. There was no reference to their faults, to misbehavior, to court records. There was genuine interest both on the part of the children and their leaders, and both groups seemed to enjoy themselves equally.

The experiment provides stimulation through group activities, new experience, response, information as to the facilities and methods of securing wholesome recreation at a minimum cost and capable of being enjoyed by both old and young members of the family.

It must be pointed out, however, that in the management of such delinquent groups lie grave dangers. It is a general principle in social work that groups should not be selected on the basis of delinquency, dependency, or any pathological traits because it is almost impossible to control the moral atmosphere which tends to pervade such groups. Furthermore, there is great danger that the pleasurable activities of such groups may be interpreted by other children who are nondelinquent as rewards for delinquency and the latter may seek to alter their behavior patterns. The sounder method perhaps would be to include these children in unselected groups of so-called normal children, since all children tend to follow the group patterns. Apparently, due to very careful management, these dangers seem to have been avoided in the Chicago groups, through vigorous activity, careful selection of cases from communities whose nondelinquent children would not envy them these minimal activities, and through careful supervision.

"The Way Out." — The comment expressed by the White House Conference on Child Health and Protection regarding "the way out" is apropos here:

When the child can find near at home, with companions of his own choice, opportunity for all that his ever widening sphere of craving and interests demands, when his community, including all groups, private, municipal, commercial, holds as its greatest asset the security and development of all of its children; when the spirit of the neighborhood reflects our most ideal teaching, then will the community help to minimize those behavior problems that handicap the lives of so many children.

Our responsibility was expressed years ago by Jane Addams in The Spirit of Youth and the City Streets: "We may either smother the divine fire of youth or we may feed it. We may either stand stupidly staring as it sinks into a murky fire of crime and flares into the intermittent blaze of folly, or we may tend it into a lambent flame with power to make clean and bright our dingy city streets."

18

Social Work for Children with Criminal Activities

Introduction

No community is well organized to deal with children in trouble without a good juvenile court, because a weak court may undo the efforts of many effective services in the pattern, and because a court which confuses its functions may throw the total network of services off balance, several vital but complex questions must be explored in some detail:

(1) What is the children's court idea and wherein lies its significance?

(2) How may the court's principles and objectives be translated into procedures and services?

(3) How should the court fit into a pattern of community services?

(4) How and why are courts so often in difficulty?

(5) What are the strategic points for community action in strengthening a court?

In brief, the core of the children's court is a basic, revolutionary concept which is suggested as a guide for work with those who offend, attack, or seek to destroy the larger community or some of its members. The concept is simply this: We ought to recognize that the offender is really somebody whose very offense is a sign of needed help. Our response, therefore, should be to understand the specific meanings and causes of the antisocial or anti-individual outbreak and to offer help and remedies suited to the etiology and to the individual. Not "to make the punishment fit the crime"; but "to make the assistance and remedy suit the offender." Not "to do something *to* a child because of what he *has done*"; but to do "something *for* a child because of what he *is* and *needs*."

All of this did not spring, fully developed, from the convictions and experience of the early experimenters in a number of cities, nor was it completely elaborated by the Chicago pioneers who actually phrased and won backing for the first full juvenile court law in 1800. The philosophy itself, and ways of implementing it, may be said to have evolved over a long period. At times, in fact, pragmatic considerations predominated, only to be followed by humanitarian and legal rationale. There were thus both ancient ideas and recent experience behind the formulation by the committee of the Chicago Bar Association when it said:

> *The fundamental idea of the Juvenile Court Law is that the State must step in and exercise guardianship over a child found under such adverse social or individual conditions as develop crime. It proposes a plan whereby he may be treated, not as a criminal or one legally charged with crime, but as a ward of the State, to receive practically the care, custody and discipline that are accorded the neglected and dependent child, and which, as the Act states, "shall approximate as nearly as may be that which should be given by its parents."*

Behind this was long tradition in the criminal law of what was called "age of responsibility," i.e., children of certain ages were not considered able to understand the consequences of their acts and therefore were not punishable for them. The dividing line varied with the century and the culture, of course, and there were certain "optional" age groups for whom a prosecutor could seek to prove understanding and responsibility.

Another stream of influence (about whose importance there is some controversy), relevant originally to neglect and dependency but applied later to delinquency, could be traced to the medieval assumption by the crown of supervision over the estates of minors. Transferred later to so-called chancery courts, this responsibility evolved into the notion that king or state, as *parens patriae*, acting as "a wise, affectionate and careful parent," assumed the protection of all infants or at least saw to it, as A. Delafield Smith has said, that they were "parented" or cared for. The origins should not be depicted only in legal terms, however. In the eighteenth and, particularly, the nineteenth century, religious and humanitarian reformers had begun to provide special and separate institution facilities for children, as it became clear that the mixed almshouse was a hazardous environment for child development. They were influenced, particularly late in the nineteenth century, by the obvious inaccuracy of considering child victims of parental misfortune or mistreatment as, themselves, unworthy and degenerate a characterization of other almshouse residents. Special institution programs led to foster home placements and aftercare services. Then Massachusetts pioneered in providing visiting agents to supervise the way in which children so placed were treated. It was natural to add, in 1869, that agents could appear "in behalf of children" when there was a court hearing to commit a child.

Separate institutions, supervision, and aftercare were soon followed in a number of places by provision for separate trials and (later) separate detention. The earlier unofficial probation services of the 1840s could now become specialized and incorporated into law—as a natural evolution from the legal tradition of the use of the suspended sentence in its several variations.

Thus, there were current, at the end of the nineteenth century, in the form of social objectives, legal philosophy, court procedure, and community practice, the components of the major reform represented by the first juvenile court law. The participants in this great innovation had invented the idea of a nonstigmatizing, noncriminal status and the word "delinquency" (already in use) was soon applied to it. It seemed reasonable to hope that the separation of children from adults and a sincere effort on the part of judges to be helpful, in themselves, would be effective. It should cause no surprise that these pioneers did not foresee all of the organizational, administrative, and professional problems yet to be faced by the juvenile court movement.

Because the complexities of delinquency were not yet well understood, the problem of criteria for disposition did not loom large, and the invention of adequate helping and reformative devices seemed a reasonable task. Because social work, psychology, and psychiatry were just beginning, their relationships to the court and the best structure for teamwork were hardly issues. Since the early atmosphere was quite legal and formal, and because social welfare services in modern form were little developed, the concern that the court might ignore due process and become a social agency was yet to be faced. And because there was, as yet, little experience with success and failure, it was not yet realized that the choice of judge or probation officer could be crucial in the implementation or defeat of the court's objectives.

With hindsight, the problems were of course inevitable. The "criteria" for justice can be much clearer if the judge is to apply rules which are meant to suit penalty to offense than if he is charged with finding a helping plan appropriate for a given child. His task is complicated further by the assumption that the child's rights are always protected. As we have noted, this must ultimately mean that similar circumstances result in similar treatment, but how is this to be achieved while knowledge is so incomplete? Courts eventually came to see that psychological and psychiatric clinics might add to the social investigations of probation officers and contribute to dispositions. As the treatment needs were clarified, the standards of probation were raised and access to a variety of institutions and community treatment facilities also became important. Where such facilities did not exist, courts were tempted to create them, not always foreseeing that the court might thus become an administrative and treatment agency which had not yet adequately integrated its legal function.

This latter trend was accentuated by the lack of social welfare services in many counties throughout the country early in the twentieth century. As child welfare programs were created (particularly so-called mothers' pensions or widows' pensions), it seemed natural to turn to courts to administer them. Programs for handicapped children were also so assigned. On the one hand, this emphasized the court's helping orientation and nonpunitive role. On the other hand, and too often, it unnecessarily converted a request for social services into a court process, a stigmatizing process. The later development of broader social welfare programs confronted courts with the difficult problem of deciding which of their activities were central to their roles and which were historical accidents, better reallocated. Inevitably there were those who would now convert the children's court to a judicial agency, narrowly defined, while others were convinced that the court would never meet its responsibilities unless certain minimum diagnostic and treatment activities were assured under its own aegis.

National Picture

Juvenile courts now serve approximately 400,000 to 800,000 cases annually, depending on whether traffic matters are included in the tabulation. The totals are for children ages 10-17, an age range most appropriate for national statistics, even though courts do work with younger children and do not end children's court jurisdiction at the same maximum age. More than half the courts, in fact, have jurisdiction until the eighteenth birthday, while some stop at age 16 and others at 17. The trend, nationally, is to raise the age limits of juvenile court jurisdiction. A few states include youths to 21 within the scope of children's courts, but the jurisdiction is concurrent with criminal courts.

Cases may be processed either "officially" or "unofficially," the exact point of differentiation varying with the state; most crucial, perhaps, is the fact of formal adjudication in the "official" cases. Approximately half of all cases, nationally, are handled officially and half unofficially, Rural areas tend toward a somewhat higher ratio of official handling, semirural areas to a slightly higher ratio of unofficial service. The urban areas are between the two.

All states have some form of juvenile court and there is basic similarity of philosophy and outlook in statutes despite differences in age jurisdiction, specification of offenses included as delinquency, and assignment of types of jurisdiction affecting children and families, other than delinquency and neglect. It is far too seldom noted, however, that only a minority of these children are, in fact, served in courts which are exclusively children's courts or juvenile courts (as they are more often called). Three states have state-wide juvenile court systems providing complete coverage (Utah, Connecticut, Rhode Island); eighty other counties have special judges for children, only half of them full time. The remainder of the some 3,000 counties in the United States are served by judges whose children's court responsibilities are discharged on a part-time basis within the framework of another court. These judges have the task of adapting their methods and outlook to this special setting as they move into it.

A report to the 1960 White House Conference on Children listed as serious problems confronting juvenile courts the lack of judges who are truly specialists in juvenile matters, the prevalence of part time judicial service in these courts, and the tendency to excessive workloads.

There is general agreement that juvenile courts should have jurisdiction over those offenses committed by children which would be crimes in adults, i.e., felonies, misdemeanors, or other offenses. In some instances adult courts are given concurrent jurisdiction in felony cases, or juvenile courts may transfer to adult courts. In others, particularly where the punishment might be death or life in prison, criminal courts may be required to waive their rights before children's court procedure is permitted. This is, of course, one index of incomplete commitment to the juvenile court idea or a compromise to meet what some consider to be community sentiment.

Court jurisdictions are far from uniform in regard to those offenses labeled as delinquency not because they are crimes in adults but because they are deemed as antisocial or indicative of inappropriate development and, thus, of need for public intervention; specified lists of offenses vary from state to state, and a situation considered as indicative of delinquency in one may suggest neglect to another. All courts also have provision for jurisdiction over children not adequately cared for or not provided with basic necessities owing to parental or guardian failings. Here, too, definitions vary widely, particularly with reference to the relative emphasis on physical abuse alone as contrasted with the failure to provide specific forms of care and service. Some courts, under dependency jurisdiction, in effect administer social services and authorize expenditure of welfare and health funds.

Many states include in their statutes broad provision for jurisdiction over adults who "contribute to the delinquency or neglect of a minor." This is a provision which might be used in a variety of ways but is often not called upon at all; serious acts which would "contribute" to delinquency are, in fact, also in the realm of criminal courts. Transfer to such courts is to be preferred both to avoid overloading children's courts with criminal cases and because individual rights are better protected where there are specific charges (assault, cruelty, etc.) which go beyond the difficult-to-establish allegation about "contributing to delinquency." Where children's courts do act in these cases, standard-setting groups consider it sound for them to limit their jurisdiction to offenses committed against children by adults with a continuing relationship to them.

In addition, in every state one court or another has jurisdiction over appointment of guardians, termination of parental rights, adoption, custody of mentally ill children, support, separation, divorce, paternity determination, intra family assault, and so on. These jurisdictions are usually dispersed in probate courts, county courts, circuit courts, and elsewhere. Some of the jurisdictions may be assigned to juvenile courts. While these matters are beyond the scope of our present discussion, it is relevant to note that the Standard Family Court Act of the National Council on Crime and Delinquency proposes that all such jurisdiction, including marital actions, be placed in one family division. Obviously, any assignment of such jurisdictions should facilitate close ties between children's court work and the proceedings involved, since the evidence is overwhelming as to the close interrelationship between broader family problems and child delinquency and neglect.

As we have already suggested, the national juvenile court picture is not encouraging in many respects: personnel inadequacies, staff shortages, resource lacks, structural defects, procedural problems, statutory limitations. These difficulties have many origins. First, the task is basically complex and both knowledge and professional skills are far from complete. Next, there are the honest differences of opinion as to the proper emphasis and direction for the court. Third, some communities are simply not able to solve the problems of financing and staffing which are involved in strengthening a court. In fact, the national increase in court caseloads has inundated some courts and led to compromises.

Despite all of this, and on the positive side, the juvenile court goal is not being abandoned. Higher courts consistently support the basic constitutionality of the approach. Some states have made notable progress in increasing the qualifications and numbers of professional staff. Nationally, juvenile court judges, on the one hand, and probation leaders, on the other, have been working to supply the knowledge and skill which have been lacking. Increasing support has come from a variety of professional groups and from the federal government. Recently formulated statements of standards and goals are particularly helpful. Finally, and most important, the juvenile court idea remains consistent with our basic heritage and attitude toward children; the reforms which are proposed tend to fit within the framework of juvenile court philosophy.

Given this situation, it seems appropriate (a) to seek more specific definition of the place of a court in the community's total approach to children in trouble, and then (b) to examine each phase of the court process and structure with a view to specifying the direction and conditions for reform. The remainder of the chapter is devoted to these tasks.

Children's Court in the Community Pattern

Enough has already been said of the history of juvenile courts to suggest the reasons for an excessively expansive concept of their functions. These courts developed where other social services did not exist and they had to create such services in order to do their own jobs. Inevitably, they were then turned to when new programs had to be housed. Their judges, influential and highly respected public servants, as well as leaders in the efforts to secure facilities, often became the initiators, planners, or coordinators of broad community efforts.

Historical perspective does not, however, justify perpetuation of an unbalanced view which sees the juvenile court as the hub or nexus of community services to children. Far too often, community efforts at prevention and treatment are organized from the court's perspective and guided by its needs, whereas sound planning would demand another vantage point.

First, the court is not primarily a preventive agency and should neither be credited with a decrease in delinquency nor held to account for its increase. Enough has been said in earlier chapters to make the point that the causation of delinquency is, basically, a matter of the world and the national scene, community atmosphere, family life, peer-group experience, and individual personality dynamics. While a court has some part in social control, it cannot affect basic causal factors of this kind in significant fashion. The evidence suggests that it is not even a major deterrent?

Nor should we expect a judge's lecture from the bench to modify a child's value system or to alter a personality pattern which is rooted in lifelong experience. Therefore, it is no reflection on the competence or dedication of juvenile court judges to suggest that the courtroom per se is not a rehabilitation center. For, although it may become a traumatic experience, the courtroom hearing is generally brief and transitory and, to the child, part of a total process which includes a variety of new and salient exposures, including arrest, detention, and parental reactions.

What, then, are the court's appropriate functions? Why the view that the community system of services has an unbridgeable gap unless it includes a strong and soundly employed children's court?

The core role of the court. Most deviant behavior in a community is absorbed in or handled by the family, schools, churches, and medical facilities. Some is assigned to the special channel of the court, as a matter of policy, because action is contemplated which seriously affects the child's status and may deprive him of liberty. Such action is contemplated in instances of behavior so dangerous and disruptive as to cause public concern (conduct defined as illegal or criminal in adults); when a child's behavior is considered a likely precursor of such illegal conduct; or (in so far as children are involved) when the behavior causes serious damage to self, family, peers, or community. The last category, in particular, is a flexible one reflecting the status at a given time of the community's evaluations of deviant conduct in children and of the need for public intervention. It is the schools and the child care, child protection, medical, and religious agencies which are the major forces in conveying to court and to legislature the status of such evaluations and, thus, their priorities as to court concern. Two questions are foremost in the minds of agencies and community institutions as they seek to define when and how they wish to use the court:

1. Are we dealing with phenomena which are beyond the scope of a service lacking access to potent sanctions?
2. Since our service to this particular case demands some infringement on custody, guardianship of the person, or parental rights, what legal procedural

measures are necessary both to assure our right to arrange the service and to protect the child's legal rights—avoiding unnecessary and arbitrary infringement?

Part of the definition of the place of a children's court in the community pattern is based on consideration of what shall occur before the decision is made that there must be legal recourse in order to render a service to a child. The remainder of the definition involves the situation after the court's intervention.

A juvenile court is inevitably involved in both levels of *case finding*: the kind which is concerned with early deviance not yet in the defined province of any particular service as well as the kind assigned to it by statutory directive. In fact, citizens, teachers, police officers, representatives of child care agencies, and others often come to the court for the purpose of clarifying whether a situation.

Children's Court in a Community System-Relevant Dimensions

Is or should be in the former or the latter category. Obviously, the court may contribute to the necessary processing at that point only if it has an adequate intake structure. While the nature of the legal, social work, and psychological skills on which intake must draw will be elaborated at a later point, it is appropriate to note that, like all case finding, intake may lead to the giving of information or advice, to referral, to brief service, or to complete court processing. Located, so to speak, in the court "vestibule," it should be a brief service. And, situated in the pre-judicial phase of the court's work, its direct service should remain *voluntary* and should not involve formal judicial decisions.

An alert judge or intake worker is also well located for that case finding which is a by-product of the work on the case at hand. Thus, a delinquency hearing may disclose the health problem of a sibling, or a neglect procedure may produce evidence of the delinquency of a neighborhood boy.

These matters should obviously be channeled to the appropriate agencies again, on a voluntary basis.

Case finding is also accompanied by *situation finding.* Probation officers and judges will become aware, constantly, of gaps in community provision, of problems in the educational system, and of conditions hazardous to child development. It is difficult to accept the notion that a court should be an isolated, judicial, decision making mechanism which ignores such things. Rather, most courts would agree to the need for a pattern of organization which permits assembling of data and experience, ensures periodic internal assessments of such material, and provides for prompt reporting of observations and concerns, as appropriate, to police, government officials, schools, health services, churches, and the public at large.

Case evaluation accompanies all of the court's case finding, whether it is of the brief screening variety which determines that the family should go elsewhere or the more complete evaluation which guides brief service in intake or leads to the courtroom. Information desk and petition-writing personnel have responsibilities for some of these functions, although major responsibility belongs to probation and other intake personnel.

Court intake asks, primarily, "Should the case be referred to the courtroom, helped here, or referred out?" The determination may be routine (certain cases must get to the courtroom) or very complex.

The judge in the courtroom is called upon to answer another kind of case evaluation question, "Does the court have jurisdiction?"

We have, elsewhere, referred to the case evaluation in the courtroom as the special skill of the court, the monopoly of the court and, indeed, its *unique* function in the total community system of services. The reference is of course to adjudication which is largely a legal evaluation and involves both issues relating to jurisdiction and issues relating to facts.

Unlike those situations in which people may be offered and will accept service on a voluntary basis and those others in which total context creates some built-in sanctions (the relief investigator and his client), there are some human circumstances, we have seen, in which society adopts the right to impose measures whatever the attitude of the individual. The applicable circumstances are defined by statute as interpreted by court opinions. It is the special purpose of adjudication to determine whether situations as alleged and as defined in the statute prevail and whether social measures may therefore be initiated. So crucial, so unique, and so valuable is this special prerogative of the court that no true advocate of juvenile courts could fail to concern himself with legal definitions, court procedures, and the full preservation of legal rights. To do so is to ignore the special contribution of a court to the total pattern.

The court's *service planning* after adjudication demands a more comprehensive *case evaluation* in the form of a probation case study. This study, where appropriate, should be supplemented by clinical reports. It is our view that a social study of this kind, involving considerable invasion of privacy, should follow only after adjudication. We shall defer the question of whether the judge should (*a*) do all the service planning; (*b*) limit himself to the decision of whether or not a child is to remain in the community or be committed; (*c*) turn the planning over to a treatment authority.

In what sense is the court also a *treatment or direct service* agency? Children and families before the court may require services as varied and diverse as any that a community can provide. No court would seek to meet all or even most of the needs. It does have in probation, however, the potential of a unique service, especially suited to it. We have already defined the probation task in intake and in case evaluation prior to disposition. The service-treatment role in probation should also be quite specific; not the endless, meaningless "reporting" and checking up which it is in many places but, rather, a defined form of intervention appropriate for a definable subgroup within the court population. The "helping" professions have described some young people in trouble as most likely to be reached if served by a community treatment facility which has direct and immediate access to sanctions in this instance, the right to commit. It is these young people who should be placed on probation. Others may be assigned this disposition because there is conviction that they should be followed up for a period and reevaluated carefully prior to discharge.

In a later section we shall have occasion to discuss in further detail the probation role and the qualifications which an individual should bring to it. Particularly promising are several new group approaches and the "reporting center" idea. We shall also, subsequently, consider the relationship of probation to court clinical services. For the present we might stress that a qualified probation structure would seem to be the best way to incorporate into treatment method the court's particular advantages as an authoritative agency. Clinical skill and personnel might be included within probation for a variety of purposes. It would be difficult to make a convincing case for a separate clinical structure. It may be appropriate in a large community to create a probation office which is administratively independent and which serves several courts.

In general, a court is not the agency best equipped to manage or operate institutional or general therapeutic services, unless the community is small and the social welfare structure undeveloped. Where possible, even detention should be administered as part of a system of facilities which includes shelters, youth residences, boarding homes, and so on. This does not preclude court control of detention intake and social service, clearly a necessity for efficiency of operation, protection of individual rights, and to avoid unnecessary use of detention. Where local conditions suggest the desirability of court administration of detention because of the close tie of detention to its core role, this should be seen as a justifiable exception, rather than reason for excursions into more extensive direct-service areas.

What comes to the court. Having looked, briefly, at the heart of the court's task and at its unique role in a community system, we must hasten to add that a court cannot implement that role in isolation. It requires close ties to all major social institutions so as to be sure that there is clear understanding of what it is ready to do. It also needs these ties so as to be in tune with community evaluations of juvenile conduct. There is no system of law which can fully determine for all time the "cut-off points" for community concern about deviance in children. As part of the mainstream of community life a court must remain in tune with the culture in relation to those statutory provisions implying evaluations of the consequences of given behavior.

To discharge its responsibility in effecting what comes into court, the court needs formal ties to voluntary and public agencies and civic groups through public and voluntary coordinating and planning bodies. Its judges and probation leaders must also be active in many phases of civic life in their personal capacities.

What the community offers. Judge O. W. Ketcham of the Washington, D.C., court, using a helpful literary device, has talked of the juvenile court as a court-community compact. Certain criminal court protections are given up in the juvenile court on the "promise" that court intervention into his life "will enhance the child's welfare." A court can hardly discharge its obligations without constant attention to what the community resources on which it draws are like and what they do.

Judges and other court administrative personnel may meet their responsibilities in part through participation in planning and coordinating bodies, as suggested above. But more is involved. At the time of appointment and periodically during a term of office, top court personnel require the kind of in-service training and orientation which will acquaint them with the resources which exist and with reasonable expectations which may be held. A court should regularly receive, study, and respond to reports on the size, staffing, and effectiveness of agencies and institutions on which its own effectiveness ultimately depends, and it should plan periodic visits to such organizations.

In reacting to community needs, reporting about serious gaps, and urging new provisions a court is discharging functions which we have identified as *reporting* and *accountability*. These are responsibilities which a court holds in common with many other community agencies rather than unique roles. Implementation of accountability requires both conscientiousness and particular discipline for a court, however. Since it intervenes in individuals' lives in what is often extremely drastic and strategic fashion, the court carries the heavy responsibility of being informed about the status of agencies and programs. It must seek constantly to assure itself and the public that public intervention is followed by constructive experience rather than by community-sanctioned mistreatment and neglect. Yet, despite its interest, its visiting, and its reporting, the court must not convert itself into a supervisory body or into the guiding force in the community system. As soon as it does, its core role is distorted and the pattern suffers a major gap because it ceases to be primarily a court, albeit a special kind of court, for children.

The "community presence." The "compact" of which Judge Ketcham speaks involves two parties. A court must remain alert to the status of community values, objectives, and resource provisions. A community must constantly keep informed about the quality and operations of its court.

There is need for citizen advisory committees to the court, "watchdog" bodies of citizens, periodic over-all reviews by scholars, legislative bodies, or bar groups. Furthermore, within the limits of protecting privacy and not affecting procedures, qualified responsible officials and citizens should visit the court and express their interest in its work. Representatives of the press and mass media should also visit in order to gain understanding of the court and to reflect community interest in its work—again, only upon assurance that names will not be used and the procedure and atmosphere not interfered with.

The client's perception of the court. A discussion of the court in the community system of services is far from complete without mention of the perception of the court on the part of children and their parents who are brought to it or who should use it. To what extent are the philosophy and objectives of the court translated into a public image which reinforces the work? Do court structure, procedures, and dispositions convey the purposes and objectives which the court holds? Do young people before the court see it as perceptive and helpful or as naive and foolish? Do parents regard it as a potential ally or as a threat to their families? The factors which will determine the answers are best outlined in a more detailed examination of issues of court structure and procedure.

Looking at a Court

An institution as complex as a large juvenile court must ultimately depend for its success on its ability to create a pervasive philosophy and to bring many types of roles and individuals into harmonious activity. This fact must be kept in the forefront as we move from broad generalizations to consideration of specific aspects of court role, jurisdiction, organization, procedure, and administration.

In what follows, we shall seek to document and to specify this point by (*a*) drawing upon available guides and standards, especially the *Standard Juvenile Court Act* and the *Standards for Specialized Courts Dealing with Children*; (*b*) reporting national and local developments and opinions; (*c*) using illustrations drawn from the New York City court. This court has been reported on regularly and in some detail in recent years by observers who are agreed basically as to the court's status and needs. Our own materials have been kept current since publication of *A Court for Children.*

Our fundamental purpose, where we present New York material, is not evaluative. The New York court's jurisdiction, services, and structure are in the process of major reorganization, as this book appears, as the result of unification of probation in three lower courts under an upgraded independent office of probation and the creation of a comprehensive, statewide Family Court. Nonetheless, the illustrative material may be used to suggest a degree of detail not reported upon for most courts, making it possible to move from standards to real situations and to visualize the requirements for any urban area seeking to create an effective facility.

As background for the illustrations, it is useful to record that the Children's Court in New York had traditional delinquency, neglect, and related jurisdiction prior to the 1962 changes and was loosely tied to a support court called Family Court. Since September, 1962, children's jurisdiction is incorporated into a Family Court with comprehensive coverage, except for the exclusion of matrimonial actions. The term "delinquency" is limited to the equivalent of crimes and offenses in adults. There is broad neglect jurisdiction. A new category, children in need of supervision, covers many of those matters previously included under delinquency but not the equivalent of crimes or offenses in adults. As did the old court, the new court has an upper age limit of sixteen for original, exclusive delinquency jurisdiction, with exclusions at fifteen for crimes punishable by death and life in prison. In the neglect and in-need-of-supervision categories the upper age limit is sixteen for boys and eighteen for girls, in a compromise effort to include the "wayward" group, while a legislative committee reviews the general problem of youth jurisdiction for ages 16-21.

A total of 17,586 new delinquency and neglect petitions were processed in the New York court in 1961. The court operates in five borough branches. There are twenty-four judges who rotate among the branches and between the adjudication and disposition "parts" and the family and children's work in each. Judges are required under the new law to have ten years of legal experience. The bench will be increased to absorb the expanded family jurisdiction and new "parts" are being created.

The largest court of its kind, it inevitably requires structure and procedures more complex than those of smaller cities. It is this elaboration of structure and procedures, however, which makes the New York court a useful one to observe in relation to issues and problems. These may be obscured but are not eliminated in smaller communities where there is less specialization and more consolidation.

Doorways

According to *Standards*, individualized, nonpunitive, remedial justice requires:

A judge and a staff identified with and capable of carrying out a nonpunitive and individualized service.

Sufficient facilities available in the court and the community to insure:

a. that the dispositions of the court are based on the best available knowledge of the needs of the child.

b. that the child, if he needs care and treatment, receives these through facilities adapted to his needs and from persons properly qualified and empowered to give them.

c. that the community receives adequate protection.

Procedures that are designed to insure that two objectives are kept constantly in mind, these being

a. the individualization of the child and his situation, and

b. the protection of the legal and constitutional fights of both parents and child.

While the subject of "sufficient facilities" is for the most part explored in other chapters, we shall concern ourselves here with both the staffing and the procedural requirements of a children's court. And it is necessary to stress at once that there is more to court impact on children and parents than the organized plan of the manuals, rules, and routines developed by those in authority. Attitudes conveyed by the manners and mannerisms of personnel are an important part of the atmosphere as it affects those who must use the court. The gossip and mood of the waiting room may influence responses as much as the instructions of a judge. The "low-down" as communicated to a child in the bus en route from detention to a court hearing has much to do with how he interprets a court disposition. In the language of the social scientist, concern for strengthening court operations demands attention to factors of informal, as well as formal, organization, to staff and client culture as well as to rules and procedures.

An institution such as a children's court begins to make its impressions from the moment a parent or child enters the building. The desperate parent who has arrived determined to take some definitive action after years of difficulty with a child, or the community member who has a complaint about a neighbor, receives many of his cues and forms many of his expectations in the first few moments. It is these expectations, in turn, which condition the manner of participation in the court process.

Apart from the physical appearance of the building itself (many court buildings are certainly not designed with their tasks in mind), the behavior of "doorway" personnel can be most important. If a court is to be truly accessible to those who must use it, the information function must be conceived as an important one and the desk must be staffed by personnel who know the court well and can refer appropriately within it, as well as answer more general inquiries. The court, along with other major health, welfare, and police services, must also be prepared to be used as a general information center by citizens who may not need court services but do not know where to go. Information desk personnel therefore require reasonably good knowledge of major community agencies and their functions and must be prepared to "clear" with other information sources when they cannot answer inquiries. Information desk staff need preparation to listen to inquiries by distressed, confused, and anxious people, and to handle them with understanding and reassurance.

The New York court has been aware of the importance of its information desk and has on occasion offered consultation advice to information desk personnel through the probation department. Special orientation has been given at times. However, staff turnover, clerical shortages, the need to use these personnel in other capacities as well have generally defeated the efforts made. It is doubtful that a court's doorway is as "open" as necessary or can render the required service until information desk personnel become part of a general intake staff in a unified Bureau of Applications (i.e., a complete intake service). Some courts have achieved such a plan.

Many courts have recognized that there are case situations which may be settled through referral, without formal court action, or which may require a brief informal discussion and advice and little more. The latter may take the form of a family conference at which agreements are reached about visitation by a separated parent, a child's allowance, "coming in" time at night, or return to a clinic. The *Standards* recommends such service in a court; this kind of service accounts for many of the "informal" cases in the delinquency and neglect statistics reported by the Children's Bureau.

Appropriate as such activity may seem to be, courts are often concerned lest they renege on some of their primary obligations and offer steering or a conference with a probation officer in an intake unit when the complainant or child has the right to legal, not social, guidance and the attention of the judge himself. According to *Standards,* this may be achieved by provision of legal advice for the intake worker—who is usually a probation officer. In addition, any person should have the right to appeal to the judge from any action or decision in an intake unit. Nor should any person be deprived of the right to file a petition on any specific issue to which he is a party.

Most observers agree that New York tended in the past excessively to limit the intake function to a point where the courtroom was unnecessarily overburdened. The court created a pioneer Bureau of Adjustment in 1936, but set up a series of rules which limited the service to less than 10 percent of court cases—those cases considered "less serious." It was widely recommended that the bureau become part of a broad court intake service, offering informal, brief-contact help in some instances and serving as a channel to the courtroom when appropriate. A complete intake structure would also include the *petition desk*, which, in the New York court, has in the past been under supervision of the clerk of the court and not always attuned to the basic philosophy of the whole. Cases which did not go to the Bureau of Adjustment began their processing at the petition desk, and those bureau cases requiring petitions were also steered there. According to a recent report, "Despite efforts by the administrative officers to standardize the procedures involved in preparing petitions, there is no uniformity of quality or practice. Some clerks prepare excellent petitions; others are verbose, use archaic legal expressions, include irrelevant allegations, and even make glaring errors of fact."

Equally crucial is the fact that the discussions of petition clerks with police officers, parents, other petitioners, and children necessarily emphasize details of the offense, the item stolen or destroyed, the circumstances of sexual misconduct. For all participants, this creates a criminal atmosphere and orientation contrary to the court's purpose. The objectives are, of course, appropriate: a desire to follow correct judicial procedure and establish which allegations are to be proven before the court assumes jurisdiction. It is relevant to inquire, however, whether these ends might not be achieved in a manner more suited to the nature of the court. For, whether they come through a Bureau of Adjustment or its equivalent, or are required to go almost directly to the courtroom, all children and parents about to go before the court require preparation for the significant experience and an indication of what to expect. They need to know about procedures, legal rights, possible dispositions, the meaning of remand. They often require considerable reassurance that their rights will be respected, their story heard, and their wishes seriously considered. The court's helping intent needs to be explained time and again. Currently, the petition procedure, in this and many other large courts, is not expected to provide any of this. While it is understood that, except for the judge at the hearing, no one can properly enter into a determination of the truth of the allegations, there are serious grounds for concern that a completely clerical conception of the responsibilities assigned to, or assumed by, petition clerks may, at its doorway, negate the very intent of a children's court.

The *Standards*, the *Standard Act*, and all other guides are agreed that a court for children requires a comprehensive intake service. In delinquency and neglect the intake department should receive all complaints and conduct "investigations to determine whether (*a*) the court or its staff should take action, and, if so, what kind of action, or (b) the matter should be referred elsewhere." An intake service needs consultation with or the participation of legally trained personnel to assure the accuracy of petition writing and the screening out of cases not within the court's scope. It needs skilled probation staff, with access to clinical consultation, so as to render its brief service skillfully, oriented both to legal and to social-psychological diagnostic considerations. Its social appraisals are appropriately brief screening inquiries to determine the court's apparent fight or need to intervene, whether more might be accomplished by "informal" agreements and adjustments or through referral to another agency, the type of court proceeding apparently called for, the need for detention or emergency psychiatric observation pending ultimate disposition. Where a court appearance is to follow, preparation (in the sense described above) is a major responsibility. Where the service required may be completed through "brief service" by the intake staff, this would seem to be desirable, provided that the voluntary nature of participation is kept clear. Extensive "unofficial casework" or "informal probation" would not seem to be a sound function for a court, despite some differences of opinion and contrary practice. New York's reorganized court is evolving a comprehensive intake service as this volume goes to press.

Judge in a Courtroom

A children's court cannot be expected to have the atmosphere of a theater lounge or even a school play yard. The children present are frightened, confused, disturbed, and anxious. Petitioners from the community are often angry or hostile, and police officers may show the insensitivity of long exposure to misery. Family tensions may erupt into arguments as next steps are discussed in preparation for the hearing. In the midst of it all, lawyers confer with clients, young children cry at their discomfort, and attendants call out names on the calendar and demand order and attention.

Surely, adequate provision for reasonably attractive physical surroundings is a minimal requirement. The fact that waiting rooms are often small, crowded, improperly furnished, and not well decorated is evidence that the atmosphere of the court anteroom has not had adequate attention. Nursery rooms to care for young children exist in some court branches and are essential everywhere, since young children should not be present at neglect hearings or at the delinquency hearings of their siblings.

Even if waiting rooms are drab, however, and if court buildings are designed to inspire dignity rather than confidence and relaxation, personnel may do much to convey the respect, individual attention, and helping purposes of a court. Again, if this is appreciated, attendants and matrons are indoctrinated in court objectives and shown how they may advance them. If it is not fully understood, or if the court is overburdened and understaffed, the court attendants only add to the general anxiety and confusion, and unintentionally undermine the best of judge and probation officer efforts. People are herded into the courtroom, more apprehensive than their normal reactions would make them; even the most talented of judges finds it difficult to overcome the formality insisted upon by those attendants who hold criminal court concepts of client courtroom behavior. Whether or not the judge does overcome all of this and conveys another mood during the hearing, attendants may undo much of what he communicates by their brisk ushering of people out. The objective may be to speed the calendar, but the consequence is a mood which again poses needless obstacles as the probation officer's work proceeds.

The New York City court has not fully conquered the task of converting many types of personnel into a unified, consistent staff; many other courts are similarly unsuccessful. Nor has this court as yet found ways of building courtrooms appropriate to court functions and to the mood it seeks to establish. In some boroughs, the bench is no higher than an ordinary table, but in others the judge is as high and as distant as judges ever are. Some of the rooms do lend themselves to disposition conferences, but instead the tendency is to arrange the tables and chairs as though there were a formal "bench" available. Even the judges who seek to undo this and to communicate more intimately with those before the court for disposition discussion find the atmosphere forbidding: in addition to personnel who must participate in the conference and the attendants, who do not try to be unobtrusive, clerical workers, translators, and a group of waiting probation officers, who are not sure when they will be reached to present cases or to confer with the judge, convert the hearing into a rather public occasion. This may be inevitable to a degree in the adjudication phase, where the court must decide whether or not a finding is to be made and must consider all those involved in an incident as well as witnesses but even here one should guard against unnecessary paraphernalia or ceremonial which confuses or intimidates. A public occasion is very far from the objective at the disposition hearing, however, where there is need to talk, understand, explain, and reassure. The *judge* is the leader of the court "team" and his qualifications and characteristics do much to make a children's court, or to disappoint those who believe in its potentialities. In the language here being employed to describe basic functions essential to a total community plan, the judge may be said to have extremely important parts in the following:

a. **Community protection :** He may place a child in detention pending long-term disposition. He may commit an adjudicated child to an institution or hospital if the child's presence in the community is a hazard.

b. **Case evaluation :** He decides whether a community has the right to exercise authority.

c. **Case disposition :** Drawing upon the data and recommendations of specialists (probation officers, psychiatrists, psychologists, educators, detention personnel, etc.) as well as his own observations and evaluation, he decides what the court's "plan" for a case will be.

d. **Referral :** The judge makes the first attempt to interpret the plan, encourage optimum use by child and parent of the service offered, and, at times, ensure agency understanding of the client and the reason the disposition was made.

e. **Reporting** : The judge may be alert to shortages or inadequacies of facilities and may communicate these to responsible bodies and to the community at large.

The judge does not carry out treatment, since a treatment relationship requires time to develop and frequency of contact. His courtroom statements to parents and children may serve to communicate community opinion or to encourage maximum use of treatment opportunities.

A sound definition of role for the judge requires a balancing of legal knowledge and method with the basic knowledge and ability essential to understand reports of specialists, to choose from many alternatives, and to convey encouragement and support as he selects and interprets a disposition. He must be able to question skillfully, observe courtroom behavior, and draw inferences from it. In addition, he must know how to respect the contributions of personnel in all categories and integrate all the court's parts into an effort on behalf of children.

Protection of rights is as vital as sound dispositions, since the court may not plan where it has no jurisdiction. Judges must explain the allegations, inform parents of the right to adjournment for counsel or to summon witnesses, and avoid disposition considerations prior to adjudication.

Procedural details will not here be reviewed. The separation between *adjudication* (the judicial determination as to whether the allegation is true and, if so, where the state shall assume some responsibility) and *disposition* may be achieved by the division into two parts, or by an adjournment for probation study between the two phases. New York City uses both these methods. Some courts blur individual rights by ignoring these two separate phases.

Creative judges are able to make excellent use of their courtroom assignments. In many jurisdictions, judges are only in children's court part of the time. Others, although full-time, may be neither dedicated to the court's objectives nor qualified for its complex demands. Thus, in all juvenile courts there are judges who overemphasize the offense and lose its significance, or fail to note clues which indicate how they may help. Many lack sufficient understanding of individual behavior or skill in relating and communicating to translate an honest desire to help into effective action. Some are basically too insensitive to work with troubled people and they hurt many who come before them through ridicule, rudeness, or failure to understand and to feel with those in court. There are, too, those who are unfamiliar with educational, social welfare, and mental hygiene resources and who do not seek to equip themselves with the knowledge their task requires.

Most judges suffer to a degree from the occupational hazards involved in extreme power over others, unchallenged by defense counsel in most cases and seldom reviewed by higher courts. A few succumb in extreme form and prefer their own hunches to the reading of probation or psychiatric reports or referral for treatment. Or, if they make referrals, they precede them with long lectures or impose behavior requirements designed, in their minds, to be the important factor in change. They may "play to the gallery" as well, as though audience ratings were a gauge of court effectiveness.

There are judges who are best equipped to deal with adjudication and others gifted in the disposition phase. In contrast to outstanding judges who give leadership to community child welfare efforts, there are those who simply do not seem to know or to care.

Honest differences of opinion are current about the judge's role, but it is clear that some of the patterns ignore the court's objectives or at least fail to contribute to their realization. This situation will change only as the result of clearer court and public agreement as to the behavior which is not desirable and the qualifications to be sought as well as the establishment of an appointment or selection procedure to protect against obviously inappropriate choices.

Many strong opinions are held as to the superiority of election, appointment, or their several variations as a mode of staffing courts. Investigation discloses no preponderance of evidence in favor of any one plan. One can cite outstanding judges derived from all possible selection procedures, and at the same time point to some among their colleagues who are hardly assets to court work. Many court reformers currently support a plan whereby a highly qualified citizen-bar panel nominates a roster of qualified candidates from which either an appointing official (mayor, governor) or party nominating conventions might make selections.

Whatever the procedural format, however, it is clear that there is need for candid legal and civic appraisal and the placing of qualifications (rather than prerogatives) in the forefront. Nationally, there is need for law schools to add to the reservoir of those potentially qualified for this role by filling some of the gaps in training in this area of what is at times called sociolegal jurisprudence. They might consider the proposal of the late Judge Jerome Frank that judicial training become an advanced law school specialty. If this is too far from any immediate reality, institutes, seminars, and inservice orientation for those selected for these courts might help convert interested and qualified attorneys into judges for children.

The National Council on Crime and Delinquency has given considerable leadership to these efforts in recent years.

Case Evaluation in Probation

Court intake personnel of all kinds make brief screening decisions. The court also requires more comprehensive case evaluations, adequate to guide a decision about intervention, i.e., so-called disposition evaluations. Because a substantial number of cases remain in treatment in the court as probationers, the disposition evaluations must be designed so as to guide the work of the probation officer in the early stages of contact (i.e., serve as a case evaluation to guide treatment). What has been traditionally called the "investigation" role of the probation officer is thus seen as a case study which should draw on the best available professional knowledge and skill. Despite earlier differences of opinion, the probation field and standard setting groups now see the assignment as belonging within the scope of social casework and seek to adapt case evaluations, as prepared by caseworkers, to the particular needs of the court. Courts are recruiting trained social workers wherever possible, or are introducing social work concepts and methods into their in-service efforts.

The case evaluation study, designed to contribute to disposition planning, as well as to facilitate the launching of probation treatment where probation is the disposition selected, requires a psychosocial emphasis. *A Court for Children* stated it thus:

> *Such study must concentrate on the child's social environment and personality, in an attempt to comprehend the significance of the current situation to him and to his family. Understanding of this kind derives from careful review of social history, current social setting, personality, and interpersonal relations. It makes possible, and should ultimately be formulated in, a case evaluation, "a diagnosis," and is prerequisite to the inauguration of helping measures. Whether these are wisely selected depends on: the ability of the probation officer to understand the child, to evaluate the case data assembled, and to make valid recommendations; the willingness of the judge to consider the probation officer's formulation carefully, without necessarily being bound by it; and the extent to which "disposition" is regarded as a treatment plan based on case study and courtroom observations. The formulation finally accepted may be that of judge, probation officer, psychiatrist, supervisor, or the product of a conference. It may utilize reports of social agencies, examinations, tests and observations by other groups, as well as the court's own data. To achieve the court's aim, all these aids to understanding must be employed in a unified strategy for rehabilitation.*

These requirements indicate the possible sources of inadequate studies or studies inadequately employed. First, probation officers may not be equipped to conduct good case studies. Course work and experience under capable supervision are necessary if one is to learn adequate social study. Second, the study may be made but the position of the probation officer vis-à-vis the judge may be such that he does not end it with an evaluation, an appraisal—as well as a recommendation. Third, judges may, for various reasons, ignore the contents of studies or not even read them. (For example, following a recent incident in which the public was outraged after a gang stabbing in one city, all the "under sixteen" boys involved were committed to a training school at once.) Fourth, judges may read the reports but not be equipped to make wise use of them. Fifth, all may function well but community and court facilities may be in such short supply as to render the activity almost futile.

All of these situations prevail in a large court system and are not readily conquered. Far too often case study is a matter of mechanical filling out of headings by partially trained probation officers who have mastered professional devices superficially. Facts are assembled, but there is little analysis to provide a dynamic, living picture of a child in trouble. Plans may be proposed yet often the rationale is not given. Recommendations may be avoided or the standard proposal made that there be psychiatric study, thus reflecting the probation officer's insecurity.

Little more should be expected in any court system with inadequate job qualifications, salaries too small to prevent rapid staff turnover, poorly trained supervisors, and caseloads too heavy to permit sound work. The job definition, in fact, is often attuned to these realities and does not demand more.

Governmental and probation leadership in New York and elsewhere has dealt seriously with these problems in recent years in many ways. Higher examination requirements, matched by better salaries, have attracted more people. Where possible, graduate social workers are sought. Supervisors are released for social work training in a work-study program. In-service efforts are made. Unfortunately, constantly growing court caseloads, reflecting the general rise in delinquency, and a rate of expansion and recruitment not equal to the caseload rise have not given many major courts opportunity to consolidate, plan, or train staff.

A staff which is not sufficiently large, or is not adequately qualified or used, is a weak link which defeats the total logic of a system of service. For example, partially trained and, therefore, insecure probation officers are ready to follow most of the recommendations from court clinics, psychiatric hospital observation wards, and detention. Frequently the probation officer's only recommendation (often on the basis of little study) is that there be psychiatric study. Yet one hardly requires a full probation case study of two to three weeks' duration to arrive at the decision that psychiatric observation or study is necessary. The intent of the law, of course, is that the probation officer take responsibility for final weighing of formulations and recommendations from all sources and that he have expert knowledge of available resources. He can then make recommendations to the court independently. However, wherever probation officers are less equipped, technically, than clinic or detention personnel, funds will continue to be expended on pointless repetition.

Because clinic recommendations are, as a rule, accepted, the probation officer's job is, in fact, gradually redefined under circumstances such as these. A large portion of the officers avoid any major responsibility for suggesting a long-range disposition by recommending clinical diagnostic study unless they feel that a "minor" offense, "deserving" probation or discharge, is involved or unless there has been a pattern of recidivism, so that commitment to a training school is considered inevitable. The consequence may well be an excessive use of court clinics and detention psychiatric facilities. Without doubt, more responsible probation case studies, with opportunity for psychiatric consultation to the officer, would simplify the procedure, speed up processing, and be more economical of psychiatric time with no less satisfactory results.

There is determination almost everywhere to improve this situation. Increased recruitment of social work graduates and provision of in-service training and work-study opportunity must accompany administrative reform and job redefinitions.

The Disposition Format

We shall hold at a later point that case disposition in a children's court is a technical matter and that the judge should perhaps limit himself to the decision as between commitment and service in the community. The choice from among the variety of community-based services or away-from-home treatment facilities may be variously assigned.

Many judges do not accept what they would define as a truncated role; others agree in principle, but point to the lack of treatment "authorities" or fully qualified probation staffs. These realities make it necessary to discuss the court's disposition format. Even where the disposition specifics are assigned elsewhere, the judge probably will retain primary responsibility for the choice as between a community based or a residential service. Structure and procedure for decision making are therefore of considerable interest.

To begin: Disposition planning must follow adjudication. A court has no right to assume jurisdiction in order to arrange treatment. When the court plans a service, it should use its rights and prerogatives. It should not, however, permit any of its functions to be undertaken without formal procedure and order.

Given clear agreement that it is the judge who makes the disposition decision, a conference format would seem to be most desirable. A case conference procedure at the disposition phase would both create the informal atmosphere which is sought and permit more adequate exchange of views between those who contribute to disposition than the current, more formal, plan. It could encourage real discussion among judge, probation officer, psychiatrist (if needed for the case), counsel (if one is involved), parents, child, representatives of other agencies concerned. A conference will not develop, of course, if the judge considers himself as *the court* rather than as a team leader who wants to understand and consider all relevant views and data. In contrast to adjudication, which requires considerable procedural structure in order to guard individual rights, the disposition conference, while a hearing, should be quite informal and should take place only in the presence of those who must be involved. The decision making is the judge's and he has the right to interview a child privately, to ask people to come and go as the progress of the conference requires, to permit attorneys to examine certain relevant materials, without disclosing medical-psychiatric data, so that they may understand the ways in which the plan is meant to help. Most important, the conference permits discussion with parents and children under reasonably good conditions so as to interpret and initiate disposition plans with them.

Case Treatment in Probation

The probation officer who does not complete adequate case studies for the reasons already given is hardly qualified to make maximum use of the court's decision to assume protective supervision over a child. It takes dynamic understanding of a child, as well as ability to develop and control a relationship in a helping way, if one is to use the probation period to promote sound growth and change. There must be good knowledge and use of community resources and services as well, and this, too, is founded on both case appraisal and skill in referral.

A friendly, big brother approach, which is possible for the well meaning layman who likes young people, was once all that was sought in probation. Despite all of the advantages and the usefulness of such an approach in appropriately selected cases even today, the probation field came to understand that it is not enough. The personal and social pathology in the backgrounds of children in the court often defies all but the most skilled workers who bring specific professional preparation to the task. This view is bolstered by the recognition that the probation officer, unlike the worker in many agencies, must grapple with the problem of changing people who, initially at least, must see him unwillingly. Moreover, he must impose certain rules and limits to protect the community, whether or not these advance individual rehabilitative objectives.

It is these considerations which give emphasis to the view that the decision to assign a child for probation treatment must be based on case understanding rather than on that misdirected generosity which employs it not as the treatment of choice but as a "second chance."

The probation field is clear about these views and has made remarkable progress in the past decade in adapting social casework to treatment in the probation setting. A chief U.S. probation officer in Illinois has put it this way: "The most important role of the probation officer is that of friendly counselor, caseworker or guidance officer. To fulfill it he must be equipped to serve as caseworker The trend is towards the methods of social casework."

Even earlier, the National Conference on Prevention and Control of Juvenile Delinquency expressed broad consensus in stating:

> *Probation treatment is essentially a task of reorientation, reeducation, a process of guidance and reconditioning in which the* relationship *between probation officer and child is the vital element which effects the changes or modifications in attitudes, habit, and environment needed to bring him into closer harmony with the requirements of society.*

As the probation field has matured professionally there has been increased understanding of the central place of that relationship between probation officer and child. Lectures and even concrete services have little effect without it; advice has meaning only in the context of a relationship in which it is given; and concrete services do not contribute to rehabilitation unless the probationer can "participate in the solution of his own problems. He becomes able to deal with difficulties constructively only by dealing with them, not by blindly following the advice of others." The probationer may need emotional support and help in expressing his fears, his likes and dislikes, at one point in the helping process, while he may require tangible and concrete services at another.

Yes, much progress is being made, but probation bureaus are everywhere understaffed and qualified personnel are in short supply. According to a recent survey, while 85 percent of probation officers are college graduates, only 10 percent meet the accepted standard of graduate social work training. Large cities (population 500,000-1,000,000) have the highest proportion of trained staff 17 percent with graduate degrees in social work. The training level is lowest in smaller communities; in areas of less than 50,000 population, only 50 percent of probation officers are college graduates. Yet probation officers are the "treatment agents" for three fifths of court-adjudicated eases. At present, 30 to 40 percent of eases so served are back in court in a few years.

Some courts have lagged in their concept of probation as well, and have not provided the supervision, consultation, clerical and office facilities essential to good work with individuals. At times, rules for probationers have dominated the scene; at others, counseling efforts have been sincere but inept. Probation is, however, the court's unique treatment instrument and there is commitment to its sound development. It must refer to Big Brothers and to friendly volunteers those boys ready for such help, but it seeks to be something else. Similarly, it must refer to clinics, as needed, but does not thereby give up its own special helping method.

Heavy caseloads and a tradition of probation as policing and supervision in the narrowest sense result in an unsatisfactory situation in many cities. Many children "on probation" are seen five to twenty minutes a month, from one to four hours a year, in brief "reporting" or checking-up sessions. They are asked a few routine questions about school, church, recreation, family, and avoidance of codelinquents and are sent away until the next time. Reporting dates are often missed. Few have any sort of relationship with their officers and many are not even known to those to whom they are assigned. In exceptional eases, a favorable probation officer-child combination may lead to a warm relationship and protective supervision. Some cases reveal friendly big brother or big sister work at its best. In a good number of eases, valuable referrals for services of other agencies are made (too often unskillfully and unsuccessfully). The officer at times serves as an instrument of community control.

New York City is now one of several large communities seeking to encourage more complete development of probation as a specialized service whereas, at present, formal structures and inadequate status convert it, too often, into the instrument of the local judge. New York's integrated probation office will no longer in fact be administered by the local court. Whatever the administrative details, which must be suited to local situations, it is unlikely that probation anywhere will have its necessary professional flowering and play its full role unless its leadership is accorded high status in the court and is dedicated to developing effective probation services. To the extent that a judge or a board of judges feels equipped to make decisions about probation policy and procedure, decisions not central to the function of the judge and not deriving from his training, the program cannot evolve to make its full contribution.

Five states (New York, Indiana, Ohio, Washington, Colorado) have begun modest state subsidies toward improved probation services. Others hope to do so. A variety of educational plans are also under way. It is understood that administration, job definitions, and professional qualifications need as much attention as caseload size. As probation treatment standards are raised, it should be possible to offer probation as the treatment of choice far more often. New York City selects probation as the post investigation disposition for about half the cases. An enthusiastic probation advocate estimates that, for the country as a whole, about 90 percent of delinquents might be placed on probation in their first court experiences and 50-75 percent on the second or third appearance. Given high quality services, he would expect a success rate of 75 or 80 percent? This is, of course, a desirable goal in view of the many obstacles to successful institutional treatment and its relatively high costs as compared with even the best of probation.

New Service—Probation Reporting Centers

Many courts have used after school reporting as a rather hollow checking-up device, usually on a weekly or biweekly Basis. For some years now, the Citizenship Training program under the *Boston* juvenile court has sought a somewhat stronger impact by requiring, as a condition of probation, that boys between the ages of twelve and seventeen report five days a week from 3:30 to 5:30 P.M. An educational-counseling-recreational program is conducted. A recent ten-year study was encouraging. Other cities have borrowed the plan.

More recently, there has been interest in a promising intensification of this approach, which is being subjected to careful study. It should be said, by way of background, that the application of group methods to probation is not new, and that there have been a variety of encouraging reports since shortly after World War II. The Provo, Utah, program, under the leadership of Professor LaMar Empey, represents an introduction of a group therapeutic approach into the reporting center idea. Boys are brought directly from school on weekdays. Originally, there was emphasis on crafts, recreation, and meetings which might broaden one's perspectives and give some realistic information about the ultimate outcomes of a criminal career. Later the program was modified under the influence of the theory followed at High fields in New Jersey.

In brief, under the Highfields plan, boys reside in a home with very few facilities and no program to divert them from focus on themselves and one another. The daily work is routine. Life is concentrated on the five-day-a-week evening "guided group interaction sessions," a sociological modification of group therapy. Groups of ten meet for an hour and a half. The group "culture" shapes a "social system" in which there is a constant process of mutual interaction and evaluation. Evaluative studies show impressive results.

It occurred to Professor Empey that a nonresident version of Highfields might be valuable and his program has been reshaped in this direction. A rigorous research design provides for assignment of boys on a random basis from among two categories: those who would ordinarily be committed to institutions and those placed on probation. The boys are brought to the center (a house) five days a week and, although there are some facilities, the program is kept unstructured—to encourage spontaneous interaction. Half of the daily three-hour period is devoted to a "guided group interaction program." A Saturday work project and a summer daily work program, with the work in each instance followed by a group meeting, repeat much of the Highfields approach, on a less intensive basis, without the residential unit.

Nationwide interest has been aroused by this program, which is now being replicated in several places, and several programs which reflect aspects of both the Boston and the Provo programs have also developed (Washington, D.C.; Minneapolis, Minnesota). Traditional probation is so structured that it tends to be individually oriented, often intrapsychically. This is often necessary. Group therapeutic approaches add diversification. Given a range of diagnostic types and social meanings inherent in the delinquencies, the reporting center would seem to be a particularly promising program for those whose delinquency is related to neighborhood and peer-group culture a major subgroup before the court. At the same time, present research may also disclose certain psychiatric-diagnostic subgroups who may respond to a program of group interaction which focuses on the ways in which one copes with the rules, demands, and values of the broader society. The program also promises and this is no small consideration to avoid exposure to the negative consequences of institutionalization where it is not necessary. Since all-day reporting is also possible (one New Jersey variation) the reporting center offers considerable community protection.

It is not yet clear whether a reporting center always should be administered by a probation department; the Highfields advocates are convinced that some authoritative auspices are essential for their programs.

Court's Mental Health Services

When Chicago's juvenile court recognized that no judge alone could encompass all the skills and knowledge essential to case appraisal, it called upon Dr. William Healy to establish the first court psychiatric clinic. Other courts followed. At first devoted largely to diagnosis, such clinics gradually took on treatment responsibilities as well. Their methods and emphasis, based originally on the early psychiatry and psychology of the turn of the century, soon reflected the development and application of dynamic mental hygiene.

Today, in the light of broader community planning concerns, we must face issues which did not exist for court clinic pioneers—issues which still are not real to many American communities which lack any clinical resources and which cannot afford to be too concerned about auspices and context of what becomes available. Let us again illustrate with reference to New York.

The New York City Children's Court Bureau of Mental Health Services began in 1916 before the court had its present form. It was essentially diagnostic and sought originally to identify mental defectives. With the growth of the mental hygiene movement, its diagnostic skills were deepened, but it did not evolve its treatment role until 1937. In fact, this phase of the work was developed by a voluntary group and was not fully supported by public funds until 1942.

Despite severe limitations of resources, the New York court's Bureau of Mental Health Services has played a pioneering role in its field and over the years has demonstrated how modern psychiatric and psychological knowledge might be applied to diagnosis of delinquent children and their parents, as well as in cases of neglect. Its staff has contributed to the development and adaptation of social work treatment methods for this group. Valuable experiments were conducted in the use of group therapy with parents and children, and there were innovations in group "intake" interviews and remedial reading. A special project tested ways of introducing clinical skills into court intake and of offering consultation services to judges in emergencies, The research and writing of bureau staff members had broad influence. There were periods, too, during which the clinical staff contributed significanfiy to the in-service training of probation staff. However, for many years this clinic has lacked resources and personnel for more than a small portion of the service sought by the judges. It has also faced fundamental questions about its role. Coordination within the court has always been difficult. For this court and all courts must ask:

a) In a city with a variety of courts, should each court develop mental health services or should there be one system serving all courts? Should the clinical system perhaps also serve the adult jail, penitentiary, and detention facilities?

b) Should court clinics limit themselves to diagnosis and consultation, or is treatment an essential function for them?

c) What relationships should be developed between court-serving clinics and the hospitals or health departments?

d) In what manner should probation and clinical services be interrelated?

These are certainly relevant questions as one takes a fresh look at courts, from the perspective of total community interests. Particular doubts are raised about the efforts to create treatment clinics in a children's court. There are those who hold, for example, that the close relationship with the court represents an obstacle to the progress of treatment, since parent and child remain suspicious of court intent, hesitate in forming relationships, and are not free in their expression. Proponents of this view note the evidence that staff in this and other clinics have often tended to isolate themselves from the court program and to separate themselves, in the minds of clients, from court authority. This seemed to be a condition of effective work.

Others add that the presence of a court clinic in which the bulk of treatment is actually rendered by social workers tends to divert attention from the need to convert probation into an effective casework treatment program. Probation officers may limit themselves to emotional support, encouragement, advice, or concrete environmental services and tend to recommend case referral if a more intensive service is required. The proponent of a court-based treatment clinic cites the experience in rendering successful treatment in authoritarian settings; he holds that a child or parent should be treated under the auspices of the authoritarian agency responsible for him. Such a patient should know that nonparticipation or failure may have certain consequences. But this type of logic would lead to the creation of treatment clinics in all courts and protective agencies as well as in schools hardly the efficient way of organizing community resources. It is our view that a community would be wiser to develop a communitywide public clinical service to which courts, schools, and correctional agencies would have easy access in making referrals for *clinical treatment.* These clinics should be medically based in a health or hospital department. This view of treatment services does not preclude other clinical service and impact in a court. An experiment in the Bureau of Mental Health Services and subsequent experience in the New York court suggests that the mental health program in a court should be organized primarily as a diagnostic and consultative service. Such service ought to be available in connection with court intake, when necessary, or as requested by the judge at hearings. It should meet psychiatric emergencies which arise in the court. It should be accessible in connection with disposition conferences. Organizational considerations might suggest a city-wide division with units assigned to individual courts. Given present tendencies to ask for psychiatric studies in too routine a fashion, guides for referral will have to be developed. One experienced judge reports that he asks for clinical study in the following types of situations:

1. where there is homosexuality or a severe sexual problem (the probation officer will require guidance to deal with the case)
2. where the child's behavior has had such serious consequences that he requires help with his guilt
3. where the child's conduct seems to reflect serious emotional disturbance, so that diagnostic guidance is necessary
4. where a parent shows a history of serious mental illness or psychopathology
5. where an institution requires a psychiatric report before considering admission of a child
6. where help is needed in evolving an appropriate placement plan

The availability of a clinic service as part of the intake machinery, prepared to consult with the judge or to conduct interviews and tests as needed, on the spot, would certainly equip a court for more effective service. Indications of the need for clinical advice could lead immediately to study efforts and to emergency action, as required. For other cases, a regular diagnostic service would still be important, prepared to accept referrals considered necessary in the course of court hearings or probation contacts. Clinic personnel, for their part, need to work closely with judges and probation officers so as to suit their reports in form, language, and content to the functions of these central court personnel. They must be alert to the status of community resources so that recommendations may be realistic and meaningful.

This recommendation does not necessarily preclude clinical impact in court treatment. We have already described the probation service as rendering that direct treatment, individual and group, which takes special advantage of the authoritative nature of the court's setting and the sanctions available to it. Well-trained probation workers obtain a core of clinical knowledge and technique which guides their service. Given access to psychiatric consultation, and reasonable workloads, a probation department may duplicate that portion of the work of a Bureau of Mental Health Services which is within the province of a social worker. That portion which is more appropriately medically based, or which demands the psychiatrist's intervention, would be referred to the community-based clinics.

Voluntary Agencies in Children's Court

Early in the history of children's courts, voluntary social agencies provided the only available probation services. Later, when full-time publicly employed probation officers became part of usual court staffing, these agencies sought to adapt their programs to the new situation. They recognized that, depending on their own staffing and auspices, they could offer specific advantages to the court for cases appropriately selected:

a. They could supply volunteer "big brothers" and "big sisters" who could offer friendship, sound models for identification, individual attention, recreation, and personal help—services requiring a warm, interested adult and not a professionally trained caseworker.

b. They could serve as a channel to social service programs in the community, acting as a generalized intake for all Catholic or all Jewish family and children's agencies, for example.

c. They could serve as a channel to religious guidance and counseling if sought by clients, or voluntarily accepted by them. The court cannot, as a public agency, offer direct religious services.

d. They could be friends and supporters of the court, understanding its problems and needs and interpreting them to the community. All of the above types of activity would, of course, provide a vantage point for this role.

There has been a tendency in recent years to add casework treatment resources and accompanying psychiatric consultation to all of the patterns. This increases the adequacy of evaluation and the skill in referral by voluntary programs. The particular pattern of organization in a given court has tended to reflect community factors and the sectarian group involved.

A long-range look at the total community pattern requires that sectarian voluntary services, whatever the immediate advantages of these programs (and none doubt the value of the service rendered), be considered in relation to the whole. From such a perspective, a plan whereby a sectarian agency provides intake and treatment for its coreligionists does not represent a desirable plan, and its most effective agents are very clear about this. All clients before the court have a right to the service currently available only to the minority in some courts: the competent assembling of background data and the preparation of clients for the courtroom, access to consultation, and careful planning of interim and long-range dispositions. The development of adequate court intake services and raising of the quality of probation case studies would, of course, achieve this.

The liaison function for voluntary social agencies, big brother and big sister programs, and religious counseling remains appropriate and necessary. In some instances it requires considerable expansion to assure necessary coverage. The liaison workers might be professional or lay, depending on the specific service.

Several cautions remain necessary. It is important, first, to stress that voluntary services should not be used as though any voluntary agency offers something superior to probation. Probation treatment needs strengthening but is not inferior to some voluntary agencies. The disposition decision to be made is whether a given child is best served through a court-based relationship with a probation officer, by a caseworker in another public agency, or by a representative of a voluntary agency. The case evaluation may also suggest the desirability of a referral to an outside service (i.e., a big brother) and concomitant probation status and confacts. Legal or treatment reasons may make the case for continuing a relationship to the court after adjudication. If it is considered desirable to ask voluntary agency representatives to assume full responsibility, client and agency should be clear that this is an alternative to a court-based service and that while agency representatives may bring cases to court, they do not function as probation officers. Especially important is the guarding of rights in referrals to religious counseling or sectarian programs. Parents have a right to choices here, constitutionally, and must understand their rights to refuse referral, to choose other sectarian or nonsectarian groups, and to be served under public auspices, if they prefer.

A successful children's court is the product of agreement and clarity about function, availability of qualified personnel, and access to a diversified system of resources. Our comments on the New York City court in 1953 would apply to a large portion of such courts today.

This study has found that the New York City Children's Court, considered by some as an illustration of what a successful court should be, has only begun to move in the expected direction. A minority of children are served with both kindness and skill by those judges, probation officers, and other staff members who have understood the purpose of a children's court, are equipped to Pedorm their tasks competently, and have at the same time had available to them needed community resources. The majority of children before the court, however, receive service which does not reflect the juvenile court movement's aspirations or the kinds of help that fully qualified personnel with adequate community resources at their disposal would be able to provide. For some of the children, the court represents a well intentioned but inadequately prepared, pressured group of individuals who cannot achieve what they strive to do. For many, it is the insensitive instrument of an indifferent or hostile social world. Thus, in most instances, the Children's Court in New York City fails to act as a "good parent" or as a skilled counselor; far too often it does not even appear as a kind friend. Indeed, it is as though an ambivalent society created a new institution and then, not being sure about what it had wrought, permitted old practices and failings to continue and provided so few new resources that the institution could not flourish.

Despite the prevalence of difficulties there is widespread agreement that a community service network requires a strong juvenile court. Hence the consensus that the obstacles must be faced directly. Nor is there major controversy about the steps to be taken.

Clearly, a powerful tribunal of this kind is justified only if properly staffed and equipped. Localities, states, and professional schools are involved in a variety of efforts to improve the availability and qualifications of court personnel. Federal assistance through the support of training programs is proposed. In addition, much is being done and more will need to be done to assure the adjunctive services and the social resources on which court effectiveness depends.

There are, however, some critics who feel that this is not enough? A court is not fully successful, they remind us, unless it carefully sorts out cases in which it has no right to intervene and unless it guards rights constantly while imposing treatment through use of sanctions of various degrees of severity. This remains important even though this is, by definition, a civil and not a criminal tribunal. For these critics assert, in the words of Roscoe Pound, that the court's non adversary procedure, confidentiality, informality, flexibility, and rehabilitative aims may convert it into a "star chamber." Although the past responses to warnings and to illustrations of arbitrariness have tended to take the form of reassurance and denial, the problem does deserve serious attention. There are few appeals from a children's court. Private lawyers do not often appear and have not generally learned to play a useful role. What occurs is not known to many people except the agencies concerned. Should we not seek to determine, through adequate experimentation, whether there are ways of using public defenders in children's courts without, at the same time, converting the judge into a prosecutor or requiring the assignment of one? Certainly, whether or not defenders are provided, all in the court have the right to counsel and should be so informed. New York's new law ensures legal aid to all who need and request it.

Whether or not a public defender is assigned, the concern for individual rights also will lead more courts to such procedural safeguards as notice, the right to adjournment for witnesses and counsel, separation of adjudication from disposition phases of the process, the right not to serve as a witness against oneself, the right to cross examine witnesses, the right to appeal.

Is it necessary, as well, to restate the court's jurisdiction in a form which will make it more specific? The *Standards* does urge clear delineation in each statute of the conditions under which the state is empowered to intervene and that "whenever the State seeks to intervene, it should be required to show that those conditions do in fact exist and that its intervention is necessary to protect the child or the community or both." This does not necessarily require differentiation between "delinquent" or "neglected," since the latter distinction is often a matter of chance, depending on the time or the point of case discovery and the perceptiveness or attitude of the petitioner. One third of the states now avoid labels and the Standard Act would end labeling; it suggests a list of circumstances under which a juvenile court shall have exclusive jurisdiction.

Tappan would go beyond all of this: holding that court methods are hardly suited to a broad program of child welfare activities concentrated upon optimum child development, he would limit juvenile courts to jurisdiction over that behavior which would be unlawful for adults. All else would be in the province of social agencies. In our view, this type of policy would, however, leave the community poorly equipped. Much child behavior is serious, dangerous, and a cause for community concern even though it has no adult equivalent. At certain points, community experience with children and their parents demands authoritative intervention and potent sanctions. Given statutory spelling out of conditions and behavior known as threats to the community and to a child's well-being and procedures which require objective evidence of the existence of such conditions, it is entirely proper to find that a child requires the care and protection of the state. He need not be labeled as offender or as delinquent. This does not mean that courts should retain a type of jurisdiction (such as that over dependency or the physically handicapped) which is merely a matter of the administration of a social service.

In fact, a case is readily made for court jurisdiction where there is the equivalent of adult crime and offense, where there is a course of conduct so deviant as to occasion concern, and where a child is endangered, neglected, or abused by parents or guardians. A statute might spell these out in detail as circumstances possibly demanding the care, protection, or cognizance of the state and therefore justifying the taking of jurisdiction by the court, requiring both (*a*) that one of the specified situations be shown to exist and (*b*) that the taking of jurisdiction be shown to be necessary in the interests of child or community.

The British Inglesby Commission recently proposed raising the age of criminal responsibility to twelve. Where younger children require court intervention it would be, in their terms, for protection or discipline, not for delinquency. While it would be difficult to win wide acceptance of this view, since many very young offenders are involved in considerable offenses and neglect adjudication does at present carry some implication of parental "guilt," the purposes of the Commission are admirable. American experience would suggest as a more basic objective the giving up of labels altogether, while continuing to specify circumstances for the taking of jurisdiction.

A tendency is noted, also, to limit the courts' "remedies" in accord with the offense. In fact, the 1959 revisions of the Standard Act reserve for those involved in law violations all institutions designated for "delinquents" and include in their neglect listing a child "who is beyond the control of his parent." Recent California legislation limits commitments of certain types (Youth Authority facilities) to situations in which young people are involved in the equivalent of adult crimes. Other resources are available for the "less-serious" delinquents (county camps) and the neglected (voluntary agency institutions). New York does not permit assignment of "children in need of supervision" to training schools under its *1962 Family Court Act*.

This type of legislation is well motivated. It would avoid punitive sanctions where the child is placed under the court's jurisdiction for protective reasons not for the equivalent of crimes. Basically, however, the approach misses the objective of the court: to assume jurisdiction under specified circumstances and to suit the treatment to the child's need, not to his act. Inadequacies in institutional provision make this an attractive avenue of reform but it does not achieve long-range objectives. Statutes should not limit the flexibility of dispositions; reformers might concentrate more energetically on the suitability of the treatment network. A training school should never be conceived of as the equivalent of an adult prison.

Bibliography

ADDAMS, JANE: The Spirit of Youth and the City Streets, The Macmillan Company, 1909.

ADDITON, HENRIETTA: " The Crime Prevention Bureau of the New York City Police Department ," in Sheldon Glueck and Eleanor Glueck, Preventing Crime, pp. 215-236, McGraw-Hill Book Company, Inc., 1936.

ADDITON, HENRIETTA: City Planning for Girls, Social Service Monograph No. 5, University of Chicago Press, 1928.

BAKER, HARRY J., and VIRGINIA TRAPHAGEN: The Diagnosis and Treatment of Behavior-Problem Children, The Macmillan Company, 1935.

BEAM, KENNETH S.: "The Coordinating Council Movement," Year Book, National Probation Association (1935), pp. 200-213.

BELDEN, EVELINA: "Courts in the United States Hearing Children's Cases", U. S. Children's Bureau Publication, No. 65 (1920).

BOWLER, ALIDA C.: "Experiments in Preventing Juvenile Delinquency," Year Book, National Probation Association (1934), pp. 162-166.

BRECKENRIDGE, SOPHONISBA P., and EDITH ABBOTT: The Delinquent Child and the Home, Russell Sage Foundation, 1912.

BRIDGMAN, RALPH R.: "Parent Education," Social Work Year Book (1935), pp. 310-315.

BRONNER, AUGUSTA F.: The Psychology of Special Abilities and Disabilities, Little, Brown and Company, 1916. See particularly Chaps. I-III, "The Problem," "Method and Diagnosis," "Differential Diagnosis," pp. 1-39.

CARTWRIGHT, JANE: "Community Cooperation versus Delinquency," Year Book, National Probation Association (1932- 1933), pp. 31-35.

CHEVALIER, EMILE: "The German Youth Movement," Living Age, CCCXXIX (April 10, 1926), 99 ff.

CHUTE, CHARLES L.: "Probation in a Community Social Welfare Program," Year Book, National Probation Association (1932- 1933), pp. 20-30.

COCHRAN, HERBERT G.: "Juvenile and Domestic Relations Court," Social Work Year Book (1935), pp. 222-228.

DE KARL SCHWEINITZ: "Social Work as It Contributes to the Strengthening of Family Life," Proceedings of the National Conference of Social Work (1923), pp. 294-299.

DEARDORFF, NEVA R.: "Child Welfare," Encyclopedia of Social Sciences, Vol. III, pp. 373-380.

DICKSON, VIRGIL E.: "The Berkeley Coordinating Council," Mental Hygiene, XIII (July, 1929), 514-519.

ELLIS, HAVELOCK: "Little Essays of Love and Virtue", George H. Doran Company, 1922, Chap. I, "Parents and Children."

FERRIS, ROBERT H.: "Some Social Factors in Family Problems," Year Book, National Probation Association (1932-1933), pp. 180-188.

FLEXNER, BERNARD, REUBEN OPPENHEIMER, and KATHERINE F. LENROOT : "The Child, the Family, and the Court", U. S. Children's Bureau Publication, No. 193 (1933).

GATES, CHARLES A.: "What Should a Juvenile Court Room Look Like?" Year Book, National Probation Association (1931), pp. 1-5.

GLUECK, SHELDON, and ELEANOR GLUECK: Preventing Crime, McGraw- Hill Book Company, Inc., 1936.

GLUECK, SHELDON: "On the Causes of Crime," American Mercury, XXIX (August, 1933), 430 ff.

GROVES, ERNEST R., and GLADYS H. GROVES: Wholesome Parenthood, Houghton Mifflin Company, 1929.

HAMILTON, MARY E.: "The Policewoman", Her Service and Ideals, Frederick A. Stokes Company, 1934.

HANMER, LEE F., "Recreation," Encyclopedia of the Social Sciences, Vol. XIII, pp. 176-181. See also play, amusements, sports, playgrounds, clubs, motion pictures, etc.

HART, HASTINGS: Preventive Treatment of Neglected Children, Russell Sage Foundation, 1910.

JACKS, L. P.: Education through Recreation, Harper & Brothers, 1932.

KILLICK, VICTOR W.: "Suggestions for Parental Administration Calculated to Reduce Juvenile Delinquency," Journal of Delinquency, II (September, 1927), 194-205.

KINGMAN, JOHN M. (Editor), and EDWARD SIDMAN: A Manual of Settlement Boys' Work, National Federation of Settlements, 1935.

LASKER, BRUNO: "The Youth Movement in Germany," Survey, XLVII (December 31, 1921), 480-493.

MASON, B. S., and E. D. MITCHELL: Social Games for Recreation, A. S. Barnes & Company, 1935.

MEAD, MARGARET: Growing Up in New Guinea; Coming of Age in Samoa, William Morrow & Company, Inc., 1930, 1928.

MITCHELL, ALICE: Children and Movies, University of Chicago Press, 1929.

MOSS, JOSEPH L.: "The Relationship of the Juvenile Court to the Police," Proceedings of the National Probation Association (1926), pp. 201-206.

MOWRER, E. R.: Domestic Discord, University of Chicago Press, 1928.

MOWRER, HARRIET R.: Personality Adjustment and Domestic Discord, American Book Company, 1935.

NEUMAN, FREDERIKA: "The Effects on the Child of an Unstable Home Situation," Proceedings of the National Conference of Social Work (1928), pp. 346-353.

NEUMEYER, MARTIN H., and ESTHER S.: "Leisure and Recreation", A. S. Barnes & Company, 1936, Chap. XVIII, "Community Recreation: Semipublic and Private Agencies," pp. 324-363.

O'BRIEN, FRANK J.: "Adjusting Treatment to Diagnosis," Year Book, National Probation Association (1928), pp. 186-201.

OWINGS, CHLOE: Women Police—A Study of the Development and Status of the Women Police Movement, F. H. Hitchcock, 1925.

PANGBURN, W. W.: "Recreation," Social Work Year Book, Russell Sage Foundation, 1935.

PENDRY, ELIZABETH R., and HUGH HARTSHORNE: Organizations for Youth, McGraw-Hill Book Company, Inc., 1935.

PETTIT, M. L.: "An Experiment in the Use of Recreation in Treating Delinquents," Year Book, National Probation Association (1931), pp. 61-68, 1934.

RAYMOND, MARCEL: "The German Youth Movement," Living Age, CCCXXXIII (September 1, 1927), 417 ff.

REEDER, RUDOLPH: Training Youth for the New Social Order, Antioch Press, 1933.

RICHARDS, ESTHER LORING, "Practical Aspects of Parental Love," Mental Hygiene, X (April, 1926), 225-241.

RICHMOND, MARY: Social Diagnosis. Russell Sage Foundation, 1917.

SARGENT, ALBERT J.: "Getting Police Cooperation," Year Book, National Probation Association (1930), pp. 245-247.

SAYLES, MARY B.: The Problem Child at Home, The Commonwealth Fund, 1928.

SCHMIEDELER, EDGAR, and M. ROSA McDONOUGH: "Parent and Child", D. Appleton-Century Company, Inc., 1934, Chap. VIII, "Discipline"; Chap. IX, "Disciplinary Devices"; Chap. XVI, "The Personality of the Child."

SCHUMACHER, H. C.: "Environmental Conflicts in the Family and Social Life of the Modern Child," Hospital Social Service, XVI (October, 1927), 299.

SCUDDER, KENYON J., and KENNETH S. BEAM: Why Have Delinquents? Pamphlet, Rotary Club of Los Angeles, 1933.

SMITH, C. F.: Games and Game Leadership, Dodd, Mead & Company, Inc., 1932.

SMITH, JEANETTE A., and CAROLINE DENTON: "An Experiment in Case Work with a Group of Parents," The Family, XVI (December, 1935), 242-247.

STÄHLEN, OTTO: Die Deutsche Jugendbewegung, Deichertsche Verlagsbuchhandlung, Leipzig, 1930.

TAFT, JESSIE: "The Effect of an Unsatisfactory Mother-daughter Relationship upon the Development of a Personality," The Family, March, 1926, 10-17.

THOMPSON, CHARLES S.: "All Nations Boys' Club, Los Angeles," in Sheldon and Eleanor Glueck (Editors), Preventing Crime, McGraw- Hill Book Company, Inc., 1936.

TOWNE, ARTHUR J.: "Young-girl Marriages in Criminal and Juvenile Courts," Journal of Social Hygiene, VIII (July, 1922), 287-305.

VAN MIRIAM WATERS: "Juvenile-court Procedure as a Factor in Diagnosis," Publications of the American Sociological Society (1921), pp. 209-217.

WALTZ, HENRY W.: "The Probation Officers and Community Organization," Year Book, National Probation Association (1934), pp. 104-113.

White House Conference on Child Health and Protection: The Young Child in the Home, D. Appleton-Century Company, Inc., 1936.

WHITE, EDNA NOBLE: "Experiments in Family Consultation Centers," Social Forces, XII (May, 1934), 557-562.

YOUNG, ERLE F.: "The Coordinating Council Plan in Los Angeles County," The Journal of Criminal Law and Criminology, XXVI (May, 1935), 34-40.

YOUNG, ERLE F.: "The German Youth Movement," Sociology and Social Research, XVI (March-April, 1932), 367-379.

YOUNG, PAULINE V.: "The Social Settlement and the Changing City," Sociology and Social Research,XIX (September-October, 1935), 63-70.

Index

D

G

H

I

J

R